THE PARTY OF HUMANITY

BOOKS BY PETER GAY
IN THE NORTON LIBRARY

The Party of Humanity: Essays in the French Enlightenment N607
The Enlightenment: An Interpretation/The Rise of Modern Paganism N870
The Enlightenment: An Interpretation/The Science of Freedom N875

THE Party OF Humanity

Essays in the French Enlightenment

by Peter Gay

W · W · NORTON & COMPANY
New York · London

First published in the Norton Library 1971
by arrangement with Alfred A. Knopf, Inc.

Published simultaneously in Canada
by George J. McLeod Limited, Toronto

W. W. Norton & Company, Inc., 500 Fifth Avenue, New York, N.Y. 10110
W. W. Norton & Company Ltd., 37 Great Russell Street, London WC1B 3NU

ISBN 0-393-00607-7

PRINTED IN THE UNITED STATES OF AMERICA

5 6 7 8 9 0

To Richard Hofstadter
in friendship

ACKNOWLEDGMENTS

The essays in this volume have all benefited from the criticisms of friends and colleagues. I am grateful to my wife, Ruth, for reading the manuscript in its final version, and to Richard Hofstadter for his generous and perceptive criticisms of my work, which date back to 1953, the year in which the earliest of these pieces was written. I have learned much from my discussions with Henry L. Roberts, and many of his suggestions have found their way into this book. In addition, I want to acknowledge the critical observations of Jacques Barzun, J. Christopher Herold, Gertrude Himmelfarb, Beatrice Hofstadter, Irving Kristol, and Orest Ranum on individual essays. I owe a special debt to the late Franz Neumann, who first called my attention to Cassirer's essay on Rousseau.

All of these essays first appeared elsewhere, often in very different form. I wish to thank various journals and their editors for permission to reprint my work. "The *Philosophe* in His Dictionary" was first published in somewhat different form as "Editor's Introduction" to Voltaire's *Philosophical Dictionary*, 2 volumes (New York: Basic Books; 1962). "Voltaire's *Idées républicaines:* From Detection to Interpretation" first appeared, also in somewhat different form, in Theodore Besterman's *Studies on Voltaire and the Eighteenth Century* (Volume VI, 1958) under the title "Voltaire's *Idées républicaines:* A Study in Bibliography and Interpretation." About half of "Voltaire's Anti-Semitism" was published by the Princeton University Press in 1959 as an appendix to my *Voltaire's Politics: The Poet as Realist.* "The Unity of the French Enlightenment," which I have left practically untouched, was first published by Meridian Books in *History* #3, in August 1960. "Three Stages on Love's Way" appeared in *Encounter*, in August 1957. "Rhetoric and Politics in the French Revolution" was first printed in *The American Historical Review* in April 1961. "Carl Becker's Heavenly City" was published in the *Political Science Quarterly* in June 1957. "Reading About Rousseau" is a greatly expanded and completely rewritten version of my "Introduction" to Ernst Cassirer's *The Question of Jean-Jacques Rousseau*, which I translated and published with Columbia University Press in 1954. "The Party of Humanity" is largely new, but it contains passages from my article "The Enlightenment in the History of Political Theory," *Political Science Quarterly*, September 1954, and several reviews, especially "An Age of Crisis: A Critical View," published in *The Journal of Modern History* in June 1961.

PREFACE

THE ESSAYS collected in this volume were written over the last ten years, for a variety of audiences. I have revised them and brought them up to date, but I have made no attempt to impose on them a uniformity of tone or method. If they have unity at all, it has been supplied by their theme—ideas in eighteenth-century France—and by my attempt to write a certain kind of intellectual history.

This eclecticism is, I think, all to the good; it is, in any event, intentional. Like other historians, intellectual historians are in search of new ways to master their subject matter. In recent years, they have concentrated on two types of inquiry: the history of ideas, practiced by the late Arthur O. Lovejoy and his school; and what I might call the political sociology of ideas, practiced largely by American social historians. The first group, closely allied to historians of philosophy, has specialized in the austere analysis of "unit ideas" like the Great Chain of

Being, or in the dissection of collective terms like Romanticism. The second group, indebted to the writings of Sigmund Freud, Max Weber, and Karl Mannheim, has specialized in studying cultural clichés like the nostalgia of urban Americans for rural simplicity. While the historians of ideas, then, have dealt with the career of first-class ideas in first-class minds, the political sociologists of ideas have dealt with the career of second-class ideas in second-class minds. Whatever their subject matter, both schools have done, and continue to do, impressive work, and as this book shows, my debt to them is great.

Yet there is at least one other type of intellectual history, related to these schools but clearly distinct from them. It is less well codified than they are; hence the need for experimentation is all the greater. It does not even have a name; I should call it the social history of ideas. This kind of intellectual history is guided by a single, simple principle: ideas have many dimensions. They are expressed by individuals, but they are social products; they are conceived, elaborated, and modified amid a specific set of historical circumstances. They reflect events like war or persecution, social realities like the class system, pressures exerted by prevailing styles of thought or literary fashions. Therefore, the social historian of ideas cannot rest content with analyzing their formal logical structure. In my essay on Carl Becker's *Heavenly City*, reprinted in this volume, I warned against what I called the fallacy of "spurious persistence"—the fallacy of treating ideas as independent, unchanging entities. In fact, words like "reason" or "happiness" may persist while their meaning changes; and, on the contrary, an idea may travel through history intact in everything except its verbal form. Voltaire's contempt for the Jews can be properly understood only after we understand the culture in which he voiced it, and the purposes he hoped to realize with his slanders. Diderot's sexual libertinism is the expression of a personal need, but it is also the response to a particular civilization—eighteenth-century France, with its peculiar mixture of official Catholic ideology and relaxed sexual morality among the privileged classes. Rousseau's *Contrat social* must remain a bloodless collection of abstract political maxims until we read it as the work of a Genevan citizen addressing himself to other Genevans, and a very special kind of Genevan—a genius who could express, in the same book, a Utopian longing for perfection and a practical program for political action.

But while ideas are the products of circumstances, they cannot be exhaustively explained by these circumstances: they are not only acted upon, but they also act upon the civilization in which they were formulated. Hence the historian must not merely understand ideas through their civilization, but also civilizations through their ideas. Nor is this all. As Lovejoy pointed out long ago, ideas are a link in a great procession: they are the children, as well as the fathers, of other ideas. And finally, ideas have an inner logic, an intrinsic worth and individual character. Diderot was not merely an eighteenth-century Frenchman, a bourgeois, an ambitious man of letters, and a sensualist; he was also a Newtonian, a Stoic, and something of a Cartesian; and he was, too, the author of works that deserve to be read purely for their own sake.

To say, therefore, that the historian should attempt to grasp ideas in all their aspects is to say that he must address himself to their intellectual and social origins, their relation to other ideas, their logic, their beauty, and their function in their civilization. It is my hope that the essays in this book will be taken as a contribution to this sort of intellectual history, which is itself part of a larger enterprise in which many historians are now engaged: to see history in its living wholeness rather than in schematic subdivisions, to capture men in their actuality, and to discover, as much as is humanly possible, both the variety and the unity of the past.

PETER GAY

New York City
June 1963

CONTENTS

Part One: Voltaire

Part Two: Toward Synthesis

Part Three: Unfinished Business

"MY DEAR SIR, you don't call Rousseau bad company. Do you really think *him* a bad man?" JOHNSON. "Sir, if you are talking jestingly of this, I don't talk with you. If you mean to be serious, I think him one of the worst of men: a rascal, who ought to be hunted out of society, as he has been. Three or four nations have expelled him; and it is a shame that he is protected in this country." BOSWELL. "I don't deny, Sir, but that his novel may, perhaps, do harm; but I cannot think his intention was bad." JOHNSON. "Sir, that will not do. We cannot prove any man's intention to be bad. You may shoot a man through the head, and say you intended to miss him; but the judge will order you to be hanged. An alleged want of intention, when evil is committed, will not be allowed in a court of justice. Rousseau, Sir, is a very bad man. I would sooner sign a sentence for his transportation, than that of any felon who has gone from the Old Bailey these many years. Yes, I should like to have him work in the plantations." BOSWELL. "Sir, do you think him as bad a man as Voltaire?" JOHNSON. "Why, Sir, it is difficult to settle the proportion of iniquity between them."

—JAMES BOSWELL, *The Life of Samuel Johnson*, Saturday, 15 February 1766

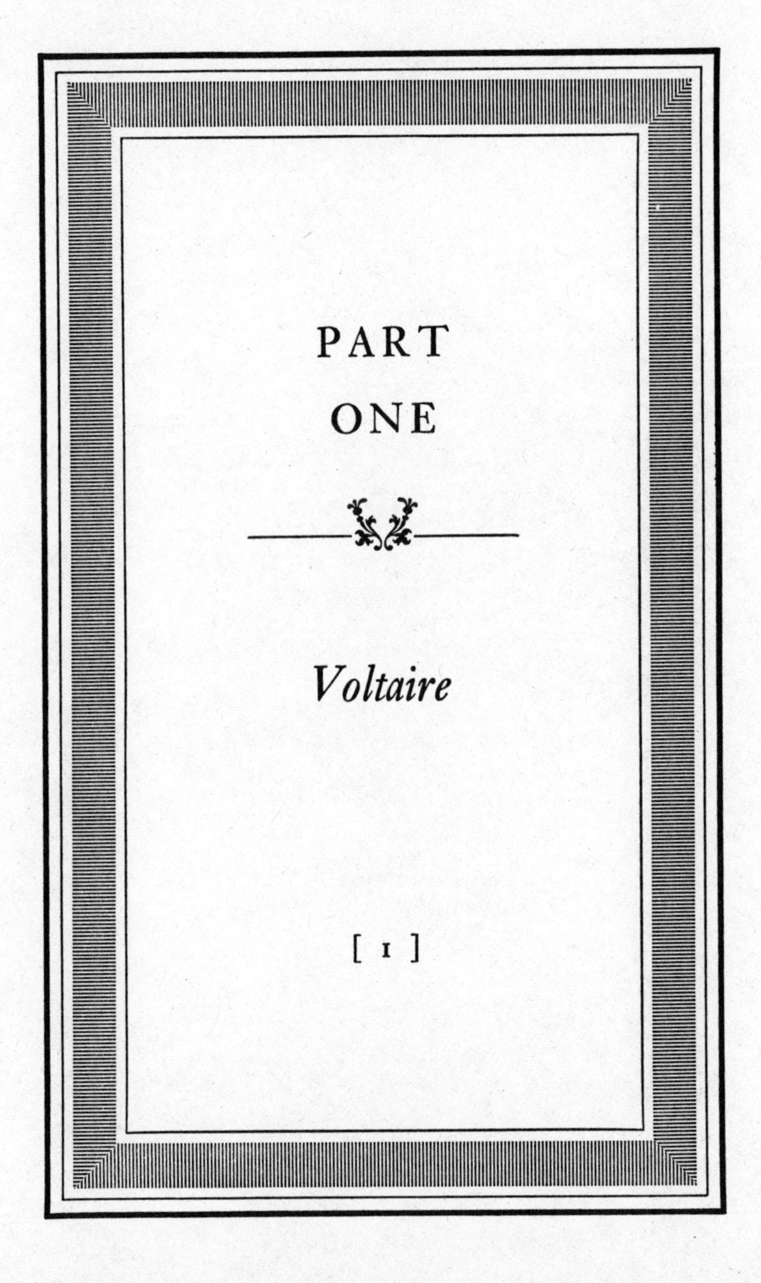

PART ONE

Voltaire

INTRODUCTION

FOR the student of the French Enlightenment the figure of Voltaire commands the center of the stage. Voltaire was not universally popular, even among the *philosophes*. Montesquieu thought him doctrinaire, Rousseau came to regard him as a menace to the peace of Geneva, while Holbach and the materialist school rejected his deist vision of the watchmaker God. Yet even his critics in the movement appreciated his originality, his versatility, his international reputation, and his social connections among the powerful. Intelligent, witty, belligerent, prejudiced, and tenaciously humane, he was the representative *philosophe*.

In part, Voltaire's power was the reward of his sheer longevity. He was born as François-Marie Arouet in Paris on November 21, 1694, in the second, less glorious half of the long reign of Louis XIV. Neo-classical culture, with Versailles as its glittering center, was in a period of slow decline:

Molière, who had died in 1673, had left no worthy successor; Racine, who lived on to 1699, had lapsed into silence. Social criticism was ineffectual: the duc de Saint-Simon muttered against the persecution of the Huguenots in the privacy of his notebooks, while Vauban's protests against rural poverty were quickly suppressed. Even Cartesianism, once a radical threat to orthodoxy, had been assimilated to the elegant Catholicism of the time by the writings of Malebranche. As a mature historian, Voltaire called the "Age of Louis XIV" one of the four great ages in the history of mankind, but in his brooding preoccupation with decay, he looked back on the period of his birth as the beginning of a literary decline which nothing, not even his own dramas, had arrested.

There was intellectual ferment during these years, but not in France. Newton's *Principia Mathematica* appeared in 1687, Locke's *Essay Concerning Human Understanding* in 1690, and Bayle's masterpiece, the *Dictionnaire historique et critique* was published in Holland in 1697. Voltaire assimilated these books into his work, and naturalized their temper and their conclusions in France. Whatever their original intentions, in Voltaire's hands they became the intellectual foundations of the Enlightenment, side by side with the classics of ancient Rome.

This is not to suggest that Voltaire encompassed all the aspects of his complex and developing movement. There were philosophic currents of which he remained unaware. He failed to appreciate Montesquieu's pioneering efforts to construct a comparative sociology of politics; he derided Rousseau's revolutionary political and educational tracts as tasteless romances; and, as a confirmed deist, he could see little merit in the materialist speculations of Holbach or the vitalism of Diderot.

Yet, Voltaire embodies the most characteristic features of the French Enlightenment—and indeed the European Enlightenment as a whole. He preached the omnicompetence of criticism and argued that nothing, least of all religion and politics, should escape the scrutiny of rational reformers. He believed that the true purpose of thought was right action, but he did not expect that all mysteries or all evils would yield to human rationality: the world, in his eyes, was a desert which man must make habitable by his efforts and endure with his humor. When he died on May 30, 1778, at the age of eighty-four, his movement dominated the *Académie française,* his causes were the causes of most educated men, his disciples were in strategic posts, and his secular philosophy was a formidable, almost irresistible rival of Christianity. The student of the French Enlightenment, wherever he wishes to end, must begin with Voltaire.

Since Voltaire is so representative, an accurate appraisal of him is a clue to the Enlightenment as a whole. If Voltaire was trivial, frivolous, foolishly optimistic, and naïvely Utopian, then the whole French Enlightenment must share the burden of these indictments. If he was something else (as I am arguing), it becomes at least thinkable that the customary interpretations of the Enlightenment need to be revised.

The most significant puzzle about Voltaire remains the relation of his character to his work, of his poses to his convictions. The facts of his life appear to be thoroughly known: a few years ago it was discovered that Voltaire had carried on a prolonged and passionate love affair with one of his nieces, but it seems unlikely that we have similar surprises to look forward to. His writings have been carefully and sensitively edited: his notebooks, his vast correspondence, and many of his major works are becoming available in reliable critical editions. We can now try to place Voltaire in his world, and to assess the relevance of his experience to his ideas.

My writings on Voltaire have been directed toward this end. In *Voltaire's Politics: The Poet as Realist* (1959), I sought to rescue him from Tocqueville's caricature, the abstract, literary salon-politician, and the more recent misconception, the principled advocate of Enlightened Despotism. I argued that Voltaire was both intensely realistic and flexibly relativistic about his political views: that he usually knew what he was talking about, and that he favored absolutism in France, despotism in Russia, constitutionalism in Great Britain, and something approaching democracy in Geneva, suiting his program to his information. In this book I make a similar point. In the first essay I treat his *Dictionnaire philosophique* as the sum of his experience, and then relate his great polemic to the culture of his time. In the second, I construct a large argument on a small point, moving from the dating of a relatively minor essay to an estimate of his character, and by implication, of the French Enlightenment as a whole. In the third essay I offer a brief study in limitations: the tension between the principle of toleration and the promptings of prejudice, between the demands of justice and the requirements of polemics. In all of them I have tried to show him as he was—a literary man who was also a political man, a humanitarian who knew how to hate.

I

THE *PHILOSOPHE* IN HIS DICTIONARY

VOLTAIRE'S *Dictionnaire philosophique* is not a dictionary. It is a polemical tract, in turn sober and witty, sensible and outrageous, sincere and disingenuous. It is sometimes angry about the wrong things, sometimes superficial in its explanations, and sometimes almost as cruel as the cruelty it lacerates. But behind the savage humor and partisan analysis stands a passion for humanity and decency, a hatred of fanaticism and stupidity, which Voltaire would not have been embarrassed to acknowledge (and which we should not be too supercilious to recognize) as moral. With its errors and its erudition, its dazzling variety of tactics and brilliant unity of style, the *Dictionnaire philosophique* is Voltaire's most characteristic work—as characteristic as its more famous companion piece *Candide*.

As a passionate, and hence personal document, the *Dictionnaire philosophique* looks in two directions—toward its author and toward its culture. On the one side, it used practically everything that Voltaire knew; on the other side, it took its particular shape because it was born in, and directed against, a Christian civilization. Voltaire was always at his best when he fashioned his work most directly from his experience. And paradoxically, it was precisely when he was most timely that he produced his most lasting work: his tragedies, which labor in a great tradition, are dead today; his polemics, even if their particular targets no longer matter, endure.

1 · The Man in His Book

When Voltaire wrote the first articles of the *Dictionnaire philosophique* in the fall of 1752, he was a glittering display piece at the court of Frederick the Great and the most famous literary man in Europe. Each new work of his was hopefully awaited by the literary world, appreciatively read by a wide public, and shamelessly pirated by unscrupulous booksellers. He turned out successes with monotonous regularity in practically every genre of the literary and journalistic repertory, arousing the awe of his friends and the envy of his competitors. He was, and he liked to think that he was, a sickly man; yet his energies and his stores of inventive imagination were inexhaustible: he was fifty-eight years old when he launched on the *Dictionnaire*, and while he drew on all his previous experience to compile it, in structure and intention it was a novel venture. Voltaire was perhaps the only man in Europe who could have written it, but he probably could not have written it much earlier.

Voltaire acquired many of the right habits early, including his pugnacious independence. His parents were solid and prosperous middle-class people with social pretensions and some claims to nobility on the mother's side. With an eye to his advancement, they sent their precocious son to *Louis-le-Grand*, a Jesuit *collège* favored by the wealthy and influential aristocrats of Paris. Their motive was tactical rather than pedagogical: they wanted the boy to become a fashionable lawyer, perhaps to rise into the nobility of the robe. *Louis-le-Grand* had the right clientele, the right social tone, and (what with the disfavor into which the Jansenists had fallen) the right political position for a family on the way up. Voltaire spent six happy years, from 1704 to 1710, at *Louis-le-Grand*, and it is here that we must seek the first roots of the book he began to write in 1752 and published in 1764.[1]

Young François-Marie Arouet disappointed both his parents and his teachers. He made friends, and in the highest social circles, but he wanted them to read his manuscripts, not his briefs. He was a remarkable student, but he was to turn the learning he had acquired from Christians against Christianity. His parents wanted him to become a lawyer, but he became a poet; his teachers wanted him to become a compliant Christian, but he became a belligerent pagan. Both the belligerence and the paganism are prominent ingredients in the *Dictionnaire*.

In the eighteenth century, an admirer of the classics did not need to be a pagan; the most distinguished classical scholars of the time were firm Christians. While the Jesuits catered to their spoiled charges and suavely tempered the severity of Christian teachings in a time when rigorous piety was out of style, they taught the Latin and Greek classics

[1] The *Dictionnaire* grew rapidly, in edition after edition. In this essay I have used the edition of 1769, the largest that can legitimately be called the *Dictionnaire philosophique*. My quotations are all from my complete translation of that edition, published in 1962.

with Christian admonitions, and used pagan doctrines and pagan myths as pedagogical gateways to higher Christian truths. The more scandalous Latin writers, like Ovid, were expurgated, and ancient philosophy was imparted with the warning that its teachings were acceptable only insofar as they anticipated, or imperfectly expressed, the sublimities of Christian doctrine. These tactics were not insincere subterfuges: the Jesuits were faithful, if modern, Christians, and the classicism they taught so well was rhetorical, literary, social. Classical education was class education: it provided delightful objects of aesthetic contemplation, interesting subjects for scholarly study, and above all, a common language for the educated. A well-placed tag from Horace, like a well-turned epigram, marked the man destined for polite society anywhere in eighteenth-century Europe. "Classical quotation," said Samuel Johnson, who was not a *philosophe*, "is the *parole* of literary men all over the world."

Voltaire's appreciation of antiquity went far beyond a hero-worship of Cicero, a quoting of Latin lines half-remembered from school-days, a playful or even serious pedantry. His rejection of Christianity—the God-man, miracles, and even specifically Christian ethics—resulted from the confluence of many streams, including modish impiety, his study of history sacred and profane, and his commitments to the procedures and theories of Newtonian physics. But his paganism was also a recapture of antique styles of thinking. Voltaire exalted modern over ancient science, and he had as little reverence for ancient metaphysical systems as he had for the system-makers of the seventeenth century. But in his concern for practical ethics, his conception of thought as a form of action, and his insistence on the sovereign rights of criticism, he was acting as an Eclectic who had synthesized the ideas of the Stoics, Epicureans, and Skeptics, and brought them up to date. In collaboration with a cosmopolitan cohort of *philosophes*, Voltaire made the Enlightenment into a movement that may be defined as ancient philosophy plus modern science.

In the *Dictionnaire*, paganism shows itself in many forms. It is decorative, as in the article "*Songes*," which opens with a quotation from Petronius. It is a polemical device, as in the article "*Julien le philosophe*," which contrasts the sober, decent humanity of the pagan emperor with the malicious fanaticism of his Christian slanderers; or as in several other articles which contrast the educated Romans, who despised and tolerated all religions, with barbarous Christians, who persecuted everyone including one another. But beyond that, paganism informs Voltaire's thinking and guides his pen in every article: it speaks through his criticism of authority, his skepticism of the miraculous, his admiration for men who suffered nobly without hope of heaven or fear of hell, his program for a humane, tolerant society, and his plea for a religion without priests, without ritual, and without nonsense. When Voltaire calls his article on "*Superstition*" a "chapter taken from Cicero, Seneca, and Plutarch," he is listing some influential spiritual ancestors.[2]

It would be naïve to portray Voltaire's education as a matter of rigid stages. Voltaire's mind was far too lively, too alert to new currents of thought, too eager to experiment with ideas or literary forms, to pick up its furnishings in

[2] Voltaire's paganism is representative of the pagan world view of the Enlightenment as a whole. I shall allude to this paganism throughout this book, and I am now completing a general interpretation of the Enlightenment that will attempt to give full weight to the affinity of the *philosophes* for ancient ways of thinking.

discrete packages: he dabbled in literature before he published his first play, he admired English philosophers before he went to England, and he introduced political ideas into his poems a quarter century before he wrote his first political pamphlet. Yet when we look back from 1752, trying to understand the man who was about to begin the *Dictionnaire*, we see each period of his life dominated by a guiding interest. Paganism was the first step in his education as a *philosophe*, literature was the second.

When we reflect on Voltaire's literary reputation, we are tempted to make Voltairian observations about the ephemeral nature of fame and the unpredictable course of taste. His plays, which now seem contrived and tedious, were hailed as masterpieces in their time. In 1718, a young worldling with an eleven-month stay in the Bastille and much fashionable versifying behind him, Voltaire produced his first tragedy, *Œdipe*, which made him famous overnight. He was hailed as the successor to Corneille and Racine. Today, *Œdipe* and his other dramatic successes have shrunk to footnotes in histories of French literature. Similarly, *La Henriade*, a long and fatiguing epic poem on Henri IV, was compared by qualified readers in the 1720's to Vergil, and is now practically forgotten. Today Voltaire is much admired, or at least much invoked, as a haggard, quixotic knight of tolerance, but outside of France his literary work, except for *Candide*, lies neglected.

Voltaire's unprecedented success as a polemicist and propagandist, of which the *Dictionnaire* is the supreme exemplar, must remain incomprehensible without an appreciation of his literary skill. The work itself says little about literature. One article, "*Critique*," tells us something about Voltaire's taste, and more about his distaste for critics who affect to despise what they cannot hope to equal. Another, a short and superficial article on literary men—"*Lettres, gens de lettres, ou lettrés*"—shows him in one of his frequent moods of self-pity but is silent on Voltaire's energetic efforts to improve the social standing, the personal dignity, and the financial lot of professional writers, including himself. Yet the fact remains that much of what Bayle had tried to do half a century before with four ponderous, tortuously written, and elaborately circumspect folios; much of what Diderot and his small army of collaborators were trying to do with an enormous encyclopedia—much of this Voltaire was trying to do with one slight book, small enough to fit into a man's pocket. The first four editions of the *Dictionnaire* advertised it to be "*portatif*." To combine a maximum of explosive power with a minimum of space, to educate without boring, and to persuade without annoying required enormous capacities in the arts of economy, selection, concealment, and entertainment. With Voltaire, such capacities resulted from the combination of natural endowment and life-long attention to the details of his craft, a craft he had begun to cultivate at *Louis-le-Grand*, and perfected in the works of the 1720's, while he was still young. He was artful enough to conceal his art, but he lavished all his literary skills on the *Dictionnaire*.

The eighteenth century was pervasively engaged with style. It was Voltaire's contemporary, the natural scientist and *philosophe* Buffon, who coined the celebrated maxim, *le style est l'homme même*. What Buffon meant by suggesting that style was the man himself was that it depended on more than artifices, graces learned in school, conventional devices, or participation in a literary tradition. It was an alliance of talent and craftsmanship, general cultivation and specific information. That is why when we speak of Voltaire's style we must begin by speaking of his knowledge. This is the burden of Diderot's perceptive remark to Catherine the Great: "What is it that particularly distinguishes Voltaire from all our young writers? Instruction. Voltaire knows a great deal, and our young poets are ignorant. The work of Voltaire is full of matter, their works are empty."[3] Clearly, what applied to poetry applied even more strongly to polemics.

In a century of voracious readers, Voltaire was remarkable for his inquisitiveness and intelligence, for the excellence of his library, the rationality of his working habits, and the energy of his research. It hardly needs pointing out that his scholarship was rarely disinterested, and the *Dictionnaire* shows that it was far from impeccable. The dates for the Bar Kochba rebellion and for Justin Martyr are incorrect; there are mistranslations. Antiquarians and classicists greatly surpassed him in their own specialties, and sometimes, when these scholars were as belligerently Christian as Voltaire was belligerently pagan, they publicly convicted him of some embarrassing errors. Yet, considering his status as an amateur and the range of his writings, his knowledge is nothing short of admirable.

It shows to good advantage in the *Dictionnaire*. Here he commands an enormous vocabulary and moves with ease from theologians' jargon or lawyers' cant to classical allusions, Italian literature, English expressions, and popular doggerel. The opening line of the first article, "*Abbé*," is a quotation from a contemporary song. Voltaire can exploit and casually refer to "the learned Fabricius," whose scholarly

[3] Denis Diderot: "Essai sur les études en Russie," *Œuvres complètes*, eds. J. Assézat and Maurice Tourneux, 20 vols. (1875–1877), III, 444.

Latin editions of the Gospels, canonical and apocryphal, were in his library; he gives his own version of Jewish history and Jewish views of Christianity by citing Basnage's voluminous *Histoire des Juifs*, a French translation of Josephus, or a compilation of Jewish writings, *Tela ignea Satanae*, by the seventeenth-century scholar Wagenseil. Sometimes his information is out of date, but usually it is derived from the most recent writers; in the article "*Religion*," he courteously and anonymously dissents from Hume's *Natural History of Religion*, which he owned in a French translation of 1759.

But, as Voltaire knew better than anyone else, a merely learned treatise, no matter how anticlerical its implications, could never touch *l'infâme;* the dry dust of learning needed the alchemy of style to be converted into a living threat to Christianity.

Voltaire's style is a celebrated but surprising instrument: it is full of concealments. It appears straightforward but is richly allusive; it appears coolly rational but is an admirable vehicle for the expression of passion; it appears disarmingly simple but contains the most powerful agents of persuasion. In his subtle analysis of Voltaire's style, Erich Auerbach points to Voltaire's "method of posing the problem so that the desired solution is contained in the very way in which the problem is posed," and to his "searchlight technique, which over-illuminates the ridiculous, the absurd, or the repulsive" in his opponent. These techniques, writes Auerbach, are not new, but Voltaire gives them special power by "his tempo."[4]

In the *Dictionnaire*, Voltaire employs his techniques with

[4] Erich Auerbach: *Mimesis: The Representation of Reality in Western Literature*, transl. by Willard R. Trask (1953), 404, 405. See also Leo Spitzer's remarkable essay: "Einige Voltaire-Interpretationen," *Romantische Stil- und Literaturstudien*, 2 vols. (1930), II, 211-43.

masterful versatility, although, impressively enough, his variety never leads him into incoherence of tone. In all his stylistic tricks and clever turns of phrase we recognize a single mind; Voltaire could never convince anyone that he had merely edited the contributions of several hands. He had a wide repertory of roles at his command, but his performances were dominated by a single, pervasive technique: irony.

Irony is more searching and more penetrating than sarcasm. It says one thing and means something else; it is thus deceptive, like a lie. But unlike a lie, which seeks only to deceive, irony seeks to clarify. The ironic effect is achieved when both actor and spectator recognize the role as role, and the deception as the path to reality. Irony says what must be said and cannot be said; it illuminates by reflected light. It is, as Goethe says, the pinch of salt that makes food palatable, but it does more: irony reveals by concealing.

Voltaire's irony consists of his adopting poses which he, and his readers, understand to be inappropriate to him, or in exploiting poses which are appropriate but dramatized for the sake of effect. These devices permit Voltaire to expose what he could never expose directly; they permit him to approach forbidden territory under cover of darkness. In a world of censorship, of ecclesiastics hunting heretics, and of influential readers demanding to be appeased, irony was an agent of twofold liberation: it freed the writer to speak the truth, and it freed the reader to see it. Voltairian irony was itself an ironic counterpoint to Jesus' assertion that the truth shall make us free.

Since Voltaire's style was never mere decoration but rather the apt expression of what he knew, his acquisition of a responsible view of the world represents an essential stage in his education. In the early 1720's, to put it simply, he learned how to say things, and after 1726 he learned what he must say. This new seriousness was not superficial; it had been hidden in the young Voltaire, the talented society wit, who had brooded on God. But it was his famous quarrel with the chevalier de Rohan, fatuous offspring of an old aristocratic house, that made manifest what had been latent. In the winter of 1725–1726, Voltaire had some words with Rohan, and in February 1726 he was lured from an elegant dinner party and beaten by Rohan's men before Rohan's contemptuous eyes. To Voltaire's dismay, his aristocratic friends turned their backs on him, and in April the government sent Voltaire once again to the Bastille, largely, it would seem, for his own protection.

The incident was a valuable if rather drastic lesson: it was a reminder that the realities of a stratified society remained realities, even for him. The heir of Racine and Vergil, the intimate of the great, the beneficiary of royal pensions, was nothing but plain Arouet once he dared to challenge the system.

This was the first benefit of his beating; his visit to England was the other. Voltaire was released from the Bastille in May 1726 and immediately embarked for England, where he stayed more than two years. The visit was of decisive importance; its echoes were to reverberate all through his life.

There used to be vigorous controversy among Voltaire scholars over this visit. Some, chiefly English, once argued that it made a man of him, and a thinker; others, chiefly French, that it only supplied him with material and confirmed religious and philosophical views he had picked up from French deists and skeptics. Today, scholars have arrived at a cosmopolitan consensus appropriate to such a cosmopolitan as Voltaire: Voltaire's English visit did not produce a conversion; his writings of the early 1720's show signs of his concern with toleration, his doubts about Christianity, his rather rudimentary interest in natural science and empirical philosophy. But his English years, nevertheless, had a profound influence on him. They were a period of urbane activity and thoughtful leisure for him, of reading and observing. England appeared to Voltaire's dazzled vision as the realization of some utopian hope. Peculiarly sensitive, after his recent humiliation, to social realities, he was delighted to see commoners honored by the state and bourgeois rising to positions of eminence; increasingly aware of literature as a craft above base propaganda or servile entertainment, he was delighted to see English writers, no matter what their social origins, rich and respected. England, he wrote to his friend Thieriot on October 26, 1726, in his newly acquired English, was a "nation fond of their liberty, learned, witty, despising life and death, a nation of philosophers."[5]

The glow of England never faded, and all his life Voltaire good-humoredly pleaded guilty to the charge of "Anglomania." English philosophers, English deists, English scientists, gave firm and informed direction to his youthful discontent, polite skepticism, and amateurish passion for politics. Some of his acquisitions bore ready fruit; when he returned from England late in 1728, he had a rich accumulation of notes and ideas for a book on English civilization. Others went underground and were fused with his later reading to produce his highly personal critique of Christianity, of which the *Dictionnaire* was the most celebrated specimen.

[5] *Voltaire's Correspondence*, ed. Theodore Besterman (1953ff), II, 37.

The *Dictionnaire*, indeed, is suffused with the warmth of Voltaire's Anglomania; like his paganism, it appears both in numerous details and in the intellectual style of the book. The imaginary dialogues which make up a good portion of the Dictionary often have Englishmen for their heroes. In "*Liberté de penser*," free expression is vigorously upheld by an English officer named Boldmind; in "*Catéchisme du Japonais*," the Japanese who defends toleration is obviously an Englishman; *L'A, B, C*, the long dialogue which Voltaire wrote in 1768 and liked well enough to include in the 1769 editions of the *Dictionnaire*, has a "monsieur A" as its most active protagonist, and he too is an Englishman. In fact, Voltaire could think of no higher praise for *L'A, B, C*, and its boldness than to call it, in a letter to Madame du Deffand, an "English roast beef."[6]

There are many echoes: memories of a meeting with Berkeley, quotations from Shaftesbury, kindly references to Quaker pacifism. But more pervasive than all these are Voltaire's intellectual debts to Locke, champion of philosophical modesty, empirical inquiry, and associationist psychology; to Newton, enemy of vain hypotheses and creator of the true system of nature; to Hume, philosophical unmasker of miracles, penetrating psychologist, and natural historian of religion; and to critical deists like Woolston. Not only "*L'A, B, C*" but the book as a whole is an English roast beef, served up with the subtlest of French sauces.

Voltaire's distillation of his English years, the *Lettres philosophiques*, came out in Paris in 1734, and was burned by the hangman as subversive and irreligious. Naturally, it was an

[6] December 26 (1768), *Œuvres complètes*, ed. Louis Moland, 52 vols. (1877–1885), XLVI, 207.

immense success, but Voltaire, who had completed the book some time before, was off on other tacks. In 1731 he had published his first major history, the *Histoire de Charles XII;* in 1732, after other plays of indifferent merit, he scored a dramatic and critical triumph with *Zaïre*, which has aptly been called "a tender" tragedy.[7] It was dedicated, with pointed bluntness, to Voltaire's English friend Everard Fawkener, "*marchand anglais.*" To dedicate a literary work to a mere commoner in an age of cringing dedications to noblemen was François-Marie Arouet's first revenge on the chevalier de Rohan. There were to be more.

But in the early 1730's, revenge was far from Voltaire's mind. He was occupied, rather, with love and with its improbable companion, scholarship. In 1733, he had become the lover of Madame du Châtelet, and in the summer of 1734, escaping possible trouble over his book on England—his "philosophical, political, critical, poetical, heretical, and diabolical letters"[8]—he moved to her *château* at Cirey in Champagne, reassuringly close to the frontiers of Lorraine. There he stayed, except for occasional trips to Holland, Prussia, and the French court, for fifteen years, until the death of his mistress.

Madame du Châtelet is such an extraordinary person, with her ungainly frame, the masculine aggressiveness of her scientific conversation, her thirst for men (which Voltaire could never hope to satisfy), her irresponsible lust for gambling, that it is all too tempting to treat her fifteen-year liaison with Voltaire as a comical interlude. It was, in fact, anything but that. The lovers worked hard, kept rigorous

[7] Gustave Lanson: *Voltaire* (n.d.), 41.

[8] Voltaire to Formont (*c.* August 15, 1733). *Correspondence*, III, 128.

hours, and collaborated in studying mathematics, making scientific experiments, and doing research in theology. Madame du Châtelet was a bluestocking, but she was not a dilettante. She translated difficult English works with competence, learned languages faster than Voltaire, knew her classical philosophy, studied Newton and Leibniz with evident comprehension, and took a professional interest in the major philosophical and theological questions that were agitating educated men all over Europe. She read hard and wrote much; some of the finest mathematicians of the century, like Maupertuis, improved her algebra and warmed her bed.

This woman was the source of great vexation, but also of great delight, to Voltaire. In her presence, with her help, or for her sake, he consolidated what he had learned and struck out in new directions. The list of his writings, or of writings nearing publication, shows the widening range of his interests and an increasing capacity for connecting the facets of his education to a central view of life. In 1738, he entered the debate between the Cartesians and Newtonians with his *Éléments de la philosophie de Newton.* In England, Newtonianism had triumphed readily; on the Continent, Descartes's physics and methods of reasoning still had overwhelming support. Voltaire was not a scientist and had only indifferent abilities as an experimenter, but with his unfailing grasp of the essential, he understood that natural science was the most significant single development in the Europe of his time and that Newton's theory of gravitation, as well as his much-discussed "refusal to make hypotheses," would become the basis of the modern world-view and the heart of the Enlightenment. During his English visit, when he had

Voltaire's interpretation of Newtonianism

witnessed Newton's funeral at Westminster Abbey and adopted the insular opinion that Newton was the greatest man who ever lived, he had still thought it possible to reconcile Newton with Descartes. Now, in the *Éléments*, neither the first nor the most rigorous, though probably the most influential popularization of Newtonian physics and Newtonian empiricism in the eighteenth century, Voltaire, for all the survival of Cartesian and Leibnizian conceptions in his thinking, made himself the prophet of Newtonianism.

The *Dictionnaire* is a thoroughly Newtonian book. Its world is a world of unchanging and unchangeable natural laws, created by a God who disdains miracles as paltry admissions of his own inefficiency or impotence; a world of basic constituents like mind or matter whose nature is unknown to us but whose obedience to eternal natural law we can understand and admire. Voltaire transcended Newton's formulations in one respect: he no longer needed to explain the observed irregularities of the solar system or of comets with Newton's notion of occasional divine intervention into the workings of the world. Mathematicians like Maupertuis, Clairaut, and d'Alembert (all acquaintances of Voltaire) were confirming and extending the truth of Newtonian theories with dramatic measurements, equations, and experiments, and fitting these irregularities into a universal system even vaster than the one Newton had conceived. Newton had been a Christian, but his scientific theories led men to a world-view irreconcilable with Christianity. Voltaire went beyond Newton, and the Newtonian scientists of Voltaire's century went beyond Voltaire into a thoroughgoing naturalism.

For Voltaire, Newtonianism was more than a scientific system: it was an intellectual method that implied a social policy. It taught us, he wrote a young man in 1741, to "examine, weigh, calculate, and measure, but never conjecture." Newton had never constructed a system; "he saw, and he made people see; but he didn't put his fancies in place of truth."[9] Such Newtonian modesty led men to focus on what they could know, and to be tolerant. If we do not, and cannot, know the essence of things (as Voltaire insists in "*Âme*," "*Bêtes*," "*Matière*," and elsewhere), we will not persecute others, who are as ignorant as we are. Thus scientific method and religious toleration, Newtonian physics and the attack on fanaticism, are aspects of a single enterprise.

The scientific revolution, then, had its rewards, but even for a deist like Voltaire it raised troublesome questions in metaphysics and ethics. He grappled with both in his years with Madame du Châtelet, first in the *Traité de métaphysique* of 1734, then in the *Discours en vers sur l'homme* of 1738, and less systematically but far more fatefully in his private correspondence with Frederick of Prussia, initiated by the crown prince with an adulatory letter in 1736. Voltaire, never a systematic thinker, gradually worked his way to a deterministic view of life (vividly reflected in the dialogue "*De la Liberté*") and a common-sense view of ethics, a kind of shorthand secular decalogue of human decency without dogmas or quibbles (repeated, in various forms and with varying emphases, throughout the *Dictionnaire*).

All this sounds rather portentous, but Voltaire's education never lacked its playful side. In the years at Cirey, he wrote some of his most famous plays and several of his delightful philosophical tales. Even his paganism found playful expression in the scandalous—or what the devout thought scandalous—defense of pleasure and luxury, the poem *Le*

[9] Voltaire to Le Cati, April 15, 1741. *Correspondence*, XI, 85.

Mondain. This poem, like almost everything else, eventually found expression in the *Dictionnaire:* the article "*Luxe*" curtly, and sensibly, defends the cultivated ease of Athens against the military rigor of Sparta, and coyly quotes two lines from *Le Mondain* as lines the author of the article has "read somewhere."

Even more significant for the *Dictionnaire* than this array of publications of the Cirey period are the writings published after it closed and the studies which never found their way into print at all. In the first group are Voltaire's two historical masterpieces, the *Siècle de Louis XIV* and the *Essai sur les mœurs*, which Voltaire undertook to prove to his mistress that history had utility as well as charm. In the second group are inquiries into the logic, coherence, dates, sources, and moral value of the Bible.

Voltaire's interest in history began early, and his epic, the *Henriade*, was the first, immature product of that interest. The *Histoire de Charles XII*, still a racy and informative book, was, for all its power, little more than the biography of a romantic adventurer. With his accounts of the reign of Louis XIV and the growth of Western civilization, he found his method and made his major contributions to the discipline of history. Voltaire was the first to make civilization the subject of historical inquiry; one of the first to be rigorously secular in his analysis of causation; and a thoroughgoing, although not always happy, critic of his sources. Voltaire's histories are histories of the "mind" of an age; they portray a network of institutions in which political forms, social ambitions, artistic production, and foreign policy all act upon one another and are, collectively and separately, more important than details of battles, court intrigues, or the history of the Chosen People.

The defects of these writings are well known—Voltaire's critics have seen to that: He lacked sympathy with ages alien to his ideal of cultivation or hostile to his theological convictions, and his persistent campaign to improve his readers often interfered with his efforts to be objective. Yet even a hasty reading of the *Dictionnaire* shows that its author has mastered the craft and the materials of history. His cautious use of Herodotus as a witness in "*Circoncision*," his skepticism of improbable tales, his relish for the revealing incident, his easy allusion to historical characters and events, his dislike of mere chronicle, and his insistence on what is important—all these show the historian at work.

In the *Dictionnaire*, to be sure, Voltaire exercises his historical skills chiefly on the Biblical Jews and the early Christians; historical analysis shades into theological criticism. When Voltaire went to Cirey, he already had a position on religion: he was in favor of toleration and simple, reasonable beliefs; he opposed fanaticism, persecution, and superstition. In a notorious early poem, *Épître à Uranie*, written in 1722 but not circulated until much later, Voltaire had attacked the idea of a cruel God and, visualizing himself as a modern Lucretius, declared war on the "Sacred lies that fill the world."[1] The *Henriade* had singled out Henri IV's tolerance as his finest virtue, while the *Lettres philosophiques* had praised the Quakers and offered as an explanation for English power and prosperity the happy coexistence of many religions. One religion, he wrote, threatens to lead to despotism, two cause religious war, but the English "have thirty, and they live happy and in peace."[2]

[1] Voltaire: *Œuvres*, IX, 359. For this puzzling and important poem, see the critical edition by Ira O. Wade: *PMLA*, XLVII (1932), 1066-112.

[2] *Lettres philosophiques*, "Ve Lettre," ed. Gustave Lanson, 2 vols. (1909), I, 74.

All these notions were the staples of advanced freethinkers for whom religious war was an anachronism, religious enthusiasm a lower-class aberration, and religious dogma a myth. But now, at Cirey, Voltaire refined his instruments of criticism and sharpened his weapons of attack: the commonplace freethinker became an accomplished Critical Deist.

Deism, which attracted many nominal Christians in the early eighteenth century, had two aspects: Constructive Deism and Critical Deism. On its Constructive side, it drew on the speculations of Christian humanists, latitudinarian clergymen, and modern Stoics. True religion, it argued, is as old as creation; it consists of a few simple maxims about the fatherhood of God, the regularity of nature, and the brotherhood of man; it preaches peace and kindness, despises ritual, sects, and intolerance; it depends for proof on the natural revelation of human reason and draws strength from the unanimity of philosophers. Chinese literati, Persian sages, Roman Stoics, and Jesus, the ethical teacher, were all regarded as deists.

This Constructive Deism is the foundation of Voltaire's positive religious convictions, and its characteristic tenets open article after article of the *Dictionnaire*. "Almost everything that goes beyond the worship of a supreme Being and the submission of one's heart to its eternal commands, is superstition"—thus begins "*Superstition*." "What is toleration? It is the endowment of humanity. We are all steeped in weaknesses and errors; let's forgive each other our follies; that is the first law of nature"—thus begins "*Tolérance*." "Every sect, of whatever kind, is the rallying point for doubt and error"—thus begins "*Secte*."

But Constructive Deism gets its cutting edge from Critical Deism, that peculiar mixture of science and hostility which undertakes to examine Christian documents to prove their absurdity, Christian history to prove its cruelty, and Christian ritual to prove its dependence on pagan rites. This is what Voltaire and Madame du Châtelet did at Cirey, with the greatest gusto and with the largest possible battery of scholarly support. They borrowed freely from Bayle's *Dictionnaire historique et critique*, used arguments from subversive manuscripts that passed slyly from hand to hand, imported Critical Deist works like Thomas Woolston's *Six Discourses on the Miracles of our Saviour*, read orthodox apologetics like La Bletterie's *Vie de l'Empereur Julien* in order to refute them, and relied heavily on dom Calmet's pious commentary, the enormous *Commentaire littéral sur tous les livres de l'Ancien et du Nouveau Testament*, which they shamelessly pillaged and ungratefully ridiculed.

The result of the lovers' exhaustive, verse-by-verse study of the Bible was a sizable manuscript by Madame du Châtelet, the *Examen de la Genèse*, which, despite the modesty of its title, is an examination of the whole Bible, from the Book of Genesis to the Book of Revelation. Voltaire's precise share in the enterprise will never be known, but it seems to have been considerable, and there is good evidence that at Cirey he wrote, or at least drafted, some of his most vehement anti-Christian writings published much later, in the 1760's, when he could operate with relative security from his strategically located *château* at Ferney.

To be sure, the *Dictionnaire* is not merely an alphabetical compilation of Critical Deist attacks on the Bible; its assault is far more comprehensive and far more varied. But again and again, the *Examen de la Genèse* reads like a first draft of a passage or an argument in the *Dictionnaire*.

Thus, to throw doubt on the veracity of the translators,

who begin Genesis with an affirmation of monotheism—"In the beginning God created the heavens and the earth"—Madame du Châtelet quotes dom Calmet to the effect that the original Hebrew text speaks of "gods." This sally from the *Examen* found its way into the article "*Genèse*" of the *Dictionnaire*, where Voltaire suggests with characteristic lightness of touch that anyone with the slightest education knows that Genesis has "gods" and not "God" in its opening sentence. Again, Madame du Châtelet ridicules the two incompatible stories of the creation of man and woman and the creation of the sun three days after light and darkness had been separated. In "*Genèse*" Voltaire raises the same objections, using Madame du Châtelet's observation that the stories demonstrate little more than an abominable ignorance of natural science.

The Bible is not only incorrectly translated and swarming with contradictions, it is also filled with immoral stories, vicious conduct held up as exemplary, foolish and puerile myths. The *Examen* makes much of Abraham passing his wife off as his sister, and the *Dictionnaire* devotes a large part of its article "*Abraham*" to this patriarchal lie. The *Examen* professes horror at David—bandit chief, murderer, and adulterer—and the *Dictionnaire* has a short but powerful article, "*David*," which repeats all these charges. Again, Madame du Châtelet condemns the Book of Proverbs as boring, repetitious, infelicitous, and inelegant in its many images, and Voltaire adopts these criticisms in his article on "*Salomon*."

The New Testament offered an equally fertile field for skepticism: the *Examen* wonders about the two contradictory genealogies of Jesus, the many apocryphal gospels, the darkness covering the earth for three hours at the Crucifixion, the reprehensible behavior of Paul in returning to the temple, and dozens of other riddles. All of them find their place in the *Dictionnaire*, especially in "*Christianisme*," significantly the longest of the articles. Behind the *Dictionnaire*, then, there stands the robust, intelligent shade of Madame du Châtelet.[3]

I say "shade," for in September 1749 this extraordinary woman died, as scandalously as she had lived, after giving birth to a girl fathered neither by her husband the marquis du Châtelet, nor by her official lover, Voltaire, but by another lover, the poet Saint-Lambert, to whom she had been driven by the demands of her passionate heart and her awkward body. Bereft, Voltaire moved to Paris, and there, late in 1749 and early in 1750, he added another dimension to his experience—politics.

His activity was neither a new interest nor a sudden caprice; he had followed diplomatic and domestic politics in Europe for over thirty years. What he had written on politics—in the *Henriade*, the *Lettres philosophiques*, and his correspondence with statesmen—showed him a hard-headed relativist, as ready to see the blessings of constitutional government as the virtues of centralized authority; Voltaire was not a doctrinaire admirer of "Enlightened Despotism." But in the political infighting in France, Voltaire was on the side of the king, and had been a royalist all his adult life. His reasons for taking this position were based not on abstract principles but on the harsh realities of French history. As a

[3] Voltaire's Cirey period was treated as a merely amorous interlude until the authoritative work of Ira O. Wade, whom I have followed here. See *Voltaire and Madame du Châtelet* (1941), *Studies on Voltaire, With Some Unpublished Papers of Madame du Châtelet* (1947), and his fine critical edition of *Voltaire's "Micromégas"* (1950).

French royalist, Voltaire opposed the privileged bodies in the state—nobility and clergy—and objected to powerful particularist and provincial tendencies which kept the country from unifying its weights and measures, rationalizing its taxes, and improving its legal procedure. The system of venality, under which military, administrative, and judicial posts were bought, sold, traded, and treated as private property, created centers of power within and against the state. These privileged groups, as Voltaire grimly noted, consumed without producing, escaped taxation, obstructed governmental efficiency, and in general resisted the most essential reforms. Voltaire's admiration for the French crown was more limited than some of his pronouncements might indicate, but he committed himself to it, for only the king and his ministers, supported by an alert public opinion, could pursue the policies the country so desperately needed.

When Voltaire came to Paris after Madame du Châtelet's death, Louis XV was embroiled with the clergy in a major struggle for power; here was a fine opportunity to express his political opinions to a large public. But it seemed that Voltaire would have to be a royalist without, and perhaps even despite, his king, for his position at court was rather ambiguous. In the mid-1740's, Voltaire had turned courtier: he had been appointed Royal Historiographer in 1745, and in the following year, after a shameless campaign, he had finally been elected to the Académie française. But he was too irreverent and too indiscreet to remain popular at court, and when he appeared in Paris in the fall of 1749, he had no close friends there. It did not matter: the fight between king and clergy was too interesting to be resisted.

The issue was taxation. The clergy, as the First Estate of France, and as a major owner of real estate, had a vast income but no obligations to pay taxes. Every five years, at the quinquennial Assembly of the Clergy, it offered a "voluntary gift" to the crown, but in 1749 Machault d'Arnouville, the aggressive finance minister, persuaded his king that this gift was not enough. Accordingly, Louis XV issued an edict imposing a five per cent income tax on all Frenchmen, including the privileged orders. In 1750, when the clergy met to consider this imposition and offered resistance, a war of pamphlets began, and Voltaire was joyfully in the midst of it. In some lighthearted sallies, Voltaire ridiculed clergymen as fat, debauched, useless, lazy; but in May or early June 1750, he wrote a full-scale political tract, *La Voix du sage et du peuple*, which moved from lampoon to a serious attack: the clergy deserved no exemptions and it should have no power in the state, either in politics or over individuals. Clerics were no better than tutors: they should be allowed to teach, but told what to teach and how to teach it.

La Voix du sage was Voltaire's first systematic statement on the political position of the clergy and on the wide gap between Voltaire's ideal and French actuality. The articles in the *Dictionnaire* that bear on these and other political questions are little more than elaborations of this first tract. Reading *La Voix du sage* side by side with such articles as "*Lois civiles et ecclésiastiques*," or "*Prêtre*," is to see the Paris of 1750 in the book of 1764.

In 1764, anticlerical ideas were becoming widespread, thanks partly to Voltaire's intervention in 1750. But in 1750, his radicalism seemed extreme and excessive even to the king in whose behalf it had been expressed. To the timorous and vacillating Louis XV, this kind of royalism concealed—or rather revealed—the most dangerous kind of anticlericalism. Unwelcome at court, Voltaire resolved to leave France. His education was complete, or nearly complete, and his ties with his old world were severed, or nearly severed. Frederick II, who had long wanted to "possess" Voltaire, now had his chance: Voltaire was willing to go to Prussia, perhaps to stay.

It seems right somehow, or even inevitable, that the *Dictionnaire* should be conceived in Prussia, in the uncertain twilight of semi-exile. All of Voltaire's experience is in the book, but it would seem that the thin air of an alien environment was the atmosphere best calculated to create, or at least confirm, the recklessness needed for his final, public break with the established order.

Voltaire at work on his *Dictionnaire* was (to borrow a phrase of Goethe's) like a "creative mirror": he brought to it not only all he had learned until 1752, but in the twelve years of its piecemeal compilation, as his radicalism deepened and grew more pointed, he added his new knowledge and his new convictions to the old store. When Voltaire published the book in 1764 he was almost seventy, but it had neither the serenity nor the resignation of an old man's mind behind it.

The *Dictionnaire philosophique* was born in the summer of 1752, in the impious ambiance of Frederick's Prussian court.[4] By September, Voltaire asked a friend to send him "the Bible dictionary of dom Calmet, with all the volumes of his commentaries." This "vast collection of sacred nonsense," he wrote, "is full of remarkable things."[5] Calmet had been

[4] It remains a matter of argument whether Frederick suggested the task to Voltaire, or whether Voltaire thought it up himself. See my summary of the problem in the "Editor's Introduction," Voltaire's *Philosophical Dictionary*, I, 24-5.

[5] Voltaire to Countess Bentinck, September 29 (1752). *Correspondence*, XXI, 78.

invaluable to Madame du Châtelet in her *Examen de la Genèse;* it was only natural for Voltaire to appeal to the same authority. Through October and November 1752, Voltaire submitted his articles to the Prussian king, his first reader and most enthusiastic critic. Fired with the excitement of a daring enterprise, the approval of his companions, the memories of the Biblical studies at Cirey, and the information drawn from Calmet, Voltaire worked effectively for a while: the articles "*Abraham*," "*Âme*," "*Athée*," and "*Batême*" followed in rapid order.

Then for several years nothing went well, and the manuscript was put aside. The reasons for this intermission are not hard to find: Voltaire quarreled with Frederick in the winter of 1752, and for over three years led a wandering existence. Rejected by Potsdam, rejected by Paris, he traveled restlessly, visited friends, lamented his lot, carried on a passionate affair with his niece, and searched for a home. During his wanderings, he entered this charming story into his notebooks: "Today, 23 June 1754, dom Calmet, abbé of Senones, asked me what was new; I told him that Madame de Pompadour's daughter had died. 'Who is Madame de Pompadour?' he replied."[6] To readers of the *Dictionnaire* the name of dom Calmet is familiar enough; he appears in it as a benighted, superstitious relic of a darker age. But this is just another trick of Voltaire's ungrateful trade: Calmet was kindly, learned, and by no means unwilling to allow his impious visitor to stay in his abbey for a month and use his library.

But while an abbey was a good place to visit, Voltaire did not want to live there. In the winter of 1755, he finally discovered his natural habitat, the neighborhood of Geneva. For the next few years he busied himself with acquiring several

[6] *Voltaire's Notebooks*, ed. Theodore Besterman, 2 vols. continuously paginated (1952), 351.

properties there, and by the end of the 1750's he was settled in Ferney, a *château* on French soil near the Genevan border. He was happy again, very rich, and very purposeful. His house was far from Paris, but with its stream of distinguished visitors and its unceasing flow of correspondence, it became a kind of literary government in exile. Where Voltaire was, *there* was Paris.

These years of readjustment were profoundly unsettling. The dreadful Lisbon earthquake of November 1, 1755, and the far more dreadful Seven Years' War, which broke out in August 1756, permanently alienated Voltaire from whatever remnants of cosmic optimism he had left. He was in a state of peculiar emotional tension: the death of his mistress, the behavior of his friend Frederick of Prussia, and the natural disaster at Lisbon all depressed him deeply. Yet, settling down, repairing houses, designing gardens in a delightful neighborhood were all causes for happiness. As Voltaire observed more than once during these years, he was happy and ashamed of being happy. He tried to resolve this tension first in his poem on the Lisbon earthquake, and then in *Candide*, a book that scorns the illusions of hope but triumphs over despair.

Candide is, in many respects, a rehearsal for the *Dictionnaire*.[7] It illustrates, once again, the inner coherence and pugnacious vitality of Voltaire's thinking. In *Candide*, Voltaire coined the much-quoted phrase that we must cultivate our garden; in the *Dictionnaire* he made clear that for him the phrase meant not Epicurean detachment but humanitarian meddling. He did not neglect literature—he would never do that—but he grew more passionate about social reform. His

[7] See my edition of *Candide* (1963) and the numerous correspondences listed there.

new slogan, *écrasez l'infâme*, expressed his new intensity, and as he planned his major assault on *l'infâme*, he turned once again to the *Dictionnaire*.

He had never wholly forgotten it; even in the dark, aimless years of the early 1750's he had put thoughts into his notebooks which were either intended for the *Dictionnaire* or later found their way into it. As we read these casual entries, we encounter Asian gods, like Xaca or Fo, who haunt the pages of the *Dictionnaire;* we read the observation that "there are virtues and vices as there is health and illness," which is elaborated in "*Catéchisme chinois*"*;* we find tantalizing lists of paradoxes and contradictions that are the germs of some of the theological articles. As the supreme professional, Voltaire wasted nothing but rewrote everything. A felicitous phrase in the notebooks would not be thrown away; it would appear, still more felicitous, in the *Dictionnaire philosophique*. Thus:

NOTEBOOKS	"*Amour-propre*"
Egotism is like that part we must hide and use, which is agreeable, necessary, and dangerous.[8]	This egotism is the instrument of our preservation; it resembles the instrument for the perpetuation of the species: we need it, we cherish it, it gives us pleasure, and we must hide it.

The 1750's, then, were a time for making phrases and storing up ideas, the early 1760's a time for using them. To judge from his infrequent and circumspect allusions in his correspondence, Voltaire resumed concentrated work on the *Dictionnaire* late in 1762 and finished it early in 1764.

Everything was propitious. Voltaire was old, independent,

[8] *Notebooks*, 367.

and relatively safe. Should trouble arise with the French authorities, he could move to Les Délices in Geneva; should Genevan pastors object to his theatrical performances or political interference, he could take refuge at Ferney in France. Now, if ever, was a time to speak out. Others were speaking out, although, as Voltaire noted with some complacency, less well than he. Diderot's *Encyclopédie* was nearing completion: it was a vast undertaking with which Voltaire collaborated, which he defended, but from which he expected little. The *Encyclopédie* was too bulky, too clumsy, too adroit, too expensive, to produce the propagandistic effect he wanted to produce. Diderot, like Voltaire, hoped to "change men's ways of thinking," but Voltaire was convinced that *l'infâme* was strong, solidly entrenched, truly built on a rock. It could be blasted loose only with simplicity, clarity, brevity, and rage: as he composed his articles for Diderot, he inevitably thought of his own, one-man *Encyclopédie*. This is what he meant when he wrote in 1766: "Twenty folio volumes will never make a revolution: it's the small, portable books at thirty *sous* that are dangerous. If the Gospel had cost 1,200 sesterces, the Christian religion would never have been established."[9]

In 1762, Voltaire received a fresh piece of evidence concerning *l'infâme* in action, the Calas case. His imagination, always touched by the concrete and the dramatic, was aroused by the affair. Marc-Antoine Calas, the eldest son of an obscure Huguenot cloth merchant in the city of Toulouse, had been found hanged in his father's shop in October 1761. Jean Calas was convicted of the murder of his son, tortured, and executed in March 1762. It was widely believed that he had committed

[9] Voltaire to d'Alembert, April 5 (1766). *Correspondence*, LXI, 8.

this outrage to prevent Marc-Antoine from converting to Catholicism. When Voltaire first heard the story late that month, it struck him as a fine specimen of Christian fanaticism, no matter whether Jean Calas was guilty or innocent. Guilty, Jean Calas demonstrated the length to which a superstitious Protestant would go to prevent his son from turning Catholic; innocent, Jean Calas demonstrated the stupidity of Catholic magistrates who believed that Huguenots committed ritual murders. Gradually, Voltaire moved from his rather callous, pragmatic view of the case to a general, humane, principled critique of the French judicial system. He became convinced that Calas had been wrongfully imprisoned and wrongfully convicted, and he began a campaign to rehabilitate the old man's memory and to reform the French legal code.[1]

He never stopped learning. What the Calas case taught him was that it was not enough to expose the crimes of religion—politics and law must be reformed as well. But, conversely, to concentrate exclusively on legal reform was to treat the symptom and leave the infection untouched. Thus from 1762 on, as Voltaire wrote petitions on the Calas affair and polemics on French law, he did not forget his larger cause. The *Dictionnaire* rapidly took shape. He importuned his friends for books; in December 1762, evidently working on articles like "*Christianisme*," he asked his Paris correspondent Damilaville to send him "*presto, presto*" a recently published *Dictionnaire des conciles*. "Theology," he wrote acidly, "amuses me; that's where we find the madness of the human spirit in all its plenitude."[2] Again, in May 1763, he asked Damilaville to return

[1] See my *Voltaire's Politics* (1959), ch. 6; and from the voluminous literature, especially David D. Bien, *The Calas Affair* (1960).

[2] December 26 (1762), *Correspondence*, L, 199.

the article "*Idolâtrie*" so that he could insert it in his forthcoming *Dictionnaire*.

It took another year to complete. Finally, in June 1764, a small octavo volume of 344 pages appeared in Geneva, bearing a false London imprint. It contained 73 articles and was entitled *Dictionnaire philosophique portatif*. Its success was immediate, enormous, and predictable: Voltaire had expended all his talents on it. In September, Grimm reported in the exclusive newsletter by which he informed and entertained royal and aristocratic subscribers all over Europe that "there exists a *Dictionnaire philosophique portatif*, a volume of over three hundred pages, published through the indefatigable zeal of the patriarch of Les Délices. But this is true only for the true faithful; as for the malicious, it is proved that this great apostle had no hand in it. Anyway, the entire edition of this precious gospel is down to perhaps twenty or twenty-five copies. Lucky the man who can get one!"[3]

Voltaire gloried in his success and frantically denied his authorship, with as much vigor as he had put into the writing. In letter after letter he begged people to believe that he had not written the book, that he had not even read all of it, that evil-minded enemies were trying to get him into trouble. "I implore you to shout that I've had no hand whatever in the *Portatif*," he wrote to d'Alembert on September 7,[4] and he repeated this injunction almost daily for months.

But it could not be denied—and Voltaire would have been displeased if it could have been denied—that the *Dictionnaire* showed the master's touch on page after page. Hence Voltaire shifted to a new line: the book was nothing but a collection of harmless pieces designed for respectable publications, a collec-

[3] September 1, 1764, *Correspondance littéraire*, ed. Maurice Tourneux (1877-1882), VI, 65.

[4] *Correspondence*, LVI, 6.

tion "by several hands" to which English divines and English deists had made major contributions. This alibi was not a complete lie; rather, it was a partial truth reiterated to produce the effect of a complete lie. At least one of the articles, "*Messie*," was in fact by Voltaire's friend, the Swiss pastor Polier de Bottens[5]; at least one article, "*Idolâtrie*," was actually printed in Diderot's *Encyclopédie;* a handful of articles, such as "*Convulsions*" and "*Miracles*," were patterned closely after the Critical Deist writings of Middleton. But everyone, including Voltaire, was perfectly aware that such judicious borrowings, far from softening, only increased the revolutionary impact of the *Dictionnaire*.

The *Dictionnaire philosophique* made a great stir. The first edition was rapidly sold out, and fortunate owners passed their copies to their friends. Outraged ecclesiastics set to work compiling anti-Philosophical Dictionaries, a tribute to Voltaire's power. He was called a "ferocious beast," an enemy to Christian men, a threat to the Christian community. In September 1764, the Genevan government ordered all copies of the book seized and burned; in December, the same ceremony took place at The Hague; on March 19, 1765, the *parlement* of Paris followed suit; and on July 8, 1765, the book was proscribed by the Holy Office at Rome. Voltaire's response to the first of these condemnations was the wry remark that the Genevan government was welcome to burn a book in which he took no interest, as long as it did not burn him. He promptly began work on a second, enlarged edition.

His notoriety and fame moved him to intermittent fits of panic and, at the same time, to aggressive euphoria. For five years, from 1764 to 1769, he reprinted, revised, and enlarged

[5] On this point see Raymond Naves: *Voltaire et l'Encyclopédie* (1938), *passim.*

the book. There was a new edition in December 1764, yet another in 1765 in two duodecimo volumes, a fourth in 1767. Then, in 1769, the book appeared in its largest form: two solid volumes with 120 articles, including the long dialogue "*L'A, B, C,*" and with the new title, *La Raison par alphabet.* It was reprinted several times in the last nine years of his life, under its final title, *Dictionnaire philosophique.* As the book expanded, so did Voltaire's sympathies. Although he would have been fully entitled to intellectual retirement, he refused to live off his capital. Living in and near Geneva, in close touch with Genevan patricians, publishers, and physicians, he could not help meddling in Genevan politics. In the two decades that Voltaire was concerned with them, Genevan politics were enlivened, and embittered, by an intricate party struggle verging on civil war. A patrician party, anxious to retain the government of the small republic in the hands of an exclusive élite, faced a bourgeois party determined to broaden participation in political decisions to their own group, without however granting the lower orders, the so-called "*natifs,*" any share in the state.

In this complicated fight, Voltaire's natural allies were the patricians. They were his friends. Besides he had spent most of his life saying that the masses were incapable of casting off superstition, were unworthy of self-government. But the more he learned of Genevan history, law, and politics, the more convinced he became of the merits of the bourgeois case, and he shifted his support, which was not without weight in this republic, in accord with his new convictions. But then, in 1766, well after the third edition of the *Dictionnaire* had appeared, the *natifs* entered the scene, and to the dismay of both patricians and bourgeois, Voltaire made himself their champion. He did not become a convert to democracy but, as always in the past, he listened to his experience. These sturdy workmen, gardeners, carpenters, and watchmakers spent their leisure time reading—even reading Voltaire—and Voltaire was moved to modify his facile, snobbish assumption that the poor must be governed by lies and the fear of hell.

This shift toward radicalism, toward appreciation of the possibilities of universal enlightenment, is subtly reflected in the successive editions of the *Dictionnaire*. In the first edition, the articles "*États*" and "*Égalité*" demand government by the rule of law but appear resigned to drastic inequality as inevitable and even useful. It is only in "*Fraude*" (characteristically a dialogue, for the issue was unresolved in Voltaire's mind) that one of the speakers suggests the need for honesty with all citizens, even the lowliest. But some of the later articles take a more radical line. "*Torture*" recalls the Calas and La Barre cases in its assault on French legal practice; and "*L'A, B, C*" is even prepared to toy with the possibility that democracy is the best form of government. The Voltaire of 1769 was no longer the Voltaire of 1764.

This is the biography of the *Dictionnaire*—or almost all of it. In the last eight years of his life, from 1770 to 1778, Voltaire's inventiveness declined, but not his vigor. He was active against *l'infâme* to the last, and now published some of the Critical Deist works he had begun thirty years before. The continuing success of the *Dictionnaire* gave him a formula which he adopted, to the confusion of his later editors, in another work. In 1770, he brought out another dictionary, a nine-volume alphabetical compendium entitled *Questions sur l'Encyclopédie*. It contained and expanded some of the articles from the *Dictionnaire*, and scores of new ones, fighting the same battles over again. When he returned to Paris in February 1778, very old and very feeble, he was *l'homme aux Calas* to the thousands who acclaimed him: a social reformer, a humanitarian, a radical anticlerical. Only the cultivated remembered, or cared, that he had also written tragedies, comedies, and dramatic criticism. That this shift in the image of Voltaire should have occurred was the result of his labors of the last twenty years. The man of *Œdipe* and *Zaïre* had become the man of the *Dictionnaire.*

2 · *The Book in Its Culture*

I said at the beginning that the *Dictionnaire philosophique* is not a dictionary. The remark has its risks: it invites the witticism that the book is not philosophical either. But to make it would be to miss the significance of philosophy for the *philosophes*. For the men of the Enlightenment, philosophy was not one discipline among many but *the* discipline—the mobilization of sound thinking for the sake of right living. With repetitive and almost obsessive vehemence, the *philosophes* denigrated metaphysics and joked about system-makers. In fact, they were so preoccupied with practicality that they sometimes skirted close to philistine anti-intellectualism, a trap they avoided only by their comprehensive definition of what was practical and by the pleasure they took in the play of mind for its own sake. Yet, for all their playfulness, they viewed the task of philosophy with grim seriousness, and first in the order of priority was the destruction of error. Locke, whom Voltaire made the hero of the Continental Enlightenment, had thought it "ambition enough to be employed as an under-labourer in clearing the ground a little, and removing some of the rubbish that lies in the way to knowledge," and Voltaire's *Dictionnaire* was perhaps the most savage rubbish-clearer of the age.

Still, for the *philosophes* the epithets "Age of Philosophy" and "Age of Criticism" were not alternatives but synonyms. They accompanied the most unsparing criticism with the most persistent concern for moral and political construction; they accepted Cicero's dictum in *De officiis* that "no man not concerned with ethics can call himself a philosopher"; and for them (as for him) ethics was virtue in action.

This conjunction has often been overlooked; the *philosophes* have often been accused of being "merely negative" or "merely destructive." To be sure, some of their belligerent language makes this interpretation plausible, but the energy that animated them was a drive for knowledge and control, a restless Faustian dissatisfaction with mere surfaces. Their favorite method was analysis; their essential atmosphere, freedom; their goal, reality. The most popular metaphors of their writings were not merely metaphors of battle but metaphors of penetration: they spoke of the light that pierces corners of darkness, the blow that levels barriers of censorship, the fresh wind that lifts the veil of religious authority, the surgical knife that cuts away the accumulation of tradition, the eye that sees through the mask of political mystery-mongers. If philosophy was destructive, that was because destruction had become the precondition of construction.

I am far from suggesting that hostility or destructiveness were absent from their mode of thought; indeed, I strongly suspect that most of them, Voltaire among them, rather relished both. But negativity was not an end in itself. Disingenuous as the *philosophes* may have been in expressing regret at the necessity for war, their assumption that war was inevitable was correct enough. As self-appointed knight errants of truth, they found the makers of myth and the forces of privilege planted like grim-faced guardians before a precious hoard. And the identity of the enemy was, as it were, emblazoned on their shields: it was Christianity.

Voltaire for one always came back to that: it was to the interest of ecclesiastics everywhere to keep men in the condition of ignorant and submissive children; it was to their interest to immolate human victims, stamp out rational dissent, enforce a deadening uniformity, and reject sound science; it was to their interest to quibble about meaningless philosophical constructions and waste the time of educated men on ridiculous theological controversies. In a word, the church was the implacable enemy of progress, decency, humanity, and rationality. For the first time in history, a happy society, based on power over nature, was within the grasp of men, but Christians were exerting all their energies to obstruct its realization. The vicious interests of Christianity, Voltaire argued further, were matched by its power, cleverness, and lack of scruple. Christian notions were inculcated early and reinforced by dire threats; hence they were hard to uproot. They were handed on from generation to generation; they paralyzed the powerful and seduced the intelligent. These are the despairing themes of several articles in the *Dictionnaire*, and they dictated its author's tactics.

The battle of the *philosophes* with Christianity is a commonplace in intellectual history, but we must understand its intensity before we can really understand the *Dictionnaire*. For, despite the crystalline clarity of its writing and the immediate appeal of its wit, the book is in many respects opaque to the twentieth-century reader. Why should a popular polemic devote at least half of its space to abstruse technical questions of theology, church history, or man's knowledge of the soul? Why should Voltaire, who was not a compulsive crank but a rational man of letters, concentrate his energies and expend his venom on matters that would arouse only a small group of students today?

The answer is that the eighteenth century was very different from our own. Theology was still important and still familiar; theological controversies had far more than academic interest—they went to the heart of daily concerns, to the very meaning of existence. It is no longer fashionable to speak of the warfare between science and theology, and in truth the seventeenth and eighteenth centuries produced a finely shaded spectrum of beliefs and tolerated close alliances between scientists and theologians, God and nature, the pulpit and the laboratory. Nevertheless, the notion of two parties, of believers against unbelievers, retains much validity. A man could be a scientist and a Christian at the same time, as Newton, the greatest of them all, demonstrated. But a man could not at the same time regard Christianity as uniquely true and subject it to the kind of rationalist critique he directed against other religions; he could not at the same time think of the Jews as God's Chosen People and investigate their history as objectively as the history of ordinary nations; he could not at the same time revere the Bible as *the* Book and read it in the same way that he read all other books.

Voltaire's logical, historical, and textual exegeses were thus more than an intellectual game. The task of persuasion, to which the *Dictionnaire* addressed itself, was (as the *philosophes* would have liked to say) practical, but it was also (as Voltaire often said) far from simple. Christianity was not only a mighty but also a many-sided enemy. It had a sacred predecessor, the Jews; an authoritative text, the Bible; an ethics of humility and self-abnegation; a history filled with affecting martyrs and impressive miracles; a philosophy of science and a theory of politics. In the *Dictionnaire philosophique* Voltaire attacked them all, rather like a modern Hercules face to face with a modern Hydra.

The stakes in this attack on Christian theology were higher than the fate of theology itself: to discredit Christianity was to take a decisive step in the direction of a secular, modern civilization. The decade of the *Dictionnaire*, the 1760's, was a time of great beginnings. It marked the quickening of mechanical inventions, improvements in agricultural productivity, and the establishment of industrial discipline. It saw the beginnings of what R. R. Palmer has recently called the "Age of the Democratic Revolution," a widespread rebellion against time-honored constituted authority, a rising demand for self-government, and rudimentary essays in popular political activity. It was the decade in which Rousseau published his most revolutionary books, the *Contrat social* and *Émile*, Diderot completed his *Encyclopédie*, and Holbach deluged Europe with his atheist tracts. Voltaire had angry contempt for the first, cool respect for the second, and (as the article "*Athée*" shows) vehement disagreements with the third of these men; but Rousseau, Diderot, Holbach, and Voltaire, an improbable team of reluctant allies, were yoked together in a single enterprise: the movement for modernity.

The *Dictionnaire*, a single cannon in a sizable battery, could fire its shots from a sheltered position. Many of the resonances evoked by its arguments could be evoked because Voltaire belonged to a formidable tradition of revolutionary dissent. And yet, for all its borrowings, for all the reinforcements it received from Voltaire's contemporaries, for all its family resemblances to other works, it was, as I said at the beginning, a deeply personal book.

One characteristic that makes the *Dictionnaire philosophique* Voltairian is its duplicity. Not all the *philosophes* used Voltaire's strategies: Rousseau signed all that he wrote, and Diderot restricted much of his best work to his intimate friends. Consequently, Voltaire's transparent mendacity has often been severely criticized; it has been taken as a constitutional inability to tell the truth, or at least as a cowardly, unnecessary precaution: did not the French government engage in a good-natured charade with writers, burning an offending work in a harmless ritual designed to impress the ignorant public without frightening the author, who, in turn, denied his responsibility for a book everyone knew he had written?

But such criticisms, while they expose one of Voltaire's weaknesses, gravely underestimate the vigor and the capriciousness of French censorship. Forbidden books were effectively driven off the market, and only the adroit or wealthy could find or afford them. Since censorship was slow and arbitrary, a book approved by a royal censor might be prohibited by the *parlements* or attacked by the clergy. Booksellers were harassed, and authors intimidated. Diderot's reluctance to publish his more daring productions after his imprisonment in 1749, or the fate of Rousseau, hounded from refuge to refuge, lend weight to Voltaire's lament of 1758: "It is a real pity that we cannot tell the truth in anything touching metaphysics and even history. . . . We are compelled to lie, and then we are still persecuted for not having lied enough."[6] Voltaire's mendacity is to some degree a reflection on him, but it casts a far larger shadow on his age: a country that compels its writers to be liars has only itself to blame if its writers lie.

Not all of Voltaire's duplicity should be called lying. Much of it, as I have said earlier, was meant as irony. For his con-

[6] Voltaire to Diderot, June 26 (1758). *Correspondence*, XXXIII, 278.

temporaries, this irony was delicious, because it was adroitly executed and reassuringly familiar. Today we are in danger of overlooking the adroitness because the familiarity has faded. It may therefore be useful if I offer some program notes to his ironic self-dramatization, a short guide to his roles.

The Bewildered Believer. Voltaire often tries to discredit Christian doctrines by pitting the pronouncements of theologians against one another. In "*Arius*" he appears confused and outraged by controversies over the nature of the Trinity. This pose is doubly ironic: a sincere believer, seeking theological clarity, might well be bewildered by quarrels over "hypostasis" and "generative power," but there is not an ounce of sincere search in Voltaire. Merely by listing them, he depicts all positions on the Trinity as equally absurd and all controversies about it as equally futile. His aim is to destroy, not to understand. Again, Voltaire, probably with conscious irony, is parodying ancient Christian tactics; many centuries before, the Fathers of the Church had attracted pagans to Christianity by unmasking the unending disagreements of pagan philosophers on the most important questions.

The Clever Prosecutor. Turning Christian arguments against Christianity is first cousin to turning statements from believers against belief. As the clever prosecutor, Voltaire puts unfriendly witnesses on the stand and compels them to condemn themselves by their own words. In "*Jephthé*" he cites Judges to convict the Biblical Jews of practicing human sacrifices; in "*Conciles*" he quotes from the emperor Constantine's letter to Hosius to convict the Church Fathers of pettiness and pride. This pose, apparently so straightforward, also has its ironic overtones. Voltaire relies on his unfriendly witnesses only when they confess their own crimes or castigate the crimes of their fellow-believers, but he refuses to accept their testimony when they speak well of themselves or their brethren. As the first Christian emperor, Constantine is a hypocrite and an assassin, but Constantine berating other Christians is heard with respect, and transformed, for a brief moment, into a *philosophe*.

The Grand Inquisitor. The role of prosecutor is not free from difficulties. Its rationale, advanced in "*Jephthé*," is that we can judge peoples only by their own archives. But since neither Jews nor Christians had ever claimed to be perfect, proof of imperfection is no argument against the religion these sinners practice. To be sure, Voltaire does not rest his case against religion entirely, or even chiefly, on the sins of its devotees; he expends much ingenuity unmasking the illogic of religion itself. But he never forgets the consequences of religious beliefs and institutions; a century before Dostoevski's Grand Inquisitor, he takes the position that the effects of Christianity have been the tragic opposite of its program. This too is an ironic role: Voltaire has little use for Christian morality even at its purest, but he is willing to use the Sermon on the Mount to demonstrate how far Christians have fallen from the announced aims of Christ. Voltaire strikes this pose, at once belligerent and despairing, in the very first article: the true "*Abbé*," as the name implies, is a father, not a lazy wastrel; and what has happened to the vows of poverty and obedience? Again, he writes in "*Miracles*" that a religion based on the true miracles of Our Savior has been degraded by the fantastic and laughable claims of modern priests. Voltaire, as the reader well knows, believes neither the "true" ancient miracles nor the false modern ones, but this insincerity (which depends for its effectiveness on its transparency) does not weaken his point: even if Christianity, at the beginning, was humane and impressive, it has lost, and had to lose, all its virtues.

The Beleaguered Catholic. Few pleasures are as pure as quoting enemies against themselves, but Voltaire was quite ready to vary his tactics and quote allies against enemies. He had to be cautious, for his allies were often dangerous company: pagans, freethinkers, rakes, or Unitarians. If they were to be quoted, they must be censured, no matter how feebly; they must, as it were, be praised with faint damns. Here, Voltaire is the beleaguered Catholic, troubled by what appear to be persuasive arguments by heretics, schismatics, or infidels. In "*Antitrinitaires*" he deftly expounds the Unitarians' denunciations of the Trinity for more than two pages, and then, with bland piety and deliberate ineffectiveness, dismisses these arguments as inexcusable, since Church Councils have decided that they are wrong.

The Subversive Anthropologist. Voltaire was a real cosmopolitan, fond of England, impressed with China, attached to pagan Greece and Rome. But when he praises all these in the *Dictionnaire*, he is doing more than giving way to affection; he is using the method of invidious comparison and exploiting his own feelings: at once involved and detached, he manipulates them as though they were not his own. For "England is free and happy because it has free speech," read: "France, which has censorship, is miserably backward." For "the Chinese literati have an admirable religion free from superstitions and the rage to persecute," read: "Catholics have a despicable faith, steeped in superstition and stained with persecution." When, in "*Morale*," he scornfully denies the imputation that ancient pagans had no morality, he is not only defending his beloved Cicero and Marcus Aurelius, he is asserting their superiority over Christians, who father such ridiculous slanders but have embarrassingly little morality of their own. In "*Tolérance*" he even uses the Jews as models: the Jews in the Roman Empire, he writes, stubbornly clung to their deity, but they did not resent the gods of others. We happen to know from his correspondence that for once his praise of the Jews was sincere, but in the *Dictionnaire* his point is that the Jews, bad as they are, are far better than the Christians: "The Jews didn't want the statue of Jupiter in Jerusalem; but the Christians didn't want it in the Capitol." Reader (as Voltaire would say), draw your own conclusions.

The Intelligent Ignoramus. The great ironist of antiquity was Socrates, and his most effective pose the pose of ignorance. Voltaire, who admired Socrates without wishing to emulate him, used ignorance with similar intentions and similar results. In Voltaire's hands, ignorance was at once a working principle and a weapon. As a good Lockian and a good Newtonian, he was convinced that there is much we do not and cannot know, that we must concentrate our energies and bring what we can know to bear on the formulation of rational policies. But his insistent reiteration of ignorance is also an ironic pose: if as educated and intelligent a thinker as Voltaire is puzzled by so much, other men must be equally in the dark. Hence all dogmatic theology, all tales of miracles are thrown into doubt, for theology depends on the unknowable, miracles depend on the undemonstrable. A philosophical dictionary is in and of itself an ironic place for the pose of ignorance, and some of Voltaire's happiest inventions in the book match this larger irony. In "*Ezéchiel*" he lends his cloak of ignoramus to a learned rabbi, who expatiates at some length on obscure passages in Ezekiel and Hosea, and then confronts Voltaire: " 'But do you know what all this means?' 'No,' I told him. 'Neither do I,' said the rabbi."

The Outraged Humanitarian. Voltaire's humanitarian activities are a matter of public record, but the purity of his motives has often been questioned. Such suspicions may be petty and are certainly wrong, but they are not useless: they point to Voltaire's self-dramatization. The *Dictionnaire* is filled with humanitarian rage; much of its energy comes from diatribes in which Voltaire expends his fury on Inquisitors who burn heretics, on Calvin who "assassinated" Servetus, rulers who gaily destroy flourishing countries in aggressive wars, judges who condemn accused men to torture, scholars who denigrate the Emperor Julian, ecclesiastics who impose Lent on the poor. In "*Fausseté des vertus humaines*" he falls upon a priest who has written a book denying human virtue, thus libeling all non-Christians by implication. Does this mean, asks Voltaire, that Epictetus was a rascal just because he was a pagan? "I'll say no more about it, lest I grow furious."

Was this fury real? To judge from his notebooks and the testimony of his most intimate friends, it was; it is not put in doubt, nor is its value diminished, by our discovery that it is used by a controlled artist. Rage and pity are all the more formidable when they are eloquent; they are particularly powerful in a writer notorious for his light touch and petty malice, for in him they are a dramatic change of pace. They come as an unforgettable shock. No doubt Voltaire enjoyed his rage, but his ironic detachment from his emotion did not kill that emotion—it converted incoherent exclamations into firmly pointed polemics. Voltaire the outraged humanitarian is playing a role, but he is playing himself.

Not one of these devices was new; they were familiar instruments of controversy in an age in which Gibbon could write his celebrated footnotes, or David Hume could remark in his essay on miracles that "The Christian religion not only was at first attended with miracles, but even at this day cannot be believed by any reasonable person without one."[7] The devices derived much of their power—I cannot insist on this enough—from their familiarity: they established immediate communication with educated readers and facilitated communication with the new reading public. Unlike our own century, the eighteenth did not make a fetish of originality; it enjoyed writing "imitations" and liked to soften the strange idea by the familiar form, the radical proposal by the traditional manner. That is why Pope could define "true wit" as

> Nature to advantage dressed,
> What oft was thought but ne'er so well expressed.

That is why Voltaire, rather than inventing techniques, combined and varied known techniques.

But these techniques had never been so skillfully employed. Consider his insistent, almost painful repetition of a single word to establish an inescapable mood (in "*Histoire des rois juifs et paralipomènes*" he uses the word "assassinate" fifteen times in one sentence to convict the Biblical Jews of bloodthirsty cruelty); his witty transposition of one issue into another (in "*Catéchisme du Japonais*" he ridicules the quarrels of Christian sects over theology by depicting schools of cooking disputing over recipes); his deft injection of piquant speculation to keep interest high (the article "*Amour nommé Socratique*" is an amusing examination of homosexuality, "*Des Loix*" exalts equity over legal fetishism with a very funny story about double incest, and "*Joseph*" playfully considers various types of eunuchs); his use, rare and more enjoyable

[7] "Concerning Human Understanding," *The Philosophical Works of David Hume*, eds. T. H. Green and T. H. Grose, 4 vols. (1882), IV, 108.

for being rare, of scatological material (as in "*Ezéchiel*" and his famous "lunch"); his straight-faced sentences which begin in one key and modulate into another (the first sentence of "*Conciles*" begins "All councils are doubtless infallible," but ends "for they are composed of men")—these are Voltaire's inimitable, unmistakable signature.

Voltaire's *Dictionnaire philosophique* thus stands in a strategic mediating position between its author and its culture, and throws light on both. The culture set the author his problems and gave him his information; the author responded to his culture with his talents and his idiosyncrasies. But the book does not merely reflect its times; it also changed them. It taught generations to be critical and to laugh at the sacred. Today, to be sure, while its irreverence remains relevant and its humanity all too necessary, its specific victims no longer look so formidable. It takes historical imagination to appreciate how serious was Voltaire's fight, but then it is the fate of all successful polemics to make themselves unnecessary in the long run. That, I suppose, is the final irony of Voltaire's masterpiece.

2

VOLTAIRE'S *IDÉES RÉPUBLICAINES:* FROM DETECTION TO INTERPRETATION

> Car pour moi je ne dis mot. Je ne suis pas de la paroisse.
> —VOLTAIRE TO FRANÇOIS TRONCHIN, *December 24, 1764*

VOLTAIRE said more than once that he was not interested in politics. We need only to read him to know that this is a typical Voltairian disclaimer. It arouses, and was designed to arouse, disbelief. Voltaire was not interested in political theorizing, for he distrusted systems and dogmas in all areas of inquiry. But throughout his life he intervened in political controversies, meddling whether asked to or not, and sometimes even when entreated to mind his own business. His comments on politics are scattered through his writings, and his few specifically political works are occasional, controversial pamphlets.

Of these political pamphlets, the *Idées républicaines* holds a favored place with commentators; it is probably more frequently cited as a source of Voltaire's political ideas than any other of his writings, not excepting the political articles in the *Dictionnaire philosophique* and the dialogue *L'A,B,C.* With its vigorous assaults on despotism and clerical pretensions, its forceful defense of republicanism and the rule of law, the *Idées* has been quarried as a rich mine of Voltaire's liberal, humane, and "impractical" political philosophy.

For all its celebrity, there has always been an intriguing—and, as I shall show, an instructive—mystery about the *Idées:* precisely when did Voltaire write it? The pamphlet, an octavo brochure of 45 pages, seems reluctant to yield this secret to the reader: a characteristic eighteenth-century production, it shows neither date nor place of publication. Nor does it give the author's name: Voltaire believed in telling the whole truth only when he could not avoid it. But while the "*membre d'un corps*" speaking in the *Idées* claims to be a Genevan, he is Voltairian in style and in feeling.

While the author and the place of publication are easily identified, the date of composition and of publication offer obstacles, indeed greater ones than has been realized. The three most scholarly editions of Voltaire's *œuvres complètes* agree in assigning the *Idées* to 1762. The Kehl editors of 1785 started the fashion. Beuchot's great edition, distinguished by critical intelligence and supreme good sense, retained the Kehl date of 1762, despite the fact that in the rash of unreliable editions flooding France in the 1820's the pamphlet was dated 1765, without ceremony and without apparent justification.[1] Beuchot explained in a footnote that it "must be of

[1] Among the editions that date the *Idées républicaines* 1765 are those of Renouard (1819–1825), Lequien (1820–1826), Delangle (1828–34), and Didot (1843).

1762, year of the publication of the *Contrat social*, of which the *Idées républicaines* is a critique. It seems to me to be a mistake to have dated this pamphlet 1765."[2] A few later editions, popular and of little editorial merit, clung to 1765, but Beuchot's scholarly authority was decisive. Louis Moland, who in the 1870's began to bring out the edition of Voltaire that is now standard, found no reason to cavil at Beuchot's date of 1762—indeed, he reproduced Beuchot's footnote without comment or modification.[3] Whatever doubt may have been left was extinguished by Georges Bengesco's authoritative bibliography of Voltaire's works. Bengesco allowed himself a "?" after "1762," but in view of his assurance this was only a polite nod to modesty. "In the *Idées républicaines*," he said flatly, echoing Beuchot, "Voltaire criticizes several passages of the *Contrat social* by Jean-Jacques Rousseau; now, the *Contrat social* appeared in 1762. . . . The *Idées républicaines* must therefore be from the year 1762."[4]

With Bengesco's confirmation, Voltaire scholars seem to have accepted 1762 as a certainty. Recent bibliographical articles supplementing and correcting Bengesco's four volumes say nothing about the *Idées*, and students of Voltaire's politics, such as Havens, Maestro, and Rowe, have accepted 1762 without a murmur.[5]

But the evidence for this date is feeble, and the reasoning that guided these editors and bibliographers is flimsy. The

[2] Beuchot, 72 vols. (1829–1840), XL, 567. Beuchot notes correctly that the Kehl editors had given the subtitle wrongly as "*par un citoyen de Genève*," omitted paragraphs LI to LX, and consolidated several others. Beuchot restored the original title and text. The erroneous title and the omissions were copied by most of the later editions, and Beuchot was right to be suspicious of the scholarship of his contemporary editors.

[3] Moland, 52 vols. (1877–1885), XXIV, 413. But this is hardly

Kehl editors did not justify their choice of a date, Moland and Bengesco simply followed Beuchot, and Beuchot's argument is invalid: The *Idées* criticizes Rousseau's *Contrat social*, the *Contrat social* appeared in 1762, hence the *Idées* must be of 1762.

This line of reasoning would permit editors to be even more precise: the *Idées* contains not only criticisms of the *Contrat social*, but a condemnation of the Genevan authorities for burning it, and since we know that the *Contrat social* was burned with *Émile* on June 19, 1762, Voltaire must have written the *Idées* in the second half of 1762.[6] But is it not absurd to equate the earliest possible date of composition with the actual date of composition? It *is* absurd, but Beuchot did precisely that, and later scholars accepted it without complaint.

It would be tempting to ascribe such reasoning to naïveté or to carelessness. But such an ascription would be gratuitous and, in any case, mistaken—Beuchot was neither naïve nor careless. It is far more fruitful to ask: What presuppositions about Voltaire's character and method of working are concealed in Beuchot's reasoning? I suggest that Beuchot must have thought of Voltaire as impulsive and frivolous. These

---

decisive since Moland rarely goes beyond Beuchot.

[4] Bengesco: *Voltaire. Bibliographie de ses œuvres*, 4 vols. (1882-1890), II, 111.

[5] The one exception I have found is Paul Chaponnière, who casually refers to the *Idées* in a discussion of the events of 1765. See his *Voltaire chez les Calvinistes* (1936), 215.

[6] "We burned this book. The operation of burning it was perhaps as odious as that of writing it. There are things that a wise government should ignore. If this book was dangerous, it needed to be refuted. To burn a rational book is to say, 'We do not have enough intelligence to reply to it.'" *Œuvres* (ed. Moland), XXIV, 424.

assumptions, I think, are necessary to Beuchot, and they are widespread among writers on Voltaire. But they are wrong.

All too many biographers, encouraged by Byron's and Taine's portraits, have depicted a Voltaire, the inconstant and facile courtier, flitting from subject to subject, a *bon mot* in each hand. Beuchot and Bengesco seem to have shared this view. "Now, the *Contrat social* appeared in 1762. . . . The *Idées républicaines* must therefore be from the year 1762." *Therefore?* Some large assumptions are concealed in that word. Had Voltaire no staying power? Could he criticize a book only in the year it was published? His entire career proves that he could drop a subject and return to it years later with fresh energy.[7] Byron called Voltaire "gay, grave, sage, or wild," but the picture of Voltaire the lightheaded dilettante is an inept caricature. He was, rather, a methodical, systematic, hard-working, and thoughtful scholar. If his criticisms of the *Contrat social* were our only clues to dating the *Idées républicaines*, we could be no more specific than to conclude that he could have written the pamphlet at any time from 1762 to 1778.

Beuchot's view of Voltaire as a frivolous poet is significant because it implies other, even more damaging traits. It suggests that Voltaire was remote from harsh reality, that his understanding of the political process was inadequate and his reform program impractical. And his lack of realism, in turn, makes it plausible to see Voltaire as an abstract political thinker. In

[7] Montesquieu's *Esprit des lois* appeared in 1748, but Voltaire sniped at it for a quarter of a century. The trial of Elizabeth Canning took place in London in 1753, and Voltaire probably read about it in the same year; yet he did not mention the case until nine years later, when he needed it to point a moral about French legal procedure. His notebooks show, too, that he could allude in his old age to events that had happened long before.

fact, this conception of Voltaire still haunts students of Voltaire's political ideas; they still derive from his writings a political philosophy irrelevant to life, unconnected with specific controversies or specific policies.

Voltaire the political thinker has been unlucky in having nearly all his interpreters stress the theoretical side of his work; his ideas have been torn from their context, his political writings have usually been searched for some general political position.[8] But if there is a political thinker for whose ideas an analysis through the social and historical context is more appropriate than for Voltaire's, I do not know him. His pronouncements were deeply embedded in and sprang directly from his political experience. The Germans, noting the intimate relation of experience to poetry in Goethe, called him their *Erlebnisdichter*. Voltaire was an *Erlebnispolitiker*. To neglect this side of his character is to impoverish his thought; indeed, it is to make his thought incomprehensible.

With few exceptions Voltaire's political pamphlets grew out of controversies. The pamphlets rarely unveil their true nature to the twentieth-century reader, for they are nearly always elliptical: Voltaire seldom alludes directly to his opponent or to the point of contention. In *La Voix du sage et du peuple* (1750), to take one prominent example, he advocates undivided sovereignty and secular supremacy over all public affairs, including ecclesiastical matters. His language throughout is general: he appears to be stating principles of universal validity and of no specific application. There is not a word about the *vingtième* tax, which the French government was at this time trying to impose upon all orders of

[8] I shall cite only one of many instances: Georges Pellissier's intelligent *Voltaire philosophe* (1908). Pellissier quotes the *Idées* repeatedly, but never illuminates the meaning of the quotations by the context.

society; not a word about *chancelier* Machault, who had originated the tax and whose policy Voltaire supported with enthusiasm; not a word about the rebellious Assembly of the Clergy of 1750, which was resisting the government's claim that the state had a right to tax the church. Yet *La Voix du sage et du peuple*, although silent on the *vingtième*, Machault, and the Assembly, is precisely about these three. His contemporaries knew it, the Kehl editors knew it, and the modern student of his political ideas must once again learn it. Voltaire's universal pronouncements may have universal import, but we can comprehend it only when we understand the environment in which they originated.

We see what we seek. Beuchot and those who followed him thought of Voltaire's politics as impulsive and abstract. Hence they found few specific political allusions in the *Idées républicaines*. Its criticisms of Rousseau's *Contrat social* and of Montesquieu's *Esprit des lois*, and its defense of Rousseau's right to talk nonsense—these alone appeared to them to refer to specific events and ideas. They took Voltaire's statements about despotism, arbitrary government, the power of the clergy, the rule of law, the interpretation of the laws by the courts, the treatment of prisoners, sumptuary legislation, toleration, to be general pronouncements, applicable to all times and all places without reference to specific events. Their preconceptions about Voltaire's character seem to have been so firmly held that they overlooked the direct allusion in the *Idées* to the *Esprit des lois* which had, after all, been published as long ago as 1748—an allusion that should have demonstrated Voltaire's attention span. Instead, they took for granted that the *Idées* must have been written immediately after the last of the events specifically mentioned in it. Hence the date 1762 was almost inevitable.

Once we abandon this erroneous conception of Voltaire,

once we see him truly as an occasional pamphleteer, a practical political reformer whose motto was *Au fait!*, the pronouncements of the *Idées républicaines* take on a much more meaningful shape. And once we place the *Idées* in its historical context, we begin to discover evidence that makes it very unlikely that the pamphlet was published in 1762. The first exhibit is an argument from silence, and it concerns Rousseau. After Rousseau's *Contrat social* was burned, his friends kept him informed of developments in Geneva. Rousseau was appalled at the passivity of his supporters: a handful of his friends objected to the proceedings of the Council of Twenty-Five as precipitous and illegal, but most of the Genevan bourgeoisie, whose cause Rousseau symbolized, and whose political position the *Contrat social* embodied, did not protest. On May 12, 1763, after nearly a year of growing disenchantment, Rousseau renounced his cherished Genevan citizenship. "They were silent when they should have spoken," he wrote a year later in the *Lettres écrites de la montagne*, "they spoke when nothing remained but to be silent." It is not likely that a single paragraph in a single pamphlet would have dispelled Rousseau's despair, but it is likely that he would have known of any public defense and noted it with gratitude, especially if it had come from such a powerful and (Rousseau was certain) hostile personage as Voltaire. In the general silence, Voltaire's brief defense of Rousseau in the *Idées* would have reverberated loudly. Yet to the best of my knowledge Rousseau never mentions the pamphlet in his correspondence or elsewhere.[9] This, then, is a first indication

[9] The two leading books on Rousseau and Geneva, Gaspard Vallette, *Jean-Jacques Rousseau Genevois* (1911), and John Stephenson Spink, *Jean-Jacques Rousseau et Genève* (1934), do not mention the *Idées républicaines*.

—no more—that the *Idées républicaines* was published after 1762.

This indication is strengthened by other evidence. In the midst of a ringing, typically Voltairian denunciation of clerical power, there is this exclamation: "An ecclesiastical assembly that presumed to make a citizen kneel before it, would be playing the part of a pedant correcting children, or of a tyrant punishing slaves."[1] Making a citizen kneel—a surprising image differing, if only in intensity, from the sentences that surround it. The image turns into a concrete description once we connect it with the Covelle case. In February 1763 the Genevan Consistory (the "ecclesiastical assembly") had condemned one Robert Covelle to genuflect and listen to a reprimand as a sign of repentance for having fathered an illegitimate child. Covelle refused to kneel and was given two weeks to think it over. He took advantage of this respite to consult Voltaire, who found the affair irresistible. He ceremoniously greeted Covelle as *Monsieur le fornicateur*—a salutation which the simple Covelle appears to have taken as an honorific title—and took up his pen.[2] He published a pamphlet against genuflection, harassed his friends, and succeeded, after six years of sporadic controversy, in having genuflection (this kind at any rate) abolished in Geneva. It is reasonable to assume that the sentence in the *Idées* about kneeling is an allusion to this case.

Voltaire's preoccupation with Covelle may help us to date the pamphlet more precisely. Perhaps his most revealing allusion to Covelle comes in the *Questions sur les miracles*, first published as a series of pamphlets from July to December 1765. It is a prolonged diatribe against Christian theology, but

[1] *Œuvres*, XXIV, 415.

[2] See Chaponnière: *Voltaire chez les Calvinistes*, 210; and Voltaire's poem, *La Guerre civile de Genève*.

surprisingly Voltaire shifts to politics in the middle of the book; he presents a series of letters ostensibly written by "M. Covelle," who comments at some length on the Genevan civil strife of 1765, and uses expressions that closely resemble those of the *Idées*.[3] The patent similarities between the two works raise the question whether the *Idées*, too, reflects the Genevan situation of late 1765. A remark in the *Idées* on the peaceful settlement of disputes lends support to this thesis: "It is perhaps useful that there should be two parties in a republic, because one watches the other, and because men need watchdogs. That a republic should need mediators is perhaps not as shameful as people think; indeed, it proves that there is obstinacy on both sides; but it also proves that both sides have much spirit, much intelligence, great sagacity in interpreting the laws in different senses; and then arbitrators are needed who will clarify the laws under dispute, who will change them if necessary, and who will anticipate new changes as soon as possible."[4] There is nothing shameful in a republic's need for mediators—a revealing line of argument, for as Voltaire well knew, Genevan class and party struggles in the eighteenth century had twice reached such a pitch of bitterness that outside mediation had become necessary. And as he knew even better, in the mid-1760's mediation appeared once again to have become inevitable. On August 21, 1763, about two

[3] Compare: *Questions sur les miracles:* "pastors are not magistrates. . . . The times are gone when laymen don't dare to think, and it is no longer permitted to give us acorns when we have got bread for ourselves." *Œuvres*, XXV, 409. *Idées républicaines:* "In the times when academies were made up of pastors alone, and they alone possessed the jargon of knowledge, it was reasonable for them alone to nominate all the professors; that was the policy of acorns. But today when laymen are enlightened, the civil power should take back its right to nominate to all pulpits." *Œuvres*, XXIV, 417.

[4] *Œuvres*, XXIV, 427-8.

years before talk of mediation had become general in Geneva, Voltaire had written prophetically to Choiseul: "You'll soon hear people talk about the city of Geneva, and I believe you will be obliged to be arbitrator between the people and the magistrate, for you are guarantor of the laws of this little town."[5] Voltaire, that "creature of air and flame," as Taine had called him, knew his Genevan history. To understand the *Idées*, we must understand some of this history, too.

When Voltaire settled near Geneva in 1755, the politics of the city-state were quiet on the surface. It was a deceptive calm, for political divisions ran deep, and discontents had not been permanently appeased by earlier settlements. The intensity of these discontents was exacerbated by the smallness of the state: party leaders knew each other, and personal hatreds sharpened class resentments and political frustrations. The political public constituted a fraction of the total population—only 1,500 privileged males among the 25,000 inhabitants enjoyed citizenship rights.

Apologists for Geneva portrayed it as a haven of liberty, toleration, and equality, and its government as a happy synthesis of the best in monarchy, aristocracy, and democracy. In 1754 Jean-Jacques Rousseau, Geneva's most illustrious son, celebrated the Genevan republic for achieving a government in conformity with natural law. In the following year, Voltaire, Geneva's most illustrious visitor, surpassed Rousseau's rhapsody with a paean to the goddess of liberty, who dwelt by the glorious lake of Geneva.[6]

This impassioned rhetoric clashed with the sober reality:

[5] *Correspondence*, ed. Theodore Besterman, LII, 247.

[6] See Rousseau's dedication to the Republic of Geneva at the head of his *Discours sur l'inégalité*, and Voltaire's poem, *L'Auteur arriv-*

Geneva was an oligarchy. Its eighteenth-century constitution, a series of edicts and practices dating back to Calvin and beyond, restricted active citizenship to a select minority and divided subjects into five classes. The disfranchised majority consisted of the peasants (*sujets*), the immigrants who had obtained the right of residence but little more (*habitants*), and the native-born descendants of the *habitants* (*natifs*). The ruling minority, in turn, was divided into the *bourgeois*, either naturalized or native, who had acquired social and political rights, could enter the liberal professions, and were allowed to vote, and their descendants, the *citoyens*, who were eligible to hold office.

This cumbersome ladder of citizenship reflects Geneva's changing position as a center of immigration. With the advent of Protestantism and the persecutions under Francis I and Henry II, French refugees streamed into Geneva. They were well received, many of them were admitted to citizenship, and became members of the local élite. A hundred and fifty years later, the revocation of the edict of Nantes brought a new flood of immigrants, but now the Genevans—for the most part the descendants of immigrants—were less hospitable. Feeling threatened by the skills and talents of the Huguenots, the Genevans discouraged the newcomers from settling in the city, imposed heavy taxes upon their livelihoods, reserved for themselves the most lucrative and reputable professions, and made it nearly impossible for the new *habitants* to become *bourgeois*.[7]

---

ant dans sa terre, près du lac de Genève (March 1755), *Œuvres*, X, 364.

[7] In 1600 it had cost 80 florins to buy citizenship; around 1650, the price had risen to 500 florins, and by 1700 to 4,000 florins—an enormous sum even if inflation is taken into account. The privilege of citizenship had been obtained by 3,222 heads of families in the sixteenth century, and by only

The *habitants* found these restrictions irritating; their descendants, the *natifs*, came to regard them as intolerable. Born in Geneva, loyal to its institutions, at home in its religious and moral climate, industrious and thrifty, often prosperous, the *natifs* were treated like pariahs. Still, it was not easy to convert them into a political pressure group: the habit of docile acceptance and prayerful apathy persisted for generations. They did not raise their voices until they were helped, ironically enough, by the aristocratic Voltaire, and until violent conflict erupted within the privileged minority.

The legal division of *bourgeois* and *citoyen* caused no conflict within this minority. Both had a great deal in common—fathers might belong to the first, sons to the second group. Moreover, *bourgeois* and *citoyens* were united in preventing the *habitants* and *natifs* from destroying their monopoly of political rights and social prestige. What caused division among Genevan citizens was a struggle between two social classes, a sizable middle class and a small, powerful patriciate.

Geneva's political institutions were not designed to heal these divisions, but appeared to have been invented to permit manipulation of the state by a small oligarchy. The Genevan government consisted of a series of councils of varying size, each council fitting into the next larger council like a box into another box in a Chinese puzzle. The largest of these councils was the General Council: all *citoyens* and *bourgeois* met in it annually to elect the four syndics and other magistrates, to formulate or to ratify legislation, and to make vital decisions on foreign policy. The General Council was sovereign—the

730 in the period from 1700 to 1782. See Pierre Bertrand: *Genève et la révocation de l'édit de Nantes* (1935), *passim; Histoire de Genève des origines à 1798* (1951), 358; and Francis D'Ivernois: *An Historical and Political View of the Constitutions and Revolutions of Geneva*, transl. by John Farell (1784), 22.

"people of Geneva" spoke through it. But during the Calvinist revolution, culminating in the political edict of 1543, the real power of the "sovereign" General Council had been sharply curtailed. Two smaller Councils, the Council of Two Hundred and the Council of Twenty-Five came to divide all legislative, executive, and judicial power between them. By the mid-sixteenth century, the Council of Two Hundred elected the members of the Council of Twenty-Five, and the Council of Twenty-Five returned the courtesy by electing the members of the Council of Two Hundred. This arrangement left to the General Council chiefly the power to confirm what the smaller councils had done. It could no longer initiate legislation, and it was restricted in its election of the syndics by choosing from a list submitted to it by the Council of Two Hundred.

The impotence of the General Council came to be taken for granted in the two succeeding centuries; gradually the power of government was engrossed by a handful of leading families. A small patriciate learned to treat the government of the city almost as its private property—it named close relatives to strategic posts, stifled criticism of its actions by branding and punishing it as sedition. Some syndics remained in office for half a century or more; some members of the Council of Twenty-Five remained in office illegally even after the Council of Two Hundred had refused to re-elect them. Since the patriciate controlled the chief legislative, executive, and judicial positions, it could dictate policies, interpret the laws in its favor, prosecute its enemies, and shield its friends.

Throughout the seventeenth century, the oligarchy found little resistance. The governing families guaranteed their predominance by nepotism, bribery at elections, violating the rules of tenure, and by using force and intimidation. They were aided by the body of Genevan pastors, the Consistory. As a body of Christian ministers, the Genevan Consistory held all souls to be equal; as the ally of the patriciate, by family ties and interests, the Consistory was induced to see that some souls were far superior to others. Sumptuary laws, originally designed to limit all luxuries, exacerbated class divisions by separating Genevan citizens into castes; the enforcement of these laws was harsh only against those who were not socially prominent.

By 1700 the political predominance of the patriciate and the political emasculation of the middle class were almost complete. It was possible for one leading family to place eight of its members in the two governing councils; it was possible for the son of a syndic to sit as a member of the Council of Two Hundred although he was only sixteen. The patriciate underscored its power by its exclusiveness: by withdrawing into its own quarters in the city, by developing its own *salons*, tastes, and dress. The old custom of electing two syndics from the lower and two syndics from the upper city was silently abandoned.

This offensive display of ascendancy naturally strengthened resentment and opposition. The number of talented, wealthy, proud, and energetic citizens who were not among the privileged grew as the patriciate consolidated. The revocation of the edict of Nantes brought into the city a mass of self-reliant and intelligent burghers and a flood of new ideas. These French refugees, noted D'Ivernois a century later, "had brought with them the love of spiritual and temporal liberty, at whose shrine they had offered the greatest sacrifices."[8] They could not help resenting their degraded status

[8] D'Ivernois: *An Historical and Political View*, 23.

as mere *habitants;* "these distinctions, this marked separation, recalled to the people's remembrance the equality established by the laws; they saw it more and more destroyed by the inequality of fortunes; they at last resolved that it should not be lost."[9]

The people—that is to say, the middle class—remembered its ancient equality, and sought to recover it. Civil war broke out. Between 1700 and 1755, the year of Voltaire's arrival in Geneva, there were two minor civil wars between the middle class and the patriciate. In 1707 middle-class malcontents, under the leadership of the young patrician lawyer Pierre Fatio, demanded among other reforms the publication of all edicts, and limitations on the numbers of members one family could place in the two smaller councils. The patriciate replied by making token concessions, treating the rebels with contempt, secretly arresting, trying, and executing Pierre Fatio, and ruthlessly dispersing his followers. For the moment, the oligarchy was saved, but it had saved itself at the price of calling in foreign troops and mediators from Berne and Zurich. The second civil war lasted longer—from 1734 to 1738—was more violent, and permanently saddled Geneva with foreign mediators. In May 1738 the three mediating powers—Zurich, Berne, and France—undertook to guarantee the settlement, an implied promise (or threat) of intervention which was to grow significant once again in the 1760's.

The settlement of 1738 was dominated by verbal concessions to the middle class: recognition of the sovereignty of the General Council, and of its right to make representations to the magistrates, to accept or reject the laws, to vote taxes, to decide on war and peace, to elect magistrates. The middle class, weary of strife and anxious to get back to its main busi-

[9] Ibid. 26.

ness of making money, was delighted with the settlement: there was general prosperity in Geneva, and in prosperity political issues lose their urgency. Moreover, the middle class felt comfortably certain that the General Council's right to make remonstrances adequately safeguarded its liberties. Events were to show that neither the prosperity nor the liberties of the middle class were secure. Almost at once the patriciate successfully evaded some of the restrictions of the mediation of 1738, by refusing to publish the edicts as required and to give accused persons all the guarantees agreed to. But until the 1760's, the middle class did not feel threatened enough to make more than sporadic protests against these illegal practices. It needed the advent of Voltaire and Rousseau to mobilize discontent and to transform grumbling into political action.

Thus Voltaire's appearance, and Rousseau's reappearance, upon the Genevan scene did not cause the civil conflicts of the 1760's. Conflict was endemic, and a crisis had to erupt sooner or later. The two *philosophes* were the precipitants and the symbols, not the causes of that crisis.

The symbolic value of Rousseau and Voltaire became evident as the 1750's shaded into the 1760's. When Voltaire had first hymned Geneva, the infatuated poet had professed to see nothing but fraternity and equality.[1] He soon learned better but this did not prevent him from entering into close relations with the Genevan patriciate. He had settled near Geneva partly to be in the skillful hands of the fashionable doctor Théodore Tronchin, and he soon became friendly with other members of that remarkable patrician family. The Tronchins brought their friends, among them intellectual Genevan pas-

[1] *Œuvres*, X, 365.

tors. Voltaire's houses, Les Délices and, later, Tournay and Ferney, became the center of a brilliant social life. The Genevan patriciate was French in its training, sympathies, and culture. Voltaire was the finest flower of that culture, a splendid and lavish host, presiding over a lively household, offering good dinners, better conversation, and, best of all, superb theater. The worldly spirits of Geneva, like their famous guests, were literate, sophisticated, urbane, and, truth be told, no longer seriously Christian. Ferney was a haven of the patricians. The middle class, on the other hand, rallied around Rousseau, the sober champion of Spartan self-discipline, thrift, probity, hard work, and self-denial. Rousseau's political views, his critique of aristocracy, his doubts about artificial, polite society, well accorded with the political posture of the Genevan middle class.

The fight between Rousseau and d'Alembert over the Genevan theater—really a fight between Rousseau and Voltaire—clarified and intensified the symbolic role of the two *philosophes*. As early as 1755 the Genevan Consistory had prevented Voltaire from indulging in his favorite pastime—performing his own plays before select guests—and in the following year Voltaire struck back through d'Alembert. D'Alembert had visited Voltaire in August 1756, had met the Genevan aristocracy at Les Délices, had charmed and been charmed in turn. The result was his article on Geneva in the *Encyclopédie*, an article which maintained not only that several Genevan pastors were "perfect Socinians," but also that Geneva could benefit from tolerating what it had not tolerated before—a theatrical company. D'Alembert had cautiously admitted that allowing professional acting troupes to perform might be taking a moral risk, but he believed that the civilizing mission of the theater more than offset its dangers, which could in any event be minimized through careful supervision of the actors. Rousseau, in his *Lettre à d'Alembert sur les spectacles* (1758), righteously excoriated the theater as an intolerable, immoral institution—immoral in its personnel as much as in the lessons it inculcated. Voltaire was amazed at the spectacle of Rousseau, the author of a few mediocre plays, denouncing the theater. But the issue, although stated in moral terms, was not moral but political. The middle class, actuated perhaps as much by envy and secret desire as by righteousness, stood squarely against the patriciate's insistence upon its prerogative to eat well, talk well, and to amuse itself at exclusive spectacles.

The burning of Rousseau's *Contrat social* and *Émile* was the first act in a long drama which resulted in the blurring of the symbols: Rousseau, the symbol of the *bourgeois* cause, withdrew from the struggle; Voltaire, the symbol of the patrician cause, first abandoned that cause to support the *bourgeoisie*, and then the *bourgeoisie* to defend the rights of the *natifs*.

When the Council of Twenty-Five on June 19, 1762, ordered that Rousseau's two books be burned, it acted upon the recommendation of the *procureur-général*, Jean-Robert Tronchin. Tronchin rightly saw the *Contrat social* as a book about Geneva, and, worse, as a Genevan party pamphlet championing the middle-class interpretation of the Genevan constitution. Rousseau treated the legislature as sovereign and the magistrates as an instrument of the sovereign people; he argued that the people can revoke all laws, and that the people ought to meet periodically, upon its own initiative, rather than upon the call of the government. These views elaborated and put into universal form the constitutional interpretation developed by Genevan bourgeois ideologists throughout the eighteenth century. They directly contradicted the constitutional views of the patriciate, views which had been succinctly stated in 1734 by Jean-Jacques Burlamaqui: Geneva is a mixed state, an "aristo-democracy," resting upon the accord of the rulers (the two small councils) and the ruled (the General Council). Geneva, upon this interpretation, consisted of co-operating orders, of which the people was only one and over which the people was not supreme. Rousseau's Genevan pamphlet reiterated all the *bourgeois* contentions, and the Council of Twenty-Five, speaking for the patriciate, struck back by condemning the *Contrat social* and *Émile* as "reckless, scandalous, impious, tending to destroy the Christian religion and all governments."

In striking at Rousseau the Council of Twenty-Five was striking at the middle class as well, but the latter, too complacent, too indifferent, or too timid to act on the threat, remained silent. One notable exception was Colonel Charles Pictet, who bravely published a protest against the Council's action. For thus exercising his constitutional rights Pictet was prosecuted and convicted in July 1762; he was sentenced to make an apology and was deprived for a year of his citizenship rights and his membership in the Council of Two Hundred. The trial, which had been held without a syndic since each of the four syndics was related either to Pictet or to the *procureur-général*, reappeared as an issue in the civil strife.[2]

These were inauspicious events for Voltaire. He had run afoul of Genevan authorities before, with his theatrical representations and with books like *Candide*. The month of Pictet's condemnation was the very month in which Voltaire was beginning to publish his pamphlets about the Calas case. One

[2] See Vallette: *Jean-Jacques Rousseau Genevois, passim.*

might have expected him to have been extremely sensitive to infringements of liberty of expression, and indeed this is the time in which he is supposed to have written the *Idées républicaines*, with its generous defense of Rousseau's freedom of speech, and of free expression in general.

But the facts are quite different. When Voltaire did refer to the burning of Rousseau's books during these months, he referred to them jokingly and callously. The dog of a Diogenes has been condemned at Geneva and will have to roll his barrel elsewhere—that is the tone of Voltaire's letters, and it is not pretty. It is not surprising that Pictet held Voltaire responsible for the condemnation of Rousseau; or that Vallette, in his brilliant study of Rousseau the Genevan portrays Voltaire as persecuting Rousseau with an implacable hatred. Still, Pictet was probably wrong, just as Vallette is definitely wrong. Voltaire's callousness in the Rousseau affair was characteristic: a joke was nearly always Voltaire's response to bad news. When he first heard about the Calas case he thought not of the suffering of the Calas family but of the value the case would have for *philosophe* propaganda. Callousness, indifference—these were forms of self-defense against a hard world. His sober second thought was almost always more humane than his initial flippancy.

Indeed, by 1763 Voltaire's mockery of Rousseau had been replaced by generous partisanship, just as the inaction of the Genevan middle class had been replaced by remonstrances. The Genevan *bourgeoisie* was finally stung into action by Rousseau's abdication of his cherished Genevan citizenship. On June 18, 1763, a delegation of citizens submitted a Very Humble and Respectful Representation to the first syndic. The grievances of the Representation were the old grievances, brought up to date and made specific: the judgment against

Rousseau had been irregular and illegal; the tribunal that had condemned Pictet had sat illegally without a syndic; the confiscation of 24 copies of *Émile* from Genevan booksellers was an invasion of property rights. A week later the Council of Twenty-Five indignantly rejected the Representation and admitted no wrong-doing. The middle class, now thoroughly aroused, made further representations in August and September 1763. Voltaire, still on intimate terms with the Tronchins and other patricians, was privately on the side of the middle class and on the side of Rousseau. On June 30, 1763, he gave the Genevan news to the Duchess of Saxe-Gotha, and commented favorably on the *démarches* in behalf of Rousseau: "So here's toleration established. God be blessed!"[3] Two months later he told Choiseul: "It's pretty comical to see a whole nation ask reparation for Jean-Jacques Rousseau. They say, it's true he wrote against the Christian religion, but that's not a good enough reason to dare make out a kind of summons" against a "citizen of Geneva."[4] And to Damilaville, with whom he could be frank, he wrote: "Don't you bless God to see the people of Calvin take the side of Jean-Jacques so loudly? Let us not consider his person, let us consider his cause. The rights of mankind have never been better sustained."[5] *Let us not consider his person, let us consider his cause*—Voltaire the empirical political pamphleteer was extracting the universal meaning from the specific event: he was rising above personal distaste to the defense of a cause.

The patricians, his friends, did not see the matter in this light. The Council of Twenty-Five contemptuously rejected all representations, and on August 20, 1763, about seven hundred citizens—almost half the total political public—pre-

[3] *Correspondence*, LII, 155.

[4] August 21, 1763, ibid. 247.

[5] August 23 (1763), ibid. 249.

sented a new petition to the first syndic, politely but firmly insisting that its representations were well founded and should be heard. The Council of Twenty-Five replied on September 5 with a startling doctrine: the small council, it argued, had a *droit négatif*—a veto power over representations. It could decide not only whether to act upon grievances, but also whether to listen to them. D'Ivernois denounced the patrician pretensions as tantamount to making the aristocracy into a state within the state. It was from this exchange that the parties henceforth drew their names—the patricians became the *Négatifs*, the partisans of the middle class the *Représentants*.

It seems likely that Voltaire would have joined the *Représentants* as early as the summer of 1763 if it had not been for Jean-Robert Tronchin's *Lettres écrites de la campagne*, published in September 1763, and Rousseau's far more celebrated reply, the *Lettres écrites de la montagne*, of December 1764. Tronchin's brochure was an urbane and moderate defense of the *Négatif* position: without the *droit négatif*, without extraordinary powers over criminals, order in the state would give way to anarchy. It was hardly possible for Voltaire to repudiate his friend directly; and when a year later Voltaire read Rousseau's reply, it seemed hardly desirable. Rousseau's *Lettres de la montagne* were a brilliant defense of his own writings, and they cogently justified the actions and the constitutional interpretation of the *Représentants*. They denied the *Négatifs*' claim to a veto power, and demonstrated the continuous violations by the patriciate of the mediation of 1738.

All of this Voltaire could probably have accepted. But casually and almost incidentally Rousseau attacked Voltaire's irreligious writings, and named him as the author of the *Sermon des cinquante*, a violently anti-Christian diatribe which Voltaire had up to now tried to fob off on La Mettrie, who had obligingly died in 1751. Whatever chance for a meeting of minds might have existed, Rousseau's act of telling the truth, which appeared to Voltaire an act of denunciation, finally spoiled it. Voltaire retaliated with the vile *Sentiments des citoyens*, probably the low point in his career. It is a pious attack on Rousseau as an anti-Christian, seditious, violent madman who deserves capital punishment.

Geneva was not the only iron in Voltaire's fire. At the time he wrote the *Sentiments des citoyens*, his *Dictionnaire philosophique* had just appeared and had been condemned in France as well as in Geneva; he was more daring in his anticlericalism than ever before; he was engaged in the delicate negotiations which were to result in the clearing of Calas's name early in 1765. Hence Voltaire may have believed it expedient and even essential to silence Rousseau, the traitor to the *philosophes*' cause. But these extenuating circumstances do not extenuate. And they do not explain what needs explaining: that Rousseau's and Voltaire's political opinions concerning Geneva were closer than ever.

The *Lettres de la montagne* had put new energy into the sagging lines of the Genevan middle class. In January 1765 the General Council first threatened to strike and then showed its displeasure with the magistrature by electing the syndics by small votes—700 or more rather than the usual 1,400. Late in February 1765, while middle-class representations were raining upon the stubborn *Négatifs*, Rousseau had bid farewell to Genevan politics, and the road was now open for Voltaire to assume his new role of champion of the Genevan middle class.

There had been a double evolution: the *bourgeoisie* had

come to see Voltaire as the defender of unpopular causes. He had defended Covelle against the Genevan Consistory, he was defending Calas against the *parlements* in France. The *Traité sur la tolérance* of 1763, so eloquent in praise of toleration and so moderate in its treatment of Christian churches, and the vindication of Calas on March 9, 1765, were milestones in the rapprochement of the Genevan *bourgeoisie* and Voltaire. On the other side, he had gradually come to accept the case of the *Représentants*. Middle-class opposition to his private theatricals weighed little in the face of *bourgeois* opposition to arbitrariness. The Genevan patriciate was cultivated and urbane but it was also vain, exclusive, capricious, and tyrannical. D'Ivernois was right when he said that although Voltaire's "connections were entirely amongst the rich, his sentiments were too elevated to permit him to espouse their petty passions."[6]

Throughout the spring and summer of 1765 tensions increased in the city, and Voltaire's radicalization progressed rapidly. In October leading *Représentants*, among them D'Ivernois and Du Peyrou, Rousseau's good friend, sought out Voltaire at Ferney. Voltaire's correspondence mirrors these visits, and his certainty that the patriciate no longer deserved his support. On October 11 he wrote to D'Argental, his oldest and closest friend, "on more than one occasion the Council has acted against all the laws; it is far from deserving (as I had long thought) the protection of the French government."[7] With few exceptions, the Genevan patriciate was "composed of sixteenth-century pedants. There is much more intelligence and reason in the other citizens. For the rest, anyone who wishes may visit me, I'm not asking anybody."[8] This last dis-

[6] *An Historical and Political View*, 187.

[7] *Correspondence*, LIX, 116.

[8] October 28, 1765, ibid. 144.

claimer was most significant—Voltaire professed to be passive in a situation in which he was more active than any other outsider. On October 16 he predicted to Damilaville that the quarreling in Geneva would soon lead to an explosion. "It is absolutely necessary," he enjoined his friend in Paris, "that you and your friends spread the word in public that the Citizens are in the right against the Magistrates: for it is certain that the people desires only liberty, and that the magistrature aspires to absolute power. Is there anything more tyrannical, for instance, than to destroy the freedom of the press? And how can a nation call itself free, when it is not permitted to think in writing? . . . Whoever has power in his hands wants to be despotic: the craze for domination is an incurable disease."[9]

Voltaire the aristocrat had learned that the Genevan aristocracy could not be trusted; the radical author of the *Dictionnaire philosophique* had learned that the Genevan authorities cared for freedom of expression only if it was anti-Catholic; the enemy of Rousseau had learned that his cause was the cause of Pictet and even of Rousseau.

Both in the city and in Voltaire's letters the excitement mounted. On November 1, 1765, the General Council met to elect the magistrates for the following year; the members refused to accept any of the nominations that had been submitted to them. A month later Voltaire tried to minimize this action in a letter to D'Argental; the General Council, he wrote, had merely asked for new candidates. But it was a strike, and violence or outside mediation were imminent; what Voltaire had shrewdly predicted in August 1763 was now about to take place. There was one other solution: private mediation by Voltaire. And, assuring everybody that

[9] Ibid. 127.

he would not think of meddling, he meddled happily; telling everybody who would listen that as a foreigner, an invalid, and an old man, he could not think of political action, he forgot his status, his health, and his age, and tried to solve the Genevan impasse.

"That a republic should need mediators is perhaps not as shameful as people think," is what Voltaire had said in the *Idées*. In November 1765, the *république* of Geneva, faced with anarchy, was in fact being offered the choice of two kinds of mediators—Voltaire, the private man of letters, the influential good neighbor, or the three guaranteeing powers, Berne, Zurich, and France. Which of these Voltaire is referring to is impossible to know. But that in the *Idées* he is addressing himself to the situation of November 1765 now appears highly likely.

This likelihood increases as we follow Voltaire's activities in November. Throughout that month, Voltaire received emissaries from both *Négatifs* and *Représentants* at Ferney, and sought to reach an accommodation of outstanding problems, usually over dinner. How deeply Voltaire was involved in these negotiations is evident from his persistent denials that he is doing anything at all. On November 13, he wrote to D'Argental and begged him to insinuate to the duc de Praslin, the French foreign minister, that he, Voltaire, was neutral in the Genevan imbroglio and wholly passive. "As a good neighbor, I must exhort them all to peace when they come to see me; I limit myself to that."[1] A week later he found it necessary to write to Praslin directly. "There are big things at stake" in Geneva, Voltaire wrote, and modestly signed his letter "*ce vieux Suisse*."[2]

But the old Swiss was up to his elbows in politics, and his

[1] Ibid. 180.

[2] Ibid. 197.

Genevan associates were not deceived. On November 13, the day he had sent his disclaimer to D'Argental, he sent a longer, more circumstantial, even less convincing disclaimer to Jacob Tronchin, a member of the Council of Twenty-Five: he respected and honored Geneva, Voltaire wrote, and he denied any attempt on his part to arouse the *bourgeoisie*. He was giving dinners at which some leading citizens had met some of the magistrates. "I told them that I regarded Geneva as a big family in which the magistrates are the fathers, and that this family should be reunited after a few disagreements."[3] Voltaire believed nothing of the sort, but as an old diplomat he doubtless told his dinner guests just that. With them, as now with Tronchin, he breathed good will and unwonted self-effacement: "I am far from believing that I could be useful; but I foresee (and I may be wrong) that it won't be impossible to reconcile people."[4]

The *Négatifs* were alarmed: their old friend seemed to have turned into a stubborn supporter of the *Représentants*. His peacemaking could only lead to concessions to the middle class, for Voltaire was not without credit in Paris. As one Genevan patrician wrote to a friend on November 21, 1765: "He proposes, he is prejudiced, and he listens to nobody. He cannot help but do us harm with the best of intentions."[5] On the same day the Council of Twenty-Five politely begged Voltaire to mind his own business.

In trying to keep Voltaire from doing something he had set his mind on, the Council was in the position of Canute trying to hold back the waves. Voltaire was launched; he kept on doing what he had been and denied that he was doing. On November 25 he wrote to Damilaville that a number of

[3] Ibid. 178.
[4] Ibid.
[5] Quoted by Chaponnière, *Voltaire chez les Calvinistes*, 219.

magistrates and citizens had asked him to devise a plan of pacification, and on the same day he sent this plan to D'Argental for his perusal. He had taken the liberty, he wrote, to propose accommodations. "There are a few articles on which one could come to terms in a quarter of an hour; there are others demanding more time, and above all more information, than I have." Unlike Rousseau, he wanted to smooth the waters. "I have put on paper a little plan of pacification which seems to me clear and very easily understood by those who are not up on the laws of the *parvulissime république de Genève*."[6] He asked D'Argental to read it; to show it to two lawyers in Paris to make sure that the plan did not violate public or international law, and then to a selected group of French officials. Only after the plan had been fully approved in Paris would Voltaire show it to the Council of Twenty-Five. As soon as the French mediator should arrive in Geneva, he added cautiously, he would withdraw. "I only prepare the way of the Lord."[7]

This "little plan of pacification" is both a statement of the issues at stake in Geneva and of Voltaire's opinions concerning them. It was written in the middle of November 1765, shortly before the Genevan magistrates asked the guaranteeing powers to step in, and is therefore an authentic political document, a partisan pamphlet. And it bears a startling resemblance in argument, opinion, and even vocabulary to the *Idées*.[8]

[6] *Correspondence*, LIX, 211.
[7] Ibid.
[8] The *Propositions à examiner pour apaiser les divisions de Genève* were first printed by Fernand Caussy in the *Revue bleue*, V^e^ série, IX (January 4, 1908), 13-15. The quotations in the left-hand column are from these pages. Voltaire's *Idées républicaines* are in *Œuvres*, XXIV, 413-32.

Propositions à examiner pour apaiser les divisions de Genève	*Idées républicaines*
The *Représentants*' "first grievance" is that the Council of Twenty-Five, "have promised to have the complete collection of laws printed in accord with the settlement of the mediation, but this necessary code has not yet appeared." Voltaire supports this complaint as reasonable.	"A criminal code is absolutely necessary for citizens and magistrates. Then the citizens would have no complaints about verdicts, and the magistrates would not fear incurring hatred."
Second grievance: "Citizens are subjected to arbitrary imprisonment without hearing." Voltaire argues here, as he does in his other legal writings of these years, that it is better for a guilty man to escape than for an innocent man to be punished—the *Représentants* thus have a good case in his judgment.	"The law that permits imprisoning a citizen without a preliminary inquiry and without judicial formalities would be tolerable in times of turmoil and war; it would be cruel and tyrannical in times of peace." One true virtue of a good republic, he notes with an obvious reference to Geneva, is security of person: "In a true republic, everyone works for himself with confidence, since he is sure of the ownership of his goods and his person."
Third grievance: "In cases in which the syndics are disqualified because they are related [to one of the parties], or for other reasons, the Council of Twenty-Five will not let the	While there is no precise counterpart to this grievance in the *Idées*, Voltaire does briefly analyze the constitutional issue at stake. He quotes Rousseau: "The guardians of the executive

Propositions

citizens, convoked in the General Council, name a new temporary . . . syndic, to preside on that occasion."

This was not merely a general constitutional point, touching on the relation of citizens to magistrates, but a specific reference to the case of Rousseau's defender, Pictet. Here Voltaire thought the *Représentants* had overreached themselves and were inviting disorder. He proposed that whenever a judge disqualified himself his immediate inferior could take his place. Thus justice would be dealt out without disruption or delay.

Idées

power are not the masters of the people, but its officials; it may name them and dismiss them when it pleases; it is not up to them to negotiate but to obey."

Voltaire comments on this: "It is true that the magistrates are not the masters of the people; it is the laws that are masters; but the rest is absolutely false; it is false in all states, it is with us. When we are met, we have the right to reject or approve the magistrates and the laws proposed to us. We don't have the right to dismiss the officials of the state 'when we please;' that right would be the code of anarchy." Voltaire thus rejects Rousseau's position for the same reason that he rejects the *Représentants*': he considers both exaggerated versions of popular sovereignty. Continuity of administration must be secure. However, Voltaire's casual reference to the power of Genevans to reject the magistrates proposed to them is characteristic of *Représentants*' interpretation of the General Council's action of November 1, 1765; it is reminiscent of the "Dixième lettre" of the *Questions sur les miracles:* "We can

Propositions	*Idées*
	accept you or reject you: hence we are your sovereigns."
Fourth grievance: "That when the citizens (who are sovereign legislators) make a representation to the Council of Twenty-Five which has the executive power, this representation can be rejected purely and simply."	"Civil government is the will of all, carried out by one or by several, by virtue of the laws which all have produced."
This point, as Voltaire knew, was the touchiest. It insisted that since the citizens were sovereign legislators (a view rejected by the *Négatifs*), they had every right to have their petitions treated seriously. Voltaire proposed a compromise which would preserve the sovereignty of the people and the executive privileges of the Council: "Would it be appropriate to decree that the Council of Twenty-Five should carry the demand of the citizens to the Council of Two Hundred, and that then the first syndic will convoke the General Council in the following cases: When seven hundred citizens, supported by the decision of three lawyers of a University of their choice, come to demand either the interpretation of a point of law	It is precisely Geneva's small size that makes political action (such as petitions) feasible for all citizens: "It seems that in a small republic the people should be listened to more than in a large one, because it is easier to make a thousand people listen to reason than forty thousand." A thousand—a figure strikingly close to the number regularly attending the sessions of the General Council. "When a law is obscure, all must interpret it, because all have promulgated it: unless they have expressly charged several men with interpreting the laws."

Propositions	*Idées*
they find obscure, or the extension of a law they find insufficient, or (which will probably never happen) the execution of a law that has been neglected?"	

These resemblances are not the only hints that the *Idées* grew out of Voltaire's Genevan experience. Some of his most abstract pronouncements seem to have emerged directly from political controversy. I say "seem," because the relation of these statements to his experience are somewhat less certain than the correspondences between the *Idées* and the *Propositions*. "Pure despotism is the punishment for men's bad conduct. If a community of men is subdued by an individual or by a few, that is obviously because it had neither the courage nor the ability to govern itself."[9] This is the opening sentence of the *Idées*, and it can be read not only as a call to arms against all despotism, but as an exhortation to the middle class of Geneva. Again: "We have restored our municipal government practically to the point it had reached under the Romans, and it has been given luster and firmness by that liberty, purchased with our blood. We have never known that odious and humiliating distinction between nobles and commoners, which originally meant nothing but lords and slaves. Born all equal, we have remained so; and we have given the dignities, that is to say, the public burdens, to those who seemed to us best equipped to sustain them."[1] This sounds like a statement of fact, but it is really a statement of principle contrary to fact, a view of the Genevan constitution and of

[9] *Œuvres*, XXIV, 413.

[1] Ibid.

Genevan society as it would be if the *Représentants* got their way.

Several paragraphs of the *Idées* attack sumptuary laws, which Voltaire deemed tolerable only in poor and uncivilized states. These attacks may represent Voltaire's personal love of luxury, his desire to live his life without interference from authority. But they may represent, too, an attack on the patriciate, which had introduced sumptuary legislation.

Or take this paragraph: "If a republic was founded during religious wars, if during these troubles it has expelled from its territory the sects that were enemies to its own, it has behaved wisely, for at that time it thought of itself as a country surrounded by persons stricken with the plague, afraid that the plague would be imported. But when such times of dizziness are over, when tolerance has become the ruling dogma of all sensible people in Europe, isn't it ridiculous barbarism to ask a man who has just established himself and brought his wealth to our country, 'Monsieur, what is your religion?' Gold and silver, industry, talents—all these have no religion."[2] What was Voltaire thinking of when he wrote this passage? He had long been annoyed by the law that prevented Catholics from becoming Genevan citizens. And in August 1765, he was annoyed by an absurd incident: a representative of Catherine II, who was recruiting Genevan girls to teach French in Russia, was expelled and the girls were compelled to return, presumably because it was feared that good Calvinists might be tainted in a Russian Orthodox environment.[3] Voltaire was probably thinking of both.

[2] Ibid. 418.

[3] On this incident see Voltaire to d'Argental, September 23 (1765), *Correspondence*, LIX, 89, and Voltaire to Prince Gallitzin (*c.* November 1, 1765), ibid. 158.

The *Idées* makes some strong pleas for freedom of expression—there is that defense of Rousseau, and above all there is a much-quoted paragraph: "In a republic worthy of the name, the freedom to publish one's thoughts is the natural right of the citizen. He may use his pen as he uses his voice: he must no more be prohibited from writing than from speaking; and the offenses committed with the pen should be punished like the offenses committed with the word: such is the law of England, a monarchical country, but where men are freer than they are elsewhere, because they are more enlightened."[4]

Voltaire's advocacy of free expression is one of the campaigns for which he is most celebrated. But it is striking to see how many well-known passages on this theme come from the autumn of 1765. In the thirteenth letter of the *Questions sur les miracles*, written in October or November 1765, Voltaire expressed himself almost word for word as he had in the *Idées*, including the flattering reference to England.[5] His letter of October 16, 1765, to Damilaville, already quoted, makes the same point in similar language.[6] Nor does it seem to me an accident that one of the articles added to the 1765 editions of the *Dictionnaire philosophique* was the dialogue entitled "*Liberté de penser.*"

This is the evidence that suggests how and when Voltaire wrote his *Idées républicaines*. It is not extravagant to visualize him in November 1765, deeply involved in Genevan affairs, dining with members of both parties, inquiring into Genevan

[4] *Œuvres*, XXIV, 418.

[5] The passage, too long to be quoted here, deserves to be read in conjunction with *Idées républicaines*. See *Œuvres*, XXV, 417-20.

[6] *Correspondence*, LIX, 127.

history and constitutional precedents, asking the *Représentants* to supply him with a list of their grievances and their legal and moral justifications, dashing off the *Questions sur les miracles*, revising the *Dictionnaire philosophique*, consulting with the "brothers" about what new steps to take against *l'infâme*, re-reading, perhaps for the tenth time, the *Contrat social*—and, in the midst of this whirl of satisfying activity, composing a party pamphlet, a collection of apothegms that will be useful to his new friends, the *Représentants*, and, perhaps, to humanity as a whole.

The *Idées*, we may now say with confidence, was written in November 1765, and printed in the same month or perhaps early in December. But was all this detective work necessary, especially since there is an obvious piece of evidence pointing to the same conclusion? In Grimm's *Correspondance littéraire* we find under January 15, 1766, the following notice: "The genius who lives at Ferney finds this a good moment to say his word about the quarrels that are dividing the republic of Geneva. He has published, continuing to hide himself from us, a little work of forty-five pages large octavo, *Idées républicaines 'par un membre d'un corps'* [sic]. This is not a humorous work. It contains very sensible ideas, and without entering into the Genevan bickering, it proposes very wise solutions. It takes up several passages of the *Contrat social* of M. Rousseau, and the *Esprit des lois* of *président* de Montesquieu. What he says of the latter will not be a success in Paris. In any case, the vigilance of the police deprives us of all these morsels. In general, it is sound philosophically."[7]

Grimm's review is remarkable in several ways. It identifies

[7] *Correspondance littéraire*, ed. Maurice Tourneux, VI, 474-5.

the author of the *Idées* correctly and without hesitation. Perceptively, Grimm also identifies its subject: the quarrels which divide Geneva; without entering into the details of these quarrels, Voltaire offers some sage solutions and some sensible ideas in general—what could be a fairer summary of the *Idées?* Grimm's notice is even more remarkable in its failure to have any effect on Voltaire-specialists. Bengesco had not overlooked it, but it had not impressed him. He knew that Grimm was not always reliable, and that eighteenth-century publishers were so mendacious that a three-year-old pamphlet might well be sold as a brand new production. But Grimm was not only right, he even supplied hints which would permit later students to confirm his view of the *Idées* as "new" in January 1766: with the shrewd eye of a trained observer he describes the pamphlet as being about the "bickering" in Geneva. That is why I went through the detective work: I wanted to establish not merely the date of a pamphlet, but the character of the pamphleteer.

This view of Voltaire, the *Erlebnispolitiker*, should solve most of the remaining controversies about his political thought. He was not a dogmatist but an opportunist; he was never a consistent supporter of any particular form of government. He was a moderate constitutionalist in England, Holland, and Geneva, a vigorous royalist in France, and an advocate of absolutism in Prussia.

This variety was not the result of complaisance: he did not simply say what his correspondents wanted him to say. If that were true, Faguet's charge that Voltaire's mind is "a chaos of clear ideas" would be just. But it is unjust. It is true that Voltaire contradicted himself: he lived too long, wrote too much, expressed opinions about too many matters, published opinions too casually held, not to be inconsistent at times. But his political aims show a complete consistency. The rule of law, freedom of speech, a humane legal code, and a tolerant religious policy—these were desirable everywhere. But Voltaire was too good a historian to forget that institutions cannot be simply transplanted from one country to another. England had a vigorous tradition of parliamentarianism, hence the strengthening of the legislature was the road to freedom; France's legislative bodies had fallen into desuetude or had become spokesmen for class interests, hence in France the road to freedom lay in the strengthening of the king's ministers. While Voltaire held his political values from the beginning of his life to the end, he understood that the forms in which they could be realized were various. Therefore he developed a flexible, pragmatic political program.

His flexibility is apparent in his treatment of that most troublesome of eighteenth-century problems, the lower orders, and once again the *Idées* supplies us with a clue to his thinking. After discussing the virtues of republicanism and obstacles to equality, Voltaire comments: "Should those who have neither land nor house in a society have a voice in it? They have no more right to that than a clerk paid by merchants has to conduct their business: but they may become associates, either by having rendered services, or by paying for their association."[8] Subjects who become citizens by paying for their citizenship—an odd observation if it is taken as a statement of principle. Constance Rowe, in a recent book on Voltaire's politics, tries unsuccessfully to make sense of it as just such a general statement: "In *Republican Ideas* the French philosopher declared that citizens who possess neither lands nor houses have no more right to a voice in public affairs than

[8] *Œuvres*, XXIV, 425.

have hired clerks the right to direct the business of their employers. Nevertheless, and the following adjoinder is typical of his unfailingly progressive outlook: '. . . they can have the status of associate, either by rendering special services or by paying for their association.' "[9] Unfailingly progressive outlook? nothing of the sort. It is the view that would have been taken by a liberal-minded *Représentant* toward the Genevan *natifs*, for we remember that a few *natifs* could buy their citizenship at an exorbitant price. Voltaire's comment is thus not a reflection of a progressive outlook, but of a specific political position.

It was a position he did not hold for long—indeed, even without Grimm's statement of January 1766, this comment of Voltaire's would have revealed that the *Idées* could not have been written after the spring of 1766, for by April and May of that year Voltaire had given up the case of the *Représentants* and gone over to the disfranchised *natifs*. His reasons for this further radicalization—a move to the left that even Rousseau at his most radical had never undertaken—were complex: pique at the bourgeoisie, for the bourgeoisie had become frightened by Voltaire's daring and repudiated his efforts in December 1765; frustration with the negotiations, for the French resident in Geneva as well as the French plenipotentiary during the mediations of 1766 to 1768 treated Voltaire politely without permitting him to participate in the mediation. But his sense of justice, too, had been aroused. The *natifs* sent representatives to Voltaire probably late in March and early in April 1766. He asked for information, historical and constitutional, and by mid-April he was their advocate. His former allies, *Négatifs* and *Représentants*, shook their heads: Voltaire was really a nuisance, and wholly incorrigible.

[9] *Voltaire and the State* (1955), 108.

His association with the *natifs* lasted from 1766 into the 1770's; it was an invaluable step in his political education. If he had written the *Idées* in 1762, it would have been more conservative, if he had written it after 1766, it would have been more radical than it actually was. Most of his pronouncements about the masses were made in the 1760's. We have some earlier ones; the *Henriade* of the 1720's and the notes to the *Henriade* written in the 1730's and 1740's have some rather disdainful comments about the fickle, uneducable, brutal *canaille*. But his most celebrated remarks, the ones that are usually quoted, were made to La Chalotais in 1762 and 1763, to Damilaville in 1766, and to Linguet in 1767. When we put his comments together we find that they show an increasingly friendly, less condescending attitude toward ordinary people. In an important letter to Linguet, Voltaire carefully distinguished between those who used only their brawn and those whose labors forced them to reflect and to extend their enlightenment.[1] It was a distinction that is implicit in all his thoughtful comments on the masses: the peasants, especially the Catholic peasants, are hopelessly caught in ignorance and superstition; urban workers, especially Protestants, are surprisingly well educated and given to reading. If we peruse his late writings with care, we shall sometimes find facile comments about the *canaille:* he was occasionally petulant even in his old age. But on the whole we can observe an evolution, and an evolution directly connected with his experience.

[1] See especially Voltaire's letters to Damilaville of March 19 and April 1 (1766), *Œuvres*, XLIV, 247-8, 256; and the letter to Linguet, March 15, 1767, *Œuvres*, VL, 163-4. See also Pellissier, *Voltaire philosophe*, 269-70.

Indeed, toward the end of 1768, Voltaire wrote a long dialogue, *L'A,B,C,* in which he allowed one of the speakers to say: "Let's look at the facts. I'll admit to you that I could easily put up with a democratic government. . . . I enjoy seeing free men making the laws under which they live, as they have made their houses. It pleases me to see my mason, my carpenter, my blacksmith, who helped me build my lodging, my neighbor the farmer, and my friend the manufacturer, all rise above their craft, and know the public interest better than the most insolent Turkish emissary. In a democracy, no day laborer, no artisan, need fear either annoyance or contempt. . . . To be free, to have none but equals, that's the true life, the natural life, of man."[2]

Before we dismiss this outburst as mere rhetoric, let us recall Voltaire's Genevan experience. It is authentic Voltaire, with its opening injunction (Let's look at the facts!) and its slightly condescending tone (*my* mason, *my* carpenter). And it sounds like the statement of a convert to the cause of the *natifs,* who perhaps lacked polish and suavity, but who were fit to govern themselves. This defense of democracy may not be Voltaire's final opinion; it doubtless represents an extreme. But if *L'A,B,C* had been written in 1765, Voltaire either would not have made the statement at all, or would have refuted it briskly.

This, then, is what we may learn from dating the *Idées républicaines* 1765 instead of 1762. For Voltaire reform had many faces, but the principles he favored and the principles he opposed remained unaltered through his life. Therefore, we

[2] I have translated this dialogue and printed it in my edition of Voltaire's *Philosophical Dictionary,* 2 vols. (1962), II, 497-606. The passage quoted here is on pp. 539-40.

can discover a real continuity in his political philosophy. And we can discover something else: that the specific origin of his political ideas does not destroy their universality. It is precisely their origin that gives their universal form its richness and, above all, its realism.

3

VOLTAIRE'S ANTI-SEMITISM

WITH ITS cosmopolitan spirit, its cultural relativism, and its doctrine of toleration, the Enlightenment converted the Jew from a victim into a problem. For over a thousand years, the attitude of Christians toward Jews had been rather uncomplicated. In pious histories the Jews were the sacred nation that had given Jesus to the world, but in popular belief they were the treacherous tribe that had killed Christ. There were pockets of toleration and even instances of kindness throughout the Middle Ages and the early modern period, but for the most part, Jews performed vital and disreputable tasks, and were punished for being indispensable. Their protectors usually treated them with disdain and subjected them to extortion, the populace engaged in sporadic outbursts of persecution, and nascent states in search of unity compelled them to convert to Christianity or expelled them from their territory. Not all Jews were martyrs, not all ghettos seemed prisons to those who lived in them, but the position of Jewry remained one of tense isolation for over a thousand years.

This position raised troublesome questions for the *philosophes*. As philosophers critical of accepted beliefs, they could hardly be expected to echo the credulous anti-Jewish tales of common men. As ideologists of humanitarianism, they posed as (and often were) a professional association devoted to rescuing the victims of society. As radical educational theorists who believed that man's mind at birth is a blank slate, the *philosophes* could see the Jew, whatever his behavior as an adult, as basically good. As observers of society, they were in a position to recognize the Jews' supposed concentration on unsavory occupations as a reflection, not on the Jews, but on the civilization that compelled them to be clothes dealers and usurious bankers. The ideology of the Enlightenment made it possible to look upon Jews at least with sympathy, and at best with esteem, and in fact some of the *philosophes* explored these possibilities. Voltaire was not one of them.

It is significant for our judgment of Voltaire's attitude that philo-Semitism was a live option for the men of the Enlightenment. Locke, whose writings on toleration had immense influence not only in Britain but on the Continent as well, had been unequivocal. "Nay," he wrote in his *Letter Concerning Toleration*, "Nay, if we may openly speak the truth, and as becomes one man to another, neither pagan nor Mahometan nor Jew ought to be excluded from the civil rights of the commonwealth because of his religion. . . . If we allow the Jews to have private houses and dwellings amongst us, why should we not allow them to have synagogues?"[1] This was an exceptional position, and it was shared only by exceptional

[1] *A Letter Concerning Toleration* (ed. 1950), 56-7.

men, like the deist John Toland, but it was the basis for a principled humaneness.[2]

Locke's views were elaborated in France by Montesquieu, who set standards that found belated echoes in the liberal legislation of the French Revolution. In his *Esprit des lois*, one of the most widely read books of the eighteenth century, Montesquieu assailed the Portuguese Inquisition for putting to death an eighteen-year-old Jewish girl. Posing as a Jewish writer, he composed an essay on the subject which, he said in some discouragement, was probably "the most useless essay ever written. When things as clear as this need to be proved, you are sure to convince nobody." To kill Jews for not believing what Christians believe is not merely cruel, but un-Christian as well: "You want us to be Christians, and you don't want to be Christians yourselves. But if you don't want to be Christians, at least be human beings." Ours is a century, he went on, in which philosophy is beginning to enlighten the minds of men, but if Inquisitions continue in their brutal way, the world will conclude that Christians are incorrigible savages: "We must warn you of one thing: if anyone in later ages should ever dare to say that in the century in which we lived the nations of Europe were civilized, they will offer you proof that they were barbarians."[3] Even more far-reaching than this generous outburst was Montesquieu's sociological analysis of the Jews' affinity for commerce and banking: guided by Aristotle's philosophy, the Schoolmen had condemned trade as a vile occupation. But since trade was necessary, it fell into the hands of the despised outsider, the Jew,

[2] See especially Toland's pamphlet, *Reasons for Naturalizing the Jews in Great Britain and Ireland* (1714).

[3] *Esprit des lois*, Book XXV, ch. 13, *Œuvres complètes*, ed. Roger Caillois, 2 vols. (1951), II, 746-9.

who first grew rich and then was robbed of his wealth by the most exquisite tortures. "Thus we see trade springing from the breast of vexation and despair."[4]

Locke and Montesquieu found ready disciples in Germany. The *Aufklärung* made a persistent attempt to integrate Jews into Western culture, and the leading Jewish assimilationist of the century, Moses Mendelssohn, who was himself a close student of modern philosophy, became the friend of the German *philosophes*. His lifelong friendship with Lessing was a symbol, both of the philo-Semitism of the *Aufklärung*, and of the emergence of Jews into the light of Western history after well over a millennium of isolation.

This rapprochement was not easy: the strangeness of the Jews could not be overcome by abstract good will alone. Even Lessing's cosmopolitanism was the product of years of intellectual growth. Several years before his first meeting with Mendelssohn, he had written a short comedy, *Die Juden*, which came, he said, out of his concern for a nation that had provided the world with heroes and prophets but was now supposed to be incapable of producing a single honest man. The hero of the play is an idealized stranger who performs all kinds of noble deeds, and is actuated by a selfless generosity of improbable purity. Lessing fills the play with shrewd thrusts at prejudice: the stranger insists that if a Jew cheats a Christian, it is largely from self-defense, since he lives at the mercy

[4] Ibid. Book XXI, ch. 20, *Œuvres*, II, 639. In his *Lettres persanes* (Letter LX), Montesquieu welcomes the gradual decline of anti-Jewish intolerance among the Christians. But in clear-eyed recognition of their predominant role in finance, he also writes in the same letter: "You ask me if there are Jews in France. Know that wherever there is money, there are Jews." *Œuvres*, I, 218. For a brief treatment of the Jewish question in eighteenth-century France, see Shelby T. McCloy, *The Humanitarian Movement in Eighteenth-Century France* (1957).

of powerful and hostile Christian forces. With his intelligence and quick thinking the stranger saves a baron and his daughter from all sorts of calamities. Offered the girl's hand in marriage, he finally reveals that he is a Jew. This stigma is enough reason for him to refuse the tempting offer, and for the baron to accept this self-denial with alacrity. With its final renunciation, the play is a symptom of transition: it allows the reader to feel the thrill of human sympathy without paying the price of his traditional convictions. In this sense, *Die Juden* is a step in Lessing's self-liberation, which he later attained in *Nathan der Weise*. In that play, Jewish, Christian, and Moslem parochialism are dissolved in a common humanity.

These were the intellectual possibilities open to Voltaire, but he did not exploit them. It is true that he deplored the persecutions of Jews, especially by the Spanish and Portuguese Inquisitions, but his observations on this subject sound more like the dutiful cant of a reader of Montesquieu than true sympathy.[5] Perhaps more important was his repeated suggestion to the Jews that they assimilate into Western culture by giving up their dietary laws and their "hatred" of other nations: "But what shall I say to my brother the Jew?" he wrote in a late work. "Shall I give him dinner? Yes, provided that during the meal Balaam's ass doesn't take it into its head to bray; that Ezekiel doesn't mix his breakfast with our dinner; that a fish doesn't come to swallow one of the guests and keep him in his belly for three days; that a serpent doesn't mix into the conversation to seduce my wife; that a prophet doesn't take it into his head to sleep with her after dinner, as that good fellow Hoseah did for fifteen francs and a bushel of barley;

[5] *Henriade*, *Œuvres*, ed. Moland, VIII, 136; *Sermon du Rabbi Akib*, *Œuvres*, XXIV, 281.

above all that no Jew make a tour around my house sounding a trumpet, making the walls come down, killing me, my father, my mother, my wife, my children, my cat and my dog, in accord with the former usage of the Jews."[6]

Such wry humanity—if that is the right phrase for it—was not Voltaire's predominant tone. In general, he described Jews as materialists, eminently qualified to be usurers, as greedy, iniquitous, clever, and rootless.[7] In 1726, when he lost some money in the bankruptcy of the banker Medina in England, he expressed his chagrin at his "damned Jew."[8] Similar expressions pervade his complaints against the Prussian *Schutzjude* Abraham Hirschel, with whom he had been engaged in some speculations during his stay at Potsdam and later became involved in an unsavory lawsuit.[9]

It was one thing for Voltaire to "advise" the Jews: "You are calculating animals; try to be thinking animals."[1] It was quite another to raise the question how (assuming the characterization to be accurate) they had come to be so. On this question, Voltaire, the *Erlebnispolitiker*, did not listen to his experience: in the clash of prejudice and life, prejudice pre-

[6] "Tolérance," *Questions sur l'Encyclopédie*, Part IX, 18.

[7] For examples, see: "Patrie," *Questions sur l'Encyclopédie*, Part VIII, 125; *La Pucelle*, *Œuvres*, IX, 149; *Essai sur les mœurs*, *Œuvres*, XII, 163; "Japanese Catechism," *Philosophical Dictionary*, ed. Gay, 152; "The Heaven of the Ancients," ibid. 201. See Voltaire to Cardinal Dubois, 28 (May 1722), *Correspondence*, ed. Besterman, I, 146-7; Voltaire to Darget, January 18, 1751, ibid. XIX, 53; Voltaire to de Lisle, December 15 (1773), *Œuvres*, XLVIII, 522.

[8] *Correspondence*, II, 36.

[9] For the Hirschel affair, consult Wilhelm Mangold, *Voltaires Rechtsstreit mit dem königlichen Schutzjuden Hirschel, 1751* (1905), and Besterman's appendix No. 56, "Voltaire and Abraham Hirschel," in *Correspondence*, XVIII, 263.

[1] "Juifs," *Œuvres*, XIX, 541.

vailed. Voltaire had some Jewish acquaintances, and late in life his views were challenged directly. Isaac Pinto, a highly cultured Portuguese Jew who admired Voltaire's work, protested against his remarks about the Jews by publishing a pamphlet which he sent to Voltaire with a most polite letter: "I am sending you a critique of a passage in your immortal works; I, who admire them most; I, a man made only to read them in silence, to study them and to be quiet. But since I respect the author even more than I admire his work, I consider him to be a great enough man to forgive this criticism in behalf of the truth which is so dear to him. . . . I hope at least that he will forgive me all the more since I act in behalf of an entire nation to which I belong. . . ."[2] Voltaire replied decently enough that he would alter the offending passages: "I was wrong to attribute to a whole nation the vices of some individuals."[3] Yet neither his acquaintances, nor these remonstrances, had much influence on Voltaire. He never rewrote the passages that had offended Pinto, and never recanted his crude prejudices. It was a defeat of the party of humanity inflicted by one of its own partisans.

But Voltaire's dislike of the Jews was more than merely anti-Jewish prejudice; it was a partly unconscious, partly conscious cloak for his anti-Christian sentiments. "When I see Christians, cursing Jews," he wrote in his English notebook, "methinks I see children beating their fathers."[4] Like his admirer Nietzsche, Voltaire struck at the Jews to strike at the Christians. Bossuet had made the Chosen People the center of his so-called universal history; Voltaire strove for a more

[2] (*c.* July 10, 1762), *Correspondence*, XLIX, 98.
[3] July 21, 1762, ibid. 131.
[4] *Notebooks*, ed. Besterman, 31 (in English).

genuine universality. "I'm weary of the absurd pedantry," he wrote after giving an account of the sanguinary history of the ancient Jews, "which assigns the history of such a nation to the instruction of the young."[5] Bossuet and Voltaire agreed that Judaism was the father of Christianity, but they drew opposite conclusions from this: Bossuet, that he must make Jewish history central; Voltaire, that the paternity of Christianity was only one more argument against it. The Jewish people of the Old Testament, to judge from their own records, were uncivilized, lecherous, and brutal. The heroes of the Jews, like King David, had been gangsters and murderers[6]; the collection of broken treaties, assassinations, blood feuds, adulteries, incests, recorded in the Old Testament, led Voltaire to observe drily that if the Holy Ghost was the author of this history, he had not chosen a very edifying subject.[7]

It is hardly to be expected that such purposeful history will be very accurate, and in fact, when Voltaire came to the history of the Jews, he repeatedly forgot his clearly formulated critical principles. Let one example stand for many: In the fifth conversation of his dialogue "*L'A,B,C,*" Voltaire sarcastically discusses the "art of surprising, killing, and robbing," and offers as an early instance of this despicable art the story of Dinah. According to Voltaire, the son of a Sheche-

[5] "A,B,C," in *Philosophical Dictionary*, 543.

[6] For the cruelties of the Biblical Jews, see *Sermon des cinquante*, *Œuvres*, XXIV, 441-4. The assault on King David is one of many instances of Voltaire's borrowing from Bayle, who had written a scathing attack on David in his *Dictionnaire historique et critique*. Voltaire's treatment of Jewish history is exhaustively documented in Hanna Emmrich, *Das Judentum bei Voltaire* (1930). For Diderot, whose attitude was similar, see Hermann Sänger, *Juden und Altes Testament bei Diderot* (1933).

[7] "History of Jewish Kings and Chronicles," *Philosophical Dictionary*, 307.

mite king was "madly in love" with Dinah and wanted to marry her. Dinah's brothers then proposed that the Shechemites be circumcised, so that all would become a single nation. The Shechemites agreed, submitted to the ceremony, and then, when they were asleep, Simeon and Levi fell upon and killed them all while "ten other patriarchs" robbed them. Voltaire offers no reason for this mass slaughter beyond saying that the two "lovers" had "slept together," and the reader must conclude—and is expected to conclude—that the Jews were a thieving, murdering horde.[8] Genesis, xxxiv, confirms the general outlines of this story, including the killing and robbing, but gives the reason for this terrible act, not once, but over and over again: Dinah had been raped. The prince saw Dinah and "seized her and lay with her and humbled her;" and Jacob told his sons when they came home from the field that their sister had been "defiled," and "the men were indignant and very angry, because he had wrought folly in Israel by lying with Jacob's daughter, for such a thing ought not to be done." Even after the slaying and robbing, Genesis emphasizes that all this was done "because their sister had been defiled." Thus Voltaire converts the primitive revenge of an outrage into an act of wanton and cowardly cruelty.

The very shape of these distortions reveals them to be anti-Christian, rather than anti-Jewish propaganda. Indeed, Voltaire plays the same game he had played with the Old Testament with the New Testament too, and in the same place. In the article "*Pierre*" in the *Dictionnaire philosophique*, Voltaire (hiding behind two scholars) condemns St. Peter for causing the death of Ananias and his wife Sapphira. As he tells it, Ananias had sold some property and given money to St. Peter,

[8] "A,B,C," in *Philosophical Dictionary*, 535.

but "held back a few écus for himself and his wife to pay for their necessities," without telling Peter. For this Peter made Ananias die "of apoplexy," and later did the same to Sapphira. This, Voltaire concludes curtly, "is harsh."[9] But read in the Biblical context, the incident acquires a rather different meaning. Acts, v, supports Voltaire's version of the incident, but Acts, iv, shows that he has once again omitted the central point: "Now the company of those who believed were of one heart and soul, and no one said that any of the things which he possessed was his own, but they had everything in common. . . . There was not a needy person among them, for as many as were possessors of lands or houses sold them, and brought the proceeds of what was sold and laid it at the apostles' feet; and distribution was made to each as any had need." Thus Voltaire turns primitive socialism enforced by primitive punishment into an example of priestly presumption and rapacity.

Despicable as the history of the Jews appears to Voltaire, the history of the Christians, their disciples, is even more despicable. The very relation between the two allows Voltaire to draw some devastating conclusions. Christians profess to despise the Jew—what then shall we think of a religion that urges men to imitate him? If the miracles of the Jews are childish fables; if the Book of Proverbs is a "collection of trivial, sordid, incoherent maxims, without taste, without discernment, and without plan"[1], and the Song of Songs a "fatuous rhapsody"[2]—what then shall we think of a religion that urges men to believe them to be of divine inspiration? In short, the vileness and absurdity of the Biblical Jews demonstrates the vileness and absurdity of Christianity.

[9] *Philosophical Dictionary*, 426-7. [2] Ibid. 462.
[1] "Solomon," ibid. 457.

Moreover, Voltaire showed with grim humor that the Jews of antiquity, superstitious and barbarous as he paints them, were less superstitious and less barbarous than the Christians. The ancient Jews had not believed in the immortality of the soul, or in the divinity of their Messiah.[3] When Voltaire deplores the Jews' failure to rise to such sublime ideas as the God-man or the immortality of the soul, he was of course pretending to censure attitudes he shared with enthusiasm.

Indeed, Voltaire portrayed the Jews as less intolerant than the Christians: the Sadducees among the Jews, he wrote, denied the existence of angels, even though the majority of Jews believed in them. Still, the Sadducees enjoyed all the rights of citizenship. This, he remarked without sarcasm, is a "beautiful example of tolerance."[4] The Romans tolerated the Jews because with all their stubborn clinging to their superstitions, they did not try to foist these superstitions on others: "The Jews didn't want the statue of Jupiter in Jerusalem; but the Christians didn't want it in the Capitol. . . . The Jews worshipped their God; but they were never astonished that each nation should have its own."[5]

Voltaire's anti-Jewish prejudice is thus qualified in two ways: it is in part a weapon against the Christians, and it is in part relieved by his conviction that Jews could purge themselves of their history by joining the main stream of philosophic culture. "I shall tell you frankly," he wrote to Pinto,

[3] See *Olympie*, Act I, scene 1, *Œuvres*, VI, 98n; *Essai sur les mœurs*, *Œuvres*, XI, 75; *Histoire de Jenni*, *Œuvres*, XXI, 569.

[4] *Notebooks*, 264; *Traité sur la tolérance*, *Œuvres*, XXV, 77-8. That this is his true opinion becomes evident from his intimate correspondence. See Voltaire to d'Alembert, February 13 (1764), and March 1 (1764), *Correspondence*, LIV, 102, 145, and Voltaire to Damilaville, March 4 (1764), ibid. LIV, 157.

[5] "Toleration," *Philosophical Dictionary*, 482-3.

"that a lot of people can stand neither your laws, nor your books, nor your superstitions; they say that your nation has at all times done itself much harm, and done harm to mankind. If you are a philosopher, as you seem to be, you will think like these gentlemen, but you won't say it. Superstition is the most abominable scourge in the world; it is this that has cut the throats of so many Jews and so many Christians; it is this that continues to send you to the stake in countries that are otherwise estimable. . . . Remain a Jew, since you are one . . . but be a philosopher—that is the best thing I can wish for you in this short life."[6] The Jews, for all their failings, would be part of Voltaire's good state. At times he did not seem certain whether he would extend the same privilege to pious Christians.

[6] *Correspondence*, XLIX, 132.

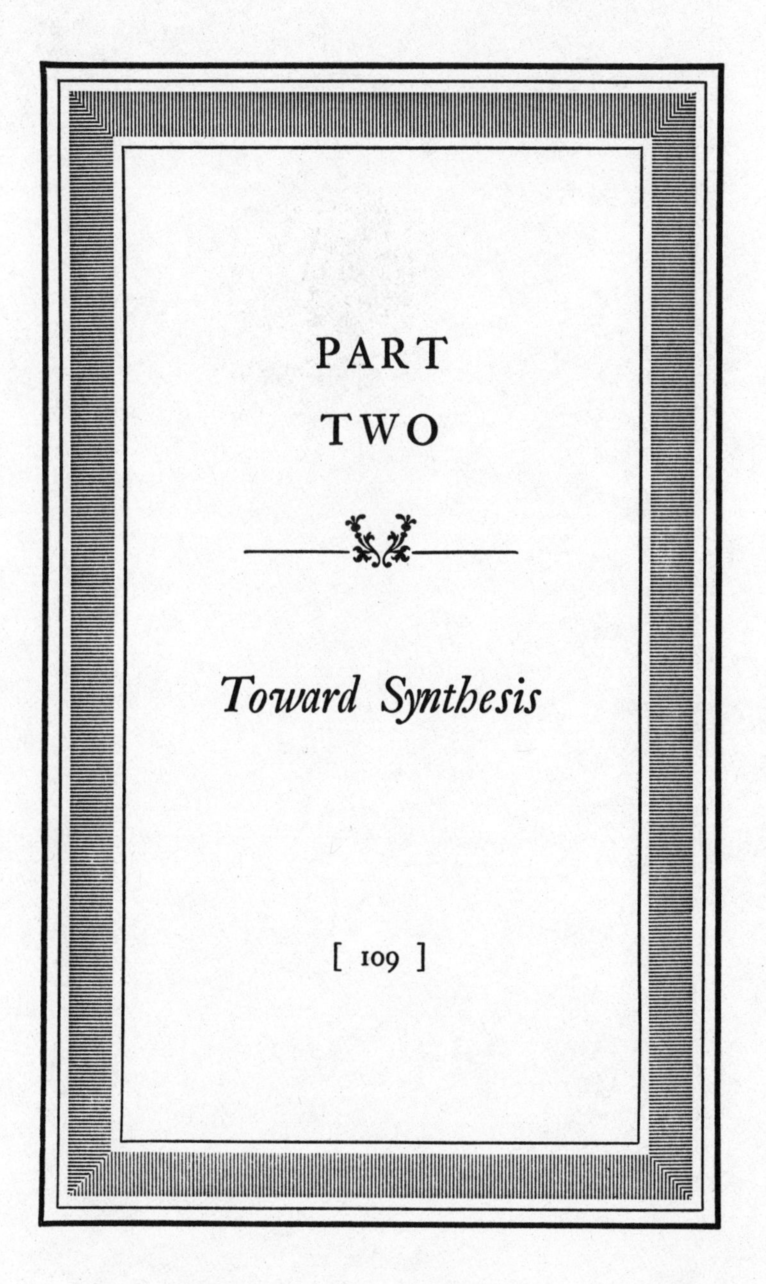

PART TWO

Toward Synthesis

INTRODUCTION

THE RAW MATERIALS of intellectual history are the ideas of individuals. Most books in the field stop short right here and confine themselves to the biography of an intellectual or to the biography of an idea in the minds of several intellectuals. Even ambitious works, like Lovejoy's history of the "great chain of being," or his book on primitivism in antiquity, rarely attempt a real synthesis. The reconstruction of a total cultural style of thought, of a climate of opinion, is generally left to the amateurs who, ignorant of the difficulties, can afford to be bold.

The reasons for this cautious nominalism on the part of professional historians are easy to understand. Large generalizations often falsify, or vulgarize, the ideas they are supposed to synthesize. Even close associates, members of a recognizable school of thought, reveal differences on close inspection. D'Alembert and Diderot were fellow *philosophes* and worked for years as colleagues on the *Encyclopédie*. They had the same enemies, fought the same battles, yet they did not agree on such fundamental issues as the constitution of matter or the place of mathematics in science. Ideas change subtly in time even within the same movement: Montesquieu's rejection of Christianity is far less thoroughgoing than Holbach's, partly because Montesquieu had written his books half a century before Holbach wrote his. Even a single thinker often eludes any single category: Diderot's religious views underwent a complex development, Voltaire changed his mind on determinism, Rousseau's world view remains the subject of lively controversy. Finally, nominalism in the history of ideas is a defense against a pretentious *Geistesgeschichte*, which hypostatizes ideas, gives them an independent life, and divorces them from all ties with their world.

Yet, it would be unfortunate if intellectual history were reduced to intellectual biography. The intellectual historian is not merely a diligent archeologist, he is a creative architect as well. We may agree that there is no such thing as a disembodied "spirit of an epoch," but ideas do possess significant similarities. They cluster in families. Each idea has its own history, its private destiny, but in certain historical moments it allies itself with others, and forms a school, or a movement that can be properly identified.

The essays in this section deal with such families, in various ways. None offers a complete synthesis of the Enlightenment—the very concentration on France prevents my drawing a complete portrait of a movement cosmopolitan in personnel and in conviction—but each is an attempt to move toward such a synthesis. The first of these essays, "The Unity of the French Enlightenment," tries to establish a common denominator below the lively variety of eighteenth-century French thought. I am convinced that its argument could be extended to the European Enlightenment as a whole.

The second essay moves toward synthesis in a rather different way. Convinced that the Enlightenment is, among other things, a thoroughgoing rebellion against Christian ethics and the Christian view of passion, I have visualized this rebellion as a dialectic which every reader of Freud will recognize. My procedure may be playful, but I am sure that it is not artificial: fundamental changes in cultural styles are always hard, slow, and attended with painful struggles within the revolutionaries themselves; my dialectical triad dramatizes the struggle and its resolution.

The last essay in this section is not, strictly speaking, about the French Enlightenment. I have included it here because it addresses itself to a question that historians of the Enlightenment have often asked: in what way, and to what extent, were the *philosophes* responsible for the French Revolution?[1] By reconstructing the mental world of the revolutionaries, I have concluded that philosophical ideas held a relatively modest place in their daily actions. This may seem like a disappointing result, but I think it is worth recording, for if there is one temptation to which intellectual historians are persistently exposed, it is to overestimate the impact of ideas, and it is useful to suggest that synthesis is possible even without exaggeration.

[1] For a well argued dissent from my position, see Crane Brinton: "Comment on Gay," *American Historical Review*, LXVI (April 1961), 677-81.

4

THE UNITY OF THE FRENCH ENLIGHTENMENT

OUR AGE is the twilight of historical clichés, in the study of the French Enlightenment as elsewhere. The comfortable generalities which welcomed us into the world of the eighteenth century have been riddled by revisionist scholarship. Even Ernst Cassirer's authoritative *Philosophy of the Enlightenment*, which remains the most impressive synthesis we have, no longer satisfies us: we have learned that the *philosophes* were more various, more political, more deeply engaged with their world than is suggested by his stately procession of thinkers who all somehow prefigured Kant.

The historian facing the monographic literature feels like a traveler in a nightmarish landscape: there is no lack of signposts, but they point with malicious delight in opposite directions. The *philosophes* were not optimists: Voltaire proclaimed life to be a shipwreck and lamented the decline of taste in his century; Holbach insisted on the viciousness and

Helvétius on the selfishness of the human animal; even Rousseau, the champion of a just Providence, defended his optimism in the most anxious and lugubrious of tones. Yet they were too active, too energetic, too deeply opposed to the Christian doctrine of man's depravity, to lapse into pessimism or pious resignation. The *philosophes* were not rationalists: Condillac, d'Alembert, and Voltaire attacked the rationalists' construction of metaphysical systems, and insisted on the limits of reason, the ignorance of humanity, and the futility of seeking certainty. Yet they despised and combated antirationalist theories of knowledge and dwelled admiringly on the achievements of scientific method. The *philosophes* battled for toleration and the humane treatment of society's victims—their humanitarian activities have withstood the scrutiny of the most hard-headed critic. Yet in their personal lives they were often intolerant and inhumane: Voltaire hounded his literary and political adversaries; d'Alembert, the enemy of censorship, peevishly asked the censors to suppress the pamphlets of his critics. The *philosophes* prided themselves on their knowledge of science: Maupertuis brilliantly confirmed and Voltaire brilliantly popularized Newton's cosmology; Diderot anticipated many discoveries in psychology and biology; the *Encyclopédie* was a massive tribute to technology and the scientific method. Yet the alert reader detects undertones of philistine aversion to scientific speculation, sometimes in the heart of the scientific camp, as in Diderot's hostility to mathematics. Perhaps the safest generality about the *philosophes* (certainly the most popular) has been that they were "cold" rationalists, contemptuous of the power of emotion, and existed in a universe stripped of love and color, devoid of any passion but sex. But for all its plausibility, this generality also dissolves under scrutiny. It would hold only if we disregarded the *philosophes*' defense of imagination, their pioneering analysis of passion, their bold creation of literary forms, and their almost unanimous infatuation with Richardson's sensibility. And we would have to rob the French Enlightenment of Rousseau and Diderot by calling them pre-Romantics—a larcenous and unjust, although widely practiced, proceeding.

I could go on listing divergences among the *philosophes:* deists against atheists, aristocrats against democrats, believers in free will against determinists. Close inspection even ruins the harmonious portrait of a friendly debate within the philosophic family—or clique, as frightened enemies called it. Voltaire collaborated with an *Encyclopédie* in which he never really believed and to whose chief editor he gave reserved and uncomprehending respect; Diderot, in return, offered reluctant tributes to the literary dictator whom he admired and distrusted as a brilliant but unstable child; Rousseau, at first welcomed by all came to reject, and to be rejected, by all. The *philosophes* moved in a highly charged atmosphere in which quarrels were bitter, reconciliations fervent, conversations intense, interests sometimes exalted but often trivial—an energetic atmosphere in which, despite all distractions, everyone worked, all the time.

It is this almost obsessive dedication to work that provides us with our escape from nominalism. For the *philosophes*, work was pleasure, obligation, consolation, fulfillment. For obvious reasons I shall resist the temptation of saying that it was salvation.

The environment in which work is performed imposes tasks, suggests styles, draws limits, and is in turn transformed by work done. Now, the *philosophes*' world (and I mean more than the censorship or the salons, I mean their total experience, including their experience of themselves) defined their task.

Let me put their situation into a formula: as men of letters at home in a world that was losing its Christian vocation, the *philosophes* felt this critical loss as a deep problem and solved it by reinterpreting and transforming their civilization. They made themselves the spokesmen for a revolutionary age in search of an interpreter.

The *philosophes* were men of letters. This is more than a phrase. It defines their vantage point, and eliminates the stale debate over their status as philosophers. As men of letters who took their craft seriously, they devoted to their writing an incessant care which is one of the secrets of their style. Their output was enormous, and they sent less to the printer than they threw away. They knew the pleasure of self-criticism, and the sweeter pleasure of criticizing others. Grimm corrected Diderot, Diderot corrected Voltaire, and Voltaire corrected everybody. Rousseau, far from tossing off his masterpieces in a fit of feverish inspiration, struggled with them for years; Voltaire rewrote untiringly, and treated first editions as drafts to be recast in the next printing; Diderot poured early versions of articles into his letters to Sophie Volland. While there is no single Enlightenment style, all *philosophes had* style.

This devotion to the art of writing gave the *philosophes* the strength that comes from membership in a respectable guild; it gave them, for all their quarrels, common interests and a common vision. No matter how varied their concerns, they were men with a single career. To attribute two careers to Voltaire—the irresponsible *littérateur* before the Calas case, the grim reformer after—is to misunderstand the unity of his life. Of course, the *philosophes*' versatility opens them to the charge of dilettantism, and it is true that they sometimes tried to teach what they had not learned—as writers will. But the range of their knowledge was extraordinary. Diderot translated works on medicine and ethics; wrote articles on crafts, industry, philosophy, theology, history, politics, classical and modern literature; rode editorial herd on a stable of willful encyclopedists; broke new paths in the bourgeois drama, in dramatic and art criticism, the novel and the dialogue. Voltaire took an informed and passionate interest in all the countries of Europe and all the countries of the mind.

Yet the *philosophes* were never so deeply engaged in politics to neglect literature, and they were never so deeply engaged in literature to neglect the society in which they lived. While they were literary men, they were neither bohemians nor alienated artists. While their view of their world was critical, and especially in religion, disruptive, they knew and loved the world they wished to change. Rousseau in some moods rejected it altogether, and asked for man's total regeneration, but it is significant that his fellow *philosophes* treated him as a madman long before his clinical symptoms became obvious. When they denounced civilization, they did so urbanely.

The *philosophes*, then, much as they wished to change it, were at home in their world. To divide the century into two sharply defined forces—the subversive *philosophes* against the orthodox—may be convenient and dramatic, but it is also much too simple. There were moments of crisis when two parties crystallized and Catholics squared off against unbelievers, but subtler and more pervasive than hostility were the ties that bound the *philosophes* to their society. They edited respectable magazines, flattered royal mistresses, wrote unexceptionable entertainments, and held responsible posts.

Nor was their attachment to the existing order based solely on calculation: they shared with literate Christians a religious education, a love for the classics of Roman and French literature, and an affection for the pleasures of cultivated leisure. Seeking to distinguish themselves, they did not wish to abolish all distinctions. When they participated in politics, they often supported one orthodox party against another: Montesquieu, the *parlements* against the king; Voltaire, the king against the *parlements*. While they helped to prepare the way for the Jacobins, they were not Jacobins themselves.

Their attachment was strengthened by their association with a spectrum of would-be *philosophes*, half-*philosophes*, or Christians liberal enough to tolerate, or even to enjoy, men whose doctrines they rejected. Hangers-on, who basked in borrowed glory or second-hand notoriety, smuggled *philosophes'* letters, arranged for theatrical claques, and offered true friendship in a quarrelsome world. Strategically placed officials stood between *philosophes* and the severities of the law, and good Christians who dabbled in higher criticism or polite anticlericalism spread philosophic doctrines in respectable circles. In brief, the *philosophes* were deeply embedded in the texture of their society.

Yet this did not prevent them from being at war with it at the same time. The *philosophes* never developed a coherent political program or even a consistent line of political tactics, but their polemics called for a France profoundly different from the country in which they lived—France after, not before, 1791. The regime could make concessions: boredom, a lost sense of purpose, could make many a bourgeois, priest, or aristocrat receptive to subversive propaganda. But aggressive deism or materialism, doctrines of the rule of law, complete toleration, and subordination of church to state—these tenets could not be assimilated by the old order. To neglect either side of their dual situation is to make the *philosophes* more revolutionary or more conservative than in fact they were.

This tension, which is yet not alienation, places not only the *philosophes* in their century, it places the century itself. To say that the eighteenth century was an age of contradictions, is to say nothing: all ages have this characteristic in common. We must be specific: eighteenth-century France was a Christian culture that was rapidly losing its Christian vocation without being fully aware of it.

"One day," writes Paul Hazard, "the French people, almost to a man, were thinking like Bossuet. The day after, they were thinking like Voltaire."[1] This is doubly wrong. The *philosophes* had much opposition among the educated and the powerful. While the writings of Montesquieu, Voltaire, and Diderot have survived, those of their adversaries have not, but survival is an unreliable guide to the intellectual map of the past: in the age of Louis XV Christianity had many a persuasive and intelligent defender. Moreover, we cannot properly speak of a "French people" in the eighteenth century. Most Frenchmen were wholly untouched by the Enlightenment and lived, as it were, in an earlier century. They believed in witches, applied spells, used home remedies long condemned by physicians, displayed a trust in authority long discarded by the educated, lived and died happily ignorant of the battles between Cartesians and Newtonians.

Yet for men sensitive or educated enough to be aware of intellectual currents, the eighteenth century was a time of turmoil. A whole complex of ideas and experiences, usually lumped together in the slippery word "secularization," came together in the reign of Louis XV to haunt thinking men. The literature of travel offered the spectacle of happy and civilized non-Christian cultures; the demands of international politics forged secular rather than sectarian alliances; the growth of

[1] Paul Hazard: *La Crise de la conscience Européenne* (1935), v.

the European economy stimulated the desire for worldly goods; the great discoveries of science suggested the appalling possibility of a universe without God.

Secularization did not mean the death of religion. Eight Frenchmen out of ten—perhaps nine—were uncontaminated by skepticism. Even the businessman or artisan, who greatly benefited from advances in technology, rarely allowed them to affect his faith. Stili, what Troeltsch has called the "Church-directed civilization" was crumbling. Christians lived by the image of hierarchy: as God, his angels, and his creatures were arranged in an order of rank, so by analogy the skies, the family, law, society, the Church, were naturally hierarchical. Now, as natural scientists demonstrated that the hierarchies of terrestrial and celestial motion, or the spheres of the heavens, were absurd, other revolutionaries were exposing the absurdity of other hierarchies.

In this time of trouble the two great hierarchical institutions, the Church and the nobility, did little to counteract this exposure. It is easy to exaggerate the worldliness of the eighteenth-century cleric or the uselessness of the eighteenth-century nobleman. Too much has been written about the atheist abbé and the idle marquis. There were many aristocrats who served their country ably, and who rose above the interests of their order to advocate truly national policies. Yet as the history of eighteenth-century France demonstrates, the French aristocracy was on the whole unwilling to make the sacrifices necessary to integrate it into a state that required some centralization of power and some revision of the tax structure. Born in an age that had given it a social function, the aristocratic caste was losing its vocation, as embittered renegades like the marquis D'Argenson did not fail to point out.

A similar loss of vocation threatened the Church. Thousands of priests fulfilled their offices with devotion; even some bishops believed in God. But in a time when natural philosophers were offering alternative explanations of the origins of man, the nature of evil, and the purpose of life, the Church needed a firmness of character, adroitness, and above all a unity that it could not muster. Many a young man of talent went into the opposition, and used the dialectical skill and classical learning imparted by his priestly instructors for their destruction.

Still, for all the impiety of the age, religion survived, and one reason for its survival was that the famous war between science and theology did not take place in the simple form familiar to us from the Whig Interpretation. The warfare began not between theology and science, but theology and some philosophical consequences drawn from science. It was not necessary to accept d'Alembert's positivism to be a good mathematician; or to be driven by Voltaire's anticlerical spleen to be a good Newtonian. Science, travel, politics, wealth, the great secularizing forces, did their work by indirection, as it were, behind the century's back.

Still they did their work, and they did it in the eighteenth century. In a celebrated book Paul Hazard has expended much learning to establish a crisis in the European conscience before 1715.[2] It is true that practically all the most aggressive ideas of eighteenth-century propagandists had a prehistory, but they did not touch a significant number of people until well after Newton's death in 1727. The typical seventeenth-century scientist was a good Christian: he was a Pascal, not a Hobbes. By separating theology from natural philosophy, or by ingeniously arguing that natural philosophy *supported*

[2] Ibid.

theology, seventeenth-century scientists concealed from themselves, as much as from others, the revolutionary implications of their work. It is a commonplace, but one all too often forgotten, that the geniuses from Galileo to Newton lived comfortably with convictions that eighteenth-century *philosophes* would stigmatize as incompatible. John Donne's famous and too much quoted lament that "new philosophy calls all in doubt," was the exceptional response of an exceptional man. In general, the imagination of the seventeenth century was unaffected, or generously expanded, by the new universe glimpsed in the new instruments. For Newton, God was active in the universe, occasionally correcting the irregularities of the solar system. The Newtonian heavens proclaimed God's glory.

This happy marriage of theism and science was not dissolved until the eighteenth century, when the discoveries of the age of genius were pushed to their logical conclusion. "Once the foundation of a revolution has been laid down," d'Alembert wrote in the *Encyclopédie*, "it is almost always in the next generation that the revolution is accomplished."[3] Several brilliant French mathematicians, d'Alembert among them, generalized Newton's laws of gravitation far beyond Newton's wishes. By the last quarter of the century, Lagrange and Laplace had established, in elegant equations, the stability of the solar system. The goal of eighteenth-century science had become evident: Newton's physics without Newton's God.

The crisis of secularization, then, was slower and subtler than we have been led to believe. It was also more pervasive.

[3] "Expérimental," in J. Lough, *d'Alembert, Selected Articles*
The Encyclopédie of Diderot and (1954), 74.

It was not confined to educated Christians, tormented by the startling conclusions of physicists. It was a problem for the *philosophes* themselves. It is not surprising that their anguish has received little attention—they covered it well with urbanity and noisy anticlericalism.

But anguish there was. The *philosophes* had two enemies: the institutions of Christianity and the idea of hierarchy. And they had two problems: God and the masses. Both the enemies and the problems were related and woven into the single task of rethinking their world. The old questions that Christianity had answered so fully for so many men and so many centuries, had to be asked anew: What—as Kant put it—what can I know? What ought I to do? What may I hope?

Science itself did not answer these questions. It only suggested—ever more insistently as the century went on—that the old answers were wrong. Now, the *philosophes* were products of Christian homes and Christian schools. If they became enemies of Christianity, they did so not from indifference or ignorance: they knew their Bible, their catechism, their Church Fathers, their apologetics. And they knew, because it had been drummed into them early, the fate that awaits heretics or atheists in the world to come. Their anticlerical humor therefore has the bitter intimacy of the family joke; to embrace materialism was an act of rejection.

The struggle of the *philosophes* was a struggle for freedom. They did not fully understand it, but to the extent that they did understand it, they knew their situation to be filled with terror and delight. They felt the anxiety and exhilaration of the explorer who stands before the unknown.

To use such existentialist language may seem like a rather portentous way of describing men noted for their sociability and frivolity. It is of course true that the *philosophes* did not suffer alone: they had the comforting company of elegant salons and of respectable philosophical forebears.

Yet even the supple Voltaire, who had been initiated into unbelief by fashionable teachers, was not free from the symptoms of this struggle. Much of his mockery was a weapon in a grim fight, and a device to keep up his own morale. Much of his philosophical rumination on free will reveals the persistence of a troublesome inner conflict.

It may not be fair to call to witness Rousseau, whose malaise was perpetual. But the shape of his suffering mirrors the suffering of his century. Nothing is more pathetic than Rousseau's attempt to rescue at least some comforting aspects of his universe from the icy blasts of Voltaire's cosmic pessimism. "All the subtleties of metaphysics," he wrote Voltaire, seeking to answer the poem on the Lisbon earthquake, "will not make me doubt for a moment the immortality of the soul or a beneficent Providence. I feel it, I believe it, I want it, I hope for it, and I shall defend it to my last breath."[4] But the edifice of Rousseau's faith was flimsily built on illogical hope: the immortality of the soul and a beneficent Providence are articles of faith to which a Christian happily subscribes, but to which the deist, nourished on scientific skepticism, has no right.

Diderot, the most ebullient of *philosophes*, the freest and most inventive of spirits, was driven from position to position and haunted by doubts. Born into a family richly endowed with priests, of pious parents and with a fanatical brother, long toying with entering the priesthood, Diderot moved from Catholicism to theism, from theism to deism, from deism to skepticism, and from skepticism to atheism. But atheism,

[4] August 18, 1756, *Correspondance générale*, ed. Théophile Dufour and Pierre-Paul Plan, 20 vols. (1924-1934), II, 324.

with its cold determinism, repelled him even though he accepted it as true; while Catholicism, with its colorful ceremony, moved him even though he rejected it as false. Writing to his mistress, Sophie Volland, he cursed the philosophy—his own—that reduced their love to a blind encounter of atoms. "I am furious at being entangled in a confounded philosophy which my mind cannot refrain from approving and my heart from denying."[5]

The materialists of course claimed to be defiantly happy at being cosmic orphans. But the question—If God is dead, what is permitted?—was not a question calculated to make men sleep easy.

I am not simply arguing that the *philosophes* were less cheerful than they appeared in their social roles—most of us are. Nor that they suffered personal crises—philosophers, especially young philosophers, often do. I am arguing that the *philosophes*' anguish was related to the crisis in their Christian civilization; that (to use different language) whatever childhood experiences made them psychologically vulnerable in adult life, their obsessions, their self-questionings, their anxieties, were poured into their religious, moral, and political speculation.

But the *philosophes*' crisis was not only a crisis felt, it was also a crisis conquered. And this brings me back to the idea of work, and to the philosophy of energy.

There are several ways of dealing with a sense of helplessness. The *philosophes* might have given way to panic, despair, or paralyzing skepticism; they might have escaped from the terrifying spectacle of an empty universe by a doctrine of

[5] Undated letter, quoted in Jean Thomas, *L'humanisme de Diderot* (ed. 1938), 49-50.

art for art's sake. Instead they overcame their anxiety by work. They escaped not from, but into reality.

The philosophy of energy was not a technical philosophical position, but a style of life. Whatever its form, it was confidence in the rational will, a humanist's pride in man's possibilities tempered by an empiricist's humility before man's limitations. Men, Voltaire said, must dare to do more than they have done. "We do not want enough," he warned,[6] and late in life he wrote to a friend, "We must battle nature and fortune until the last moment, and never despair of anything until we are good and dead."[7]

Sometimes work was an escape. The drudgery of reading proofs on an *Encyclopédie* or of correcting a king's verses were bulwarks against uncertainty, loneliness, and *Weltschmerz.* "If I were by your side, I'd complain and you would comfort me; but you are absent, and work is the only means I have of diverting my thoughts from my sufferings." Thus Diderot, depressed and alone in Paris, to his best friend Grimm.[8] "To work and think of you, that's my life." Thus Voltaire, after his disastrous stay at the Prussian court, to his niece and mistress Madame Denis.[9] Love and work: an energetic program to make an unpalatable world less unpalatable.

But work as consolation is only the most primitive level of the philosophy of energy. Its most familiar expression, which pervaded the *philosophes*' writings through the century, was the drive to assert man's power over his environment. Even

[6] *Anecdotes sur le czar Pierre Le Grand, Œuvres,* XXIII, 303.

[7] Voltaire to d'Argental, August 31 (1777), *Œuvres,* L, 263.

[8] (End of April-May 1, 1759), *Correspondance,* ed. Georges Roth (1955ff.), II, 126.

[9] September 3 (1753), *Correspondence,* XXIII, 166.

the materialists, for all their determinism, taught the virtue of rational activity and the possibility of modifying nature.

Power over nature was more than a cliché: the *philosophes* knew precisely what they meant by it. They had learned it, partly from Bacon, partly (although rather less) from Descartes, and above all from the needs and possibilities of their time. Medieval man had not abjectly resigned himself to misery or pathetic dependence on divine intervention in his behalf. Yet even sympathetic historians have conceded that the Middle Ages were an age of precarious and violent existence. Men aged young and died young; those fortunate enough to survive infancy, epidemics, or famines, were likely victims of bandits, pirates, sudden war, or brutal migrations. "Beneath all social life," Marc Bloch writes, "there was a soil of primitivism, of submission to ungovernable powers."[1]

To remedy this—to prolong life, clear the roads of assassins, keep men from starving, and give them hope of enjoying the fruits of their labors—required more than a stable political organization. It required a spiritual revolution, and the culmination of that revolution was the philosophy of the *philosophes*.

But words alone did not eliminate illness, starvation, or insecurity, scourges that continued to haunt the world of Bacon and even the world of Voltaire. French civilization of the eighteenth century still wore a half-finished look. Polish was bright, because it was new; the decline of religious fervor did not prevent occasional terrifying outbursts of hysteria, the advances of education did not eliminate brutal games, sadistic sports, or destructive riots.

[1] *La Société féodale, La formation des liens de dépendance* (1939), 116.

The survival of coarseness was related to the continuing ravages of diseases and the pressures of hunger: the uncertainty of life did not allow the generous grace of conduct that comes with true ease. The fate of the royal family—the death in rapid succession of the only son and two of the grandsons of Louis XIV—dramatically underlined the general precariousness. At the age of forty-six, Diderot, on a visit to his native town, found most of his schoolmates gone, and mused darkly on the brevity of life.[2]

Yet the *philosophes*' attitude to the blows of fate was one of defiance, not resignation. While deists continued to protest that the Lord gave, they saw no reason why they might not enjoy what he had given, and why they might not try to keep it as long as possible. In the Middle Ages, the accidents of nature had dominated man; in the eighteenth century, to use Diderot's phrase, men were seizing nature and tormenting her. Scientists were beginning to force from her reluctant lips the secrets of her operations.

Evidence for this sense of mastery is everywhere. It is in medicine, which had a place of honor among the *philosophes*. Some of them were physicians, others took an abiding interest in what La Mettrie, himself a doctor, praised as the supreme art of healing. It is, too, in Diderot's *Encyclopédie*. Its alphabetical arrangement vividly emphasizes its single-minded purpose. The anticlerical articles are not just bait to make the reader tolerate dull pieces on crafts; the articles on crafts are not just padding for daring heresies. Both have a single purpose: to reinterpret the world and by reinterpreting it, to change it. In a phrase which has become too familiar to have

[2] Diderot to Sophie Volland (August 4 or 5, 1759), *Correspondance*, II, 202.

retained its original vigor, Diderot said that he wanted his *Encyclopédie* to "change the general way of thinking."[3]

The *philosophes*, men with a single career which took a variety of forms, also had a single task which took a variety of expressions. The philosophy of energy is the glass that collects all their activities in a single focus. Diderot spoke for them all: "Everything belongs together in the human understanding; the obscurity of one idea spreads over those that surround it. An error throws shadows over neighboring truths, and if it happens that there should be in society men interested in forming, as it were, centers of shadow, soon the people will find itself plunged into a profound darkness."[4] The spreading of light operates by the same Keynesian multiplier: the *philosophes*' propaganda campaign, from the bulky *Encyclopédie* to the sprightly *Dictionnaire philosophique*, is a series of lamps from which others will find illumination and spread the light in their turn.

The *philosophes*' task cannot therefore be contained in the word *humanitarianism*. It was greater than that: the campaign to abolish torture cannot be divorced from the campaign to abolish Jesuits or to spread technological knowledge—all are part of the struggle to impose man's rational will on the environment. Nor was it simply the acquisition of knowledge. As good Baconians, the *philosophes* preached that knowledge is power, but few of them were naïve enough to believe that knowledge automatically creates virtue: their writings are filled with warnings against the misuse of intelligence or the brutalizing of learning. They did argue that since knowledge is power, ignorance is impotence. It followed that the men

[3] This famous phrase occurs in Diderot's article "Encyclopédie," in his *Encyclopédie*. See Arthur M. Wilson: *Diderot: The Testing Years* (1957), 244.

[4] "Bramines," in Lough, *The Encyclopédie*, 17-18.

who wanted to keep others in ignorance were enemies of humanity. What does one do with monsters who want to castrate mankind? All—or almost all—methods are fair against them.

The philosophers of energy face to face with their enemies: this confrontation leads us back to the beginning, for it helps to solve the puzzling contradictions that beset the interpreter of the Enlightenment. The French Enlightenment had its own history, and that history mirrors, and helped to shape, the history of the century. Something happened in Europe in the 1760's. It was the beginning of industrial society; the beginning of modern politics and the great democratic revolt against aristocratic regimes. It was a time of turmoil within the Christian world itself: witness the suppression of the Jesuits, and the outbursts of hysterical prosecutions of Huguenots and blasphemers.

In this time of trouble, the *philosophes* added to their sense of power over the environment a sense of mission. The moderate anticlericalism of a Montesquieu gave way to the belligerent cry, *Écrasez l'infâme;* democratic political ideas found a favorable hearing even from the skeptic Voltaire.[5] The *philosophes* grew more radical, more combative, more convinced than ever that they were the prophets of a new age that would rise on the ruins of the old.

As they became more violently partisan, the contradictions in their views became more obvious. As a historian, Voltaire delighted in the past for its own sake; as an aesthetician, Diderot delighted in the play of light and shade on canvas. But as prophets, both found it necessary to import moral lessons into their writings. If the old civilization must give way to the new, if men must learn to dare and to rely on

[5] See my *Voltaire's Politics,* ch. 4.

themselves, if even the uneducated are to find their place in this revolution, then *philosophes* must teach, and teach again, and teach everywhere. Cultivated men possessed by a sense of mission temper their cultivation for the sake of their mission. This will lead to inconsistencies. But these inconsistencies do not destroy, they merely dramatize, the richness and the unity of the French Enlightenment.

5

THREE STAGES ON LOVE'S WAY: ROUSSEAU, LACLOS, DIDEROT

Je ne désirais pas de jouir, je voulais savior.
—MARQUISE DE MERTEUIL, in Laclos, *Les Liaisons dangereuses*

IN 1782, Choderlos de Laclos, a *capitaine-commandant* in the French artillery, published a novel that scandalized even the jaded readers in that unpuritanical century. *Les Liaisons dangereuses*, an immediate and immense success, dwelt lovingly on the joys of sexual pursuit, the initiation of the innocent, the degradation of the pious; it analyzed with caressing care the stratagems of promiscuity and the rewards of betrayal; it introduced to the literary scene a pair of villains so spectacularly villainous, so utterly devoid of decency and so single-mindedly dedicated to evil, that only a great writer could prevent them from becoming incredible or ludicrous. Laclos's sudden emergence, his superb deftness and deep insight, startled the literary world; his earlier work, some facile verses of a mildly erotic turn, had not even hinted at the range of his talent.

It was perhaps even more startling to see that Laclos had inscribed on the title page of his novel the motto "I have seen the morals of this age, and I have published these letters," a motto taken, of all places, from Rousseau's *Nouvelle Héloïse*.

The readers of Laclos's novel must have suspected that the author was making fun of them: what could the world's most immoral novel have in common with a book that was a moral tract parading as a novel? Some critics of *Les Liaisons dangereuses* pointed out that the villains of the novel are destroyed in the end, but the *dénouement*, on a far lower level of invention than the rest of the book, was either a joke on the reader or an immoral preachment in a novel guise: the villains are punished as a result of their first, and only, display of human feeling. Again, the external similarity of Rousseau's and Laclos's novels seems to mean little: both are about love and, more specifically, about seduction, but the identity of the theme vanishes before the divergence of the treatment. Both novels, finally, are epistolary, but that form was an almost compulsory international convention, initiated by Richardson and imitated by Goethe. The conclusion suggests itself, therefore, that Laclos chose his motto in bad faith and that he was not a disciple but a parodist of Rousseau. But this conclusion, plausible as it is, is mistaken. The two novels are related to each other dialectically: they embody different stages of the French eighteenth-century mind.

The *philosophes* were above all reformers, suspicious of theoretical speculation for its own sake. But their practical demands for social and political change drove them, in spite of themselves, to reflect on the foundations of morality. Gropingly, not always wholly conscious of the revolutionary significance of their thinking, they evolved an image of the world that was distinctively modern—secular, determinist, scientific, pragmatic. They replaced the Christian world view with a non-Christian world view.

The most formidable victims of the new philosophy were Christian theology and Christian churches—many twentieth-century readers know little more about the *philosophes* than that they unmasked miracles, revelation, and priests. But the *philosophes* were not the first to attack the Christian world view, nor were they content to attack it alone. They were also trying to undermine the Christian view of man and of morality. These two rebellions were equally significant, but they were not equally successful. Christian cosmology found few intellectual defenders—seventeenth-century rationalists had tried in vain to hold the line against scientific empiricism. But Christian morality found two allies: Puritanism and the bourgeoisie. Hence the *philosophes*' assault on Christian morality was at once more subversive and less effective than their assault on Christian cosmology.

The core of Enlightenment ethics was a favorable estimate of human nature and of the human enterprise. Voltaire said that Pascal had taught men to hate themselves, while they ought to learn, instead, to love themselves. David Hume, following the Renaissance Humanists and anticipating Nietzsche, derided Christian humility and defended a reasonable pride and a measured self-love. Kant spoke for the whole Enlightenment when he called upon men to strive for autonomy.

In seeking to free man from the stigma of original sin, the *philosophes* needed to rehabilitate the emotions. Human passions might be blind, unmeasured, but they were not evil.

Above all, it was essential to reinstate sexuality in its legitimate place as a joyous, morally acceptable activity. This was a grave and risky enterprise. Catholic social ethics had always found room for the Old Adam—it had tolerated ribald songs, erotic tales, sexual epithets. The very ritual and imagery of the Church freely used sexual symbols. Chivalry celebrated emotions that the Church had condemned as mortal sins. But Catholicism had always looked upon these escapes from the denigration of sexuality as concessions to fallen humanity. These escapes were tolerated, not happily accepted. They were disguised, reinterpreted, or idealized: divorce was forbidden, but one might divest oneself of one's wife through annulment; chivalry sang love and pride, but pride was humbled and love rarely successful—sensuality, as Huizinga has shown, was transformed into the craving for self-sacrifice; courtly love was purified by the acceptable motive of loyalty and by the acceptable ending of marriage. These accommodations of Christian virtues to libidinal urges were shrewd concessions, but never more than that. Man was a vessel of wrath, sexuality was lust and concupiscence—the mark of man's folly and disobedience, not of his worthiness.

The Reformation and the increasing acceptance of bourgeois standards only accentuated this rejection of the sexual urge; in this area, as in others, the Reformation was no liberation.[1] Protestant divines deplored the flesh as they deplored

[1] I am aware that this is a simplified account of a complicated relationship. Troeltsch pointed out half a century ago that Christianity was not merely ascetic, but was very much in this world. Surely the picture of the dour Puritan who condemns all pleasure as lust is little better than a lazy caricature. At the same time, the prevailing direction of all versions of Christianity was toward a separation of aspects of human behavior that the *philosophes* were seeking to reunite.

images or colorful dress. Bourgeois laymen were more ambivalent: they could never resolve the conflict between gratification and abstention. They believed in indulgence and enjoyment, but they needed libidinal energies for the sake of accumulation and investment. Hence the invention of "respectability"—a rationalization of ambivalent sexual feelings; hence the exaggeration of the old separation of sex from love. When Protestant burghers derided priests they did so because the priest was parasitical, wasteful, unproductive.

The *philosophes*' demand for the reconstruction of sexual morality was thus not merely a pragmatic demand for greater license, but a fundamental demand for a revaluation of libidinal drives. It is fanciful to see the *philosophes* dissolutely chasing from *boudoir* to *boudoir*, or to think that all they wished for was the right to snigger at obscene pictures or to produce pornographic novels. The *philosophes* sought to break with conventional—that is to say, Christian and bourgeois—morality because in their opinion it constrained and even degraded man's nature. And in exalting man they sought to give a positive value to the strongest and most mysterious of his passions.

Rousseau's *Nouvelle Héloïse* is a timid first step in this campaign of liberation. It is perhaps the most conventional novel of seduction ever written. Conventional seems a strange word to apply to Rousseau who strove, from his first *Discours* onward, to penetrate beyond artificiality to nature. But the *Nouvelle Héloïse* is conventional in accepting Christian standards of conduct. Love is an evil passion, to sleep with the person you love is a transgression that will permanently tarnish your whole existence. Moreover, love is a passion that victimizes men. Rousseau is careful to deprive his hero of all responsibility: Saint-Preux, the middle-class tutor of gentle-born Julie, confesses to his young charge that he loves her. He knows that as a commoner he has little hope of winning the consent of Julie's aristocratic father, and he offers to leave. This moment, like the famous moment in Proust when the narrator's mother spends the night with her terrified boy, is the decisive moment of weakness from which all later weakness flows. Saint-Preux's offer to leave is like a politician's offer to resign: he knows it will not be accepted. If Saint-Preux had been a man, he would either have avowed his passion to Julie's father, or eloped with Julie, or, sensing the hopelessness of his attempt to cross class lines, he would have departed. But no—Saint-Preux is like a little boy: he wants others to make decisions for him, he wants to transgress the moral code while swooning in an aura of moral approval. He protests that his sentiments are pure, and he is speaking the truth. What he does not know—and what Rousseau does not know—is that he wants to enjoy without paying. He is largely passive, the object rather than the master of passion. "I am no vile seducer!" he exclaims. He is right: it is virginal, pure-minded Julie who seduces him. He offers to leave, she begs him to stay. He avows the harmlessness of his love, she begs him to save her from a passionate transgression—an unconscious invitation that only puts an idea into Saint-Preux's mind. When things become complicated, Julie sends Saint-Preux away and when she learns that her father has picked out a wealthy elderly husband for her, she decides to lose her virginity with her beloved tutor. "I had to kill the author of my days, my lover, or myself. Without knowing what I was doing, I chose my own misfortune."[2] What could be sweeter than to revenge

[2] *Julie, ou la Nouvelle Héloïse,* *Œuvres complètes,* ed. Bernard Guyon et al. (Pléiade ed., in progress), II, 96.

yourself on "the author of your days" by indulging yourself with your lover? For ordinary mortals, perhaps, nothing, but for Julie there is one greater pleasure, a pleasure to which she surrenders for hundreds of pages—preaching.

Throughout most of the novel, Julie takes a high moral tone and lectures everybody. It is evident from Rousseau's careful handling of her soliloquies, and from the effect which they have on her listeners, that she is not to be taken as a prude, a bore, or a compulsive talker, but as a genuine moralist. Perhaps a little apologetically, Rousseau has Julie recognize her bent by having her call herself *la prêcheuse*, but no one in the novel seems to be able to do without her sermons. Even her proud father, who forgets himself enough to strike her in a moment of fury, finally succumbs to her rhetoric and her unique moral superiority. Julie is more than moral—she is strong as well. She decides when to invite Saint-Preux into what he calls "the sanctuary of all that my heart adores" (her bedroom)[3]; she decides to have a child by her lover (a child that is, fortunately for the plot, miscarried when her father strikes her); she decides to send Saint-Preux into exile, and to marry her father's candidate, a bloodless rationalist named de Wolmar. When she finally dies after rescuing one of her children from drowning, still loving Saint-Preux, but also loving and respecting her husband, she dominates the final scene by arranging to marry Saint-Preux to her cousin Claire,

[3] This bedroom scene describes the second time they have slept together. Interestingly enough, Julie is reluctant to take full responsibility for the first occasion. In reporting on it to her cousin Claire, she blames Claire for leaving her in a critical moment, thereby making the seduction possible. But she comes through: in the same letter she collects herself and refuses to blame either Claire or Saint-Preux: "He is not guilty; I alone am guilty; all my miseries are my work, and I have no one to blame but myself." Ibid.

another patient victim of her lectures. While this scheme fails, widower, lover, and cousin join to worship the memory of this extraordinary creature.

It has often been said that Julie is a conflation of several women whom Rousseau had loved, especially Madame d'Houdetot, who did not return Rousseau's middle-aged devotion and who, although filled with pity and kindness for Rousseau, refused to become unfaithful to her own lover, the poet Saint-Lambert. Another ingredient in Julie may have been Madame de Warens, Rousseau's matronly first mistress, whom he called, appropriately enough, *Maman*, and who had gravely invited Jean-Jacques to her bed: life anticipating art, naturally on a lower level.

But Julie is more than reality purified by the writer's imagination—she is Rousseau's idea of Woman: pure, unattainable, the guardian of morality, the embracing mother who dominates the lives of others, who permits intimacy without sin, and who takes away the stain of transgression by her soothing words. That is Julie: the Woman as seen by the awed little son, the boy who is tempted to sin, and hopes to sin without losing the affection of his mother. Rousseau—and Saint-Preux—are like the forlorn little boy in the story who tells the policeman on the corner that he is running away from home, but that he is standing on the sidewalk because he is not permitted to cross the street.

Julie, of course, seems not to have proved unattainable. But that is only an illusion. Despite her loss of virginity, she is sexually unfulfilled and indeed sexually indifferent. After her first experience she reports to her cousin nothing but remorse and confesses that she yielded out of pity. When she invites Saint-Preux to her bedroom the next time, she is fulfilling an obligation: "This very evening I can fulfill my promises, and pay all at once all the debts of love"—a significant metaphor.[4] Saint-Preux enjoys love-making (that is evident from his incoherent expressions of joy) but Julie seems to see the act of love as an error, a concession to a male (who is, by his very masculinity, of cruder clay), a vulgar animal coupling that can only be enjoyed by impure souls. Julie's love affair never seems to give her a sense of liberation. When she hears the solemn words of the wedding service which unite her to the respectable M. de Wolmar, she feels herself purified. She is mistaken: she has never been defiled. She is, alas, a perpetual virgin.

Julie expresses her conventionality even more forcefully in the choices she makes: she is willing to sleep with Saint-Preux, but she will not run away to Paris with him. She rationalizes her refusal by writing him that she is torn between obligations to her parents and her love for him. And when she decides, she decides as we expect her to: instead of abandoning her home and a father whom Rousseau has described as self-willed, loutish, overbearing, and stupid, she abandons the only man whom she can ever truly love. She does not seem to feel that marrying a man she does not love is an immoral act—by her sacrifice she has maintained and sanctified the order of society. The radical Rousseau has been unwilling to tear the fabric of class relations. Perhaps the most significant incident in the novel is the death of Julie's child by Saint-Preux through her father's blow: a symbolic victory of convention over emotion, of obedience over love. The "first romantic novel" becomes a cautionary tale against love, passion, and rebellion.

Julie is pure—her purity is only intensified by her lapse;

[4] Ibid. II, 145.

Saint-Preux is weak—his weakness is only accentuated by his occasional, ineffectual acts of rebellion. Since Julie's kind of purity is a form of weakness, Julie and her lover may be said to have much in common. And they have something else in common—their overwhelming desire to purge themselves through talk. Like Doña Ana in Shaw's *Man and Superman*, they love confession. We know that Rousseau himself sought to expiate his crimes, real or imagined, by confessing the whole truth, or even more than the whole truth; and the protagonists of *La Nouvelle Héloïse* drown their guilty consciences in an avalanche of pitiless self-recrimination. It is not that the lovers seek to deal honestly with each other—that would be human and desirable. Their constant confessions are not honesty; they permit the lovers to act without assuming responsibility. Saint-Preux confesses his guilty love to Julie, hoping that his candor will bring absolution from the object of his adoration and thus permit him to go on loving. Until Julie can confess her premarital lapse to her husband, she cannot be fully happy, and she hopes that her confession will, in some miraculous way, remove the stain from her act of love. The ritualistic nature of her confession is underlined by the fact that her omniscient husband had known of her affair with Saint-Preux all along. Again, while Saint-Preux is in Paris, he falls in with a fast crowd and one morning, after a drunken night, he finds himself in bed with a courtesan. It is the very event against which Julie had warned him earlier —"I am not afraid that the senses and coarse pleasures will corrupt you"—and which Saint-Preux had promised would never happen. Now Paris is far from Vevey, Julie's home, but instead of remaining silent about the incident like a sensible man, Saint-Preux describes it to Julie in the most embarrassing detail and begs her forgiveness: "Julie, O Julie! Whom at one time I dared to call mine, and whose name I profane today! the pen escapes my trembling hand; my tears inundate the paper . . ." And then, with unconscious insight: "I can neither keep quiet nor speak. Come, honorable and dear image, come to purify and to strengthen a heart degraded by shame and broken by repentance. Uphold my courage which is extinguished; give my remorse the strength to avow the involuntary crime which your absence has permitted me to commit." Then, for two pages, a complete confession, ending with the request for punishment: "I have finished this awful account; let it no longer soil your attention or my memory. O you, from whom I await my judgment, I implore rigor; I deserve it. Whatever my punishment will be, it will be less cruel to me than the memory of my crime."[5]

I need hardly add that all these expectations of forgiveness are fulfilled, that all these lapses are condoned, and that the confessors show a depth of understanding almost unheard of outside the confessional until the advent of psychoanalysis. It is true that forgiveness is apt to be a little sententious and self-righteous—Julie gives Saint-Preux a lecture that is likely to make the modern reader squirm—but she forgives him, and that is all that he desired. So much guilt! So much desire to satisfy one's passions, and so much need to have these "low" satisfactions sanctified!

This is not sincerity, it is the cult of sincerity. Sincerity partakes of reason; it includes not only candor but also judicious silence. It is against Alceste's cult of sincerity that Philinte upholds sincerity in Molière's *Misanthrope:*

[5] Ibid. II, 294-7. Rousseau tells us in his *Confessions* that this incident was drawn from life—his life. *Œuvres complètes,* I, 354-6.

Il faut, parmi le monde, une vertu traitable;
A force de sagesse on peut être blâmable;
La parfaite raison fuit toute extrémité
Et veut que l'on soit sage avec sobriété.[6]

The cult of sincerity is the compulsive need to confess all, to eschew circumlocution, to despise politeness. In the area of social relations it results in fanaticism—the sense of superiority accompanied by the need to make others conform to one's own standards of purity. When Saint-Preux goes to Paris he finds much to censure in good society. The Parisian wit strikes him as empty rather than delightful, its courtesy as fraudulent rather than well-mannered. Saint-Preux—and through him, Rousseau—is a tiresome, and perhaps dangerous, enemy of "hypocrisy."

Satirists have always found ready material in the gap between profession and performance that is called "hypocrisy." But the searching satirist does not simply denounce hypocrisy, he sees it as a contradiction between socially acceptable and socially necessary behavior; he is concerned with exposing the contradiction rather than displaying his own purity by desiring the "hypocrite" to avow his feelings and actions. Shaw, in *Widowers' Houses*, exhibits respectable bourgeois living off slums, but he is concerned not with the sincerity of the bourgeois—what would be gained by the slum dweller if his landlord openly acknowledged the source of his wealth?—but with the social origin of his "hypocrisy."

Moreover, Rousseau's cult of sincerity—of which most of his characters are devotees—is a mask for insincerity. In seeking to undo by confession what cannot be undone, the protagonists of *La Nouvelle Héloïse* lie to themselves about their actions and about their very natures.

[6] Act I, scene 1.

Those who think of Rousseau only as a tearful romantic may be surprised by the didactic character of his novel. In fact, Rousseau deliberately designed his novel as a tract and carefully adjusted its style to his purpose. In its description of nature and of peasants' feasts, *La Nouvelle Héloïse* has an eloquent lyricism that was pioneering and that was justly influential. But in its interminable debates, it veered between carefully weighed classical antitheses that would have delighted Gibbon, and incoherent ejaculations, liberally using suspension dots and exclamation points, that are designed to convey intolerable emotional tension: "Ah, God! My mother sends for me. Whither shall I fly? How stand her looks? Why can't I hide myself in the bosom of the earth! . . . My whole body trembles and I am not in a state to take a step. . . . Shame, humiliation, severe reproaches. . . . I have deserved everything; I shall stand everything. But the pain, the tears of a disconsolate mother. . . . O my heart, what lacerations! . . . She is waiting for me, I can delay no longer. . . . She'll want to know . . . it will be necessary to tell all. . . . Regianino will be fired. Don't write me any more until further notice. . . . Who knows if ever . . . I could . . . what! lie! . . . Lie to my mother! . . . Ah! if we must save ourselves by a lie, adieu, we are lost!"[7]

Whatever the virtues of such heart-rending monologues, whatever the virtues of the novel—as a specimen of the Enlightenment's revolt against Christian morality, *La Nouvelle Héloïse* does not carry the revolt very far. Julie, it is true, does not avow herself a sinner even after her Fall, and professes a deism that has little doctrinal relation to Christianity. But in their deeper struggle with conventionality, the novel's characters surrender again and again. They have sexual re-

[7] *Julie, ou la Nouvelle Héloïse, Œuvres,* II, 306.

lations which they enjoy neither as sensual experiences nor as moral liberation; they are sincere with each other but dishonest with themselves; they think that they are free spirits, and act conventionally; the one unconventional character, Julie's husband, is a chilly manipulator of emotions, a man who plays a game with life, free because he is dead and not because he is alive; the rights of love yield before the rights of class. Rebellion there is, but it is feeble and abortive; conventional morality is victorious on all fronts. The prevailing emotion of *La Nouvelle Héloïse* is fear.

With Choderlos de Laclos's *Les Liaisons dangereuses*, the rebellion against Christian morality is carried a step further. Laclos's novel, as F.C. Green has said, is a reply to *La Nouvelle Héloïse*. But it is also more than that: it is a development of the morality of Rousseau's novel converted into its opposite. Where Rousseau is conventional, moral, and edifying, Laclos is unconventional, immoral, and destructive. In Rousseau everybody wins through losing: the sacrifice of gratification leads to purer, more exalted happiness. In Laclos, everybody loses through winning: insistence on gratification leads to restlessness, a sense of being cheated, and tragedy. Rousseau offers us the cult of sincerity, Laclos the cult of insincerity.

For a book that spends so much time on sex, there is singularly little sexual enjoyment in *Les Liaisons dangereuses*. The two chief actors of the novel, the marquise de Merteuil and her unwitting henchman, the vicomte de Valmont, are no strangers to voluptuousness. They are masters in the varieties of sexual experience. After having given her current lover a hard day, Mme de Merteuil makes up for it with an intimate night which she describes to M. de Valmont in erotic detail:

". . . my pardon was sealed on that same ottoman where you and I sealed, so gaily and in the same manner, our eternal rupture. Since we had six hours to spend together, and since I had resolved that this whole time should be equally delicious for him, I calmed his raptures and friendly coquettishness replaced tenderness. I do not believe that I have ever taken such pains to please. . . . After supper, in turn childish and reasonable, wanton and responsive, sometimes even licentious, I pleased myself to treat him like a sultan in his seraglio, where I was in turn his different favorites. Indeed, his repeated homage, although always received by the same woman, was always received by a new mistress."[8]

But neither Merteuil nor Valmont experiences sex as part of a passionate human relation. They see it as momentary gratification of the senses, and more importantly as part of an exquisite game that fascinates them far more than intercourse: the playing of a role for the sake of degrading others. The sexual act is an act of destruction, of hostility; it comes as the culmination of a long campaign, the result of far-seeing strategy, delicate tactics, clever assaults, and cleverer retreats.[9] Mme de Merteuil gets more enjoyment from deceiving the world by appearing as a prude than from having lovers. She concocts an elaborate plot that results in the disgrace of a

[8] In Choderlos de Laclos: *Œuvres complètes*, ed. Maurice Allen (1951), 55.

[9] In his interesting analysis, Martin Turnell has pointed to Laclos's constant use of military metaphors and expressions. *The Novel in France* (1950), 58, 68-9. These metaphors, which come easily to the pen, were generally favorites among the *philosophes*. It should be noted that there is some similarity of Valmont to Don Juan. Both are adolescent lovers, and Shaw's Don Juan in Hell shocks his hearers by telling them that "the sex relation is not a personal or friendly relation at all." But the two are also very different. Don Juan seeks confirmation through sex, Valmont, destruction.

sexual athlete—a man whom she regards as desirable, as a *superbe vainqueur*—rather than having an affair with him that would have pleased her physically. Similarly Valmont prefers arduous campaigns of conquest and convoluted stratagems to simple sensual satisfaction.

Most of the plot of *Les Liaisons dangereuses* centers around Valmont's successful attacks on the virtue of two women, *la présidente* de Tourvel, a pious, cool, and faithful wife, and Cécile Volanges, an empty-headed, sensual, flirtatious young virgin. Mme de Merteuil's motive in encouraging the second conquest is revenge upon the girl and her fiancé, who had apparently slighted her; her motive in discouraging the first is the fear that Valmont might discover the human emotion of real love. Valmont complicates his seduction of Mme Tourvel to an almost unbelievable degree: he plays the role of a charitable but dissolute young man whom the pious lady is to save from himself; her final downfall involves her confessor who is made an unconscious appendage to Valmont's plot; and her surrender to him must take certain ritual forms. As for his seduction of Cécile, all too easy for an experienced rake like him, Valmont adds piquant touches to his affair with her by teaching her positions and words that he would not dare, he writes, to demand from "all the girls who are professionals." As a sexually experienced man, with unlimited time, funds, and opportunities, he prefers these two tortuous conquests of unawakened and unsophisticated women (who are likely to be physically unsatisfactory) to nights with actresses, ladies of the town, or former mistresses whose talents he has good reason to remember. Valmont, like Mme de Merteuil, is not solely, or even largely, interested in sensual gratification.

But if *Les Liaisons dangereuses* is not mainly about sex, what is it about? I have said that it celebrates the cult of insincerity. Indeed, the amount of deception and plotting is staggering. Valmont lies to the women he tries to seduce, and to his friend Mme de Merteuil; Mme de Merteuil lies to everybody, resting her whole reputation on a cynical deception; Mme Tourvel lies to her husband; Cécile lies to her mother, her fiancé, and her lover. On a deeper level, the characters lie to themselves: Mme Tourvel permits herself to drift into a ruinous affair with Valmont by denying her sensuality, conscious only of her sincere desire to save the charming reprobate from himself; Cécile has no inkling of her multiple faithlessness. Even the rational, cold-blooded protagonists are not safe from self-deception: Valmont thinks he is in control of his passions, but he is, in fact, their slave. He thinks himself the freest of mortals; repudiating morality at will, he is caught in a web of compulsions that he does not understand or even recognize. Even his vile pursuit of Mme Tourvel, as Mme de Merteuil astutely reminds him, is based on emotions that he does not grasp. Most significantly, Mme de Merteuil, who thinks of herself as a chessplayer of vice, who has carefully worked out her philosophy and rationalized her resentments, falls in love with the chevalier Danceny (Cécile's suitor before Valmont, supposedly his friend, had taken over from him) and commits an imprudence that takes the game out of her hands, resulting in the death of Valmont and in her own complete ruin. And there is deception even on another level: in advertising *Les Liaisons dangereuses* as a moral novel, Laclos is lying either to his reader or to himself.

The whole novel, then, to use an old-fashioned phrase, is a tissue of lies. Even its humor depends on deception: two of the most amusing, and at the same time most chilling passages of the book (perhaps, by their very playfulness, its most immoral scenes) are based on Valmont's perverse sense of humor. Early in his pursuit of Mme Tourvel, Valmont writes to her from the bed of an actress, after a night of continuous love-making, using his mistress's back as a desk. In the middle of the letter he interrupts to make love to his actress and then resumes his writing. The action is mirrored in the letter itself, which can only be described as a long and diabolical pun: "It is after a stormy night, during which I did not close an eye; it is after having been without cease either in the agitation of a devouring ardor, or in the complete annihilation of all the faculties of my soul, that I come to seek near you, Madame, a rest which I need, and which nevertheless I do not think I shall enjoy. Indeed, the situation in which I find myself while writing to you, makes me know better than ever the irresistible power of love; I have difficulty in preserving enough mastery over myself to put my ideas in some order; and already I foresee that I shall not finish this letter without being interrupted. What! May I not hope that you will share one day the turmoil which I am undergoing at this moment? . . . Believe me, Madame, cold tranquillity, the sleep of the soul, image of death, do not lead to happiness; only the active passions can lead to it; and despite the torments which you are making me undergo, I think I can say without fear that at this moment I am happier than you. . . . I have never had so much pleasure in writing to you; never before did I feel, in this occupation, a feeling so sweet and yet so lively. Everything seems to increase my raptures: the air I breathe is filled with voluptuousness; the very table on which I am writing to you, devoted to this purpose for the first time, becomes for me the sacred altar of love; how it will grow in beauty in my eyes! I shall have traced on it the vow to love you always! Forgive me, I beg you, the disorder of my senses. I should perhaps give myself less to raptures that you do not share: I must leave you for a moment to dissipate an intoxication which grows with every moment, and which is becoming too strong for me.

I return to you, Madame. . . ."[1]

The other incident is minor, but it displays Valmont's ingenuity. One night, dining at the château of a vicomte and his vicomtesse, the latter asks Valmont to spend the night. He replies that he will do so with pleasure if he can spend the night with her. "Impossible," she tells him—her lover is in the château. Piqued by the word *impossible*, Valmont decides to persevere, and succeeds in persuading the vicomtesse. That night he finds that the vicomtesse's husband sleeps in the room to her right, her lover is lodged to her left, and he—Valmont—across the hall. After a complicated arrangement, involving trumped-up quarrels and multiple deceptions, Valmont succeeds in having his adventure.

If we consider *Les Liaisons dangereuses* in the stream of the eighteenth-century novel, if we inquire, not whether it is moral or disgusting, but what is its relation to Rousseau, we find that it is a mirror image of *La Nouvelle Héloïse*. And just as we saw that Rousseau's cult of sincerity masked insincerity, Laclos's cult of insincerity masks sincerity. For with all its lies, *Les Liaisons dangereuses* earnestly, almost desperately, tries to tell the truth. It may be objected that this is taking these scabrous adventures too seriously. But they deserve to be taken seriously—they are a departure from and a distinct advance over, most earlier treatments of love. In the Christian centuries physical love had been ignored, spiritualized, senti-

[1] *Les Liaisons dangereuses, Œuvres*, 126-7.

mentalized, or depicted with pornographic directness. Laclos was trying to probe beyond the appearance of love to its reality, and, in associating love with hostility, had been anticipated by few writers, perhaps only Racine in France. That Laclos saw the whole of love and of life can safely be doubted, but what he did see he saw sharply and pitilessly.

The never-ending plotting for physical conquest might be a search for love, a search for confirmation of manliness or of worthiness, but it could not be love itself. To the protagonists of *Les Liaisons dangereuses* it was hate. Valmont and Mme de Merteuil hate their victims, hate their world, and hate themselves. In moments of recognition they see that what they really want in this world is revenge. And this revenge can be achieved only by the degradation of others. "I have unveiled a double mystery of love and iniquity," writes Valmont to his confidante, "I shall enjoy the one and revenge the other; I shall fly from pleasure to pleasure."[2] Mme de Merteuil, in a long letter to Valmont, makes clear that in the eternal combat between Man and Woman, the latter must conquer the former since otherwise she is at Man's mercy. Women are condemned to depend on man's decency; they can liberate themselves only by supreme rationality and supreme ruthlessness. "*Il faut vaincre ou périr*"—a doctrine which makes love impossible and revenge essential.

This is the fundamental meaning of *Les Liaisons dangereuses*. The old Christian values have collapsed, and the discovery of this awesome truth has brought not true liberation but the semblance of liberation. The adolescent who has discovered that his parents are not perfect is free only to say "No"—free not to enjoy but to reject. Throughout the

[2] Ibid. 116.

novel, piety is pitted unsuccessfully against evil, and both Mme de Merteuil and Valmont openly repudiate God. But their rebellion is incomplete: they are like adolescents shaking their fists at an empty sky. The prevailing emotion of *Les Liaisons dangereuses* is rage.

Kant defined the free man as autonomous and the unfree man as heteronomous. Autonomous actions proceed from choice and deliberate judgments—they spring from needs, and aim toward ends that are recognized and understood. Heteronomous actions proceed from compulsions—they aim not at the announced goal but at a goal hidden both from the world and from the actor. A man who acts in order to prove something—to himself or to others—is not free, and the man who acts to prove that he is free is perhaps the most enslaved of all. In *La Nouvelle Héloïse* convention is accepted for the sake of acceptance—conventionality is debated and occasionally disregarded, but it always wins out without having to give reasons. The rationalizations of the protagonists are not reasons, they are excuses. In *Les Liaisons dangereuses* convention is rejected for the sake of rejection; the rationalizations offered for the violations of convention are rarely the real reasons. Neither Rousseau's nor Laclos's characters are therefore free, no matter what the appearances. They prove, if they prove anything at all, that Christian morality was proving hard to displace.

There is evidence, however, that some Enlightenment thinkers glimpsed the way to a constructive non-Christian moral code. Some of them saw that the road to freedom—that is to say, the road to maturity—lay in the acceptance of passion and in the integration of passion into a rational conduct of life. Ironically enough, Rousseau achieved this integration, which had escaped him in his novel, in his political thought. Whatever we may think of Rousseau's political Idealism, his "solution" of the conundrum of how to reconcile authority and liberty enlisted the whole man: the political enterprise of becoming worthy of a society in which the general will prevailed encouraged the natural growth of reason, grafted organically upon human emotions. To participate in the general will is an experience in which reason and the passions cooperate and ennoble each other.

Similarly, Voltaire's social thought sought to reconcile passion and reason through a gradual process of education, a slow liberation from enthusiasm (perverted and uninformed emotion), and a slow recognition of reality (the channeling and shaping of emotion through reason). Whatever the rationalism of some Christian theologians, fundamental to Christianity was the enmity of passion and salvation: a sense of guilt was to hold back desire—the Fall of Man at once created lust and gave man a weapon against it. In the Enlightenment, the dichotomy of lust versus guilt was softened into the opposition of reason to emotion, and with this softening arose the opportunity of achieving a view of man in which these opposites would be reconciled.

Perhaps the most representative example of this reconciliation, expressed in a new attitude toward sexual morality, is the work of Diderot. Among his many works, the delightful little piece, *Supplément au Voyage de Bougainville*, written in 1772, exactly midway between the publication dates of *La Nouvelle Héloïse* and *Les Liaisons dangereuses*, may be taken as typical. Diderot accepts and even exalts sexual urges, but he does so without a sense of doing anything wrong or daring; he is neither smutty nor coy, he neither gloats nor preaches. Moreover, Diderot seeks to integrate sexual life into the life of the community as well as into the life of the individual—love-making is delightful in itself and useful socially.

The success of Diderot's enterprise is proved by his daring to be conventional. That is not a paradox: the scared child does not dare to transgress the prevailing moral code, the rage-filled adolescent does not dare to conform to the prevailing moral code. Only the mature individual can judge each act on its merits—he cheerfully accepts restrictions that are rational, just as he cheerfully insists on gratification that is productive. He is neither conventional for the sake of conventionality nor unconventional for the sake of unconventionality. He knows that only *that* self-restraint is mature that is freely arrived at; it is self-limitation based on self-acceptance not self-rejection, and it alternates with enjoyment, with what is wrongly called "indulgence." Rational self-limitation is not grim, just as rational enjoyment is not frantic.

Diderot's *Supplément* began as a book-review of Bougainville's report on his world tour.[3] For his imaginative purposes, Diderot constructed a long dialogue between Tahitians and members of Bougainville's party to illuminate the ills of contemporary France. The civilized conduct of his Tahitians has sometimes been obscured by the still widely accepted myth that the *philosophes* sought to return to the life of the noble savage. Diderot's Tahitians are noble, but they are not savages. They are genuinely civilized men, and they are genuinely free. To them, Western manners and laws would be "nothing but shackles disguised in a hundred different ways. These shackles

[3] For the *Supplément*, I have used the excellent translation by Ralph H. Bowen in his and Jacques Barzun's edition of Diderot's *Rameau's Nephew and Other Works* (1956). All other translations are my own.

could only provoke the indignation and scorn of creatures in whom the most profound feeling is a love of liberty."[4]

Tahitian society, as viewed by Bougainville and as reconstructed by Diderot, is a rational social order. Its chief virtue is its closeness to man's nature: its institutions accept and use the deep promptings of human passions. There is no private property either in land or in women, but the system of production does not lead to scarcity: "When we are hungry we have something to eat; when we are cold, we have clothing to put on." The Tahitians' wants are simple, but their simplicity is not a virtue created by necessity—it is a rational code of conduct. Western civilization, driven by work and competitive values, leads to anxiety not happiness: "We have no wish to barter what you call our ignorance for your useless knowledge," the Tahitian spokesman indignantly informs the French invaders.[5]

Speaking through his Tahitians, Diderot thus defines "natural" not as primitive or animal-like, but as appropriateness. Hence sexual intercourse is facilitated but not free from sensible restrictions. Tahitian sexual relations, as Diderot describes them, had been healthy until Bougainville's party brought the scourge of syphilis; they had been openly enjoyed, without false modesty, until Bougainville's party introduced Western prudishness: "But a little while ago, the young Tahitian girl blissfully abandoned herself to the embraces of a Tahitian youth and awaited impatiently the day when her mother, authorized to do so by her having reached the age of puberty, would remove her veil and uncover her breasts. She was proud of her ability to excite men's desires, to attract the amorous looks of strangers, of her own relatives, of her own

[4] *Supplement*, in *Rameau's Nephew*, 1949.

[5] Ibid. 197.

brothers. In our presence, without shame, in the center of a throng of innocent Tahitians who danced and played the flute, she accepted the caresses of the young men whom her young heart and the secret promptings of her senses had marked out for her. The notion of crime and the fear of disease have come among us only with your coming. Now our enjoyments, formerly so sweet, are attended with guilt and terror. That man in black, who stands near you and listens to me, has spoken to our young men, and I know not what he has said to our young girls, but our youths are hesitant and our young girls blush. Creep away into the dark forest, if you wish, with the perverse companion of your pleasures, but allow the good, simple Tahitians to reproduce themselves without shame under the open sky in broad daylight."[6]

This improbable discourse reads like a deliberate, carefully worked out mockery of the Christian view of sex. It contradicts, point for point, the writings of the Church fathers.[7] In the paradise of Tahiti's innocence, Christian morality, coupled

[6] Ibid. 198-9.

[7] Consider St. Augustine's discussion of the origin of lust. He argues that lust (which he defines as the "lustful excitement of the organs of generation") did not exist before Eve's disobedience. After that disobedience, sexual intercourse has been attended with lust and hence with shame, and Augustine holds that "lust requires for its consummation darkness and secrecy; and this not only when unlawful intercourse is desired, but even such fornication as the earthly city has legalized." While the Cynics thought otherwise, and Diogenes once publicly performed intercourse, "instinctive shame has overborne this wild fancy." However, Augustine is troubled over the question as to whether generation would have taken place without sin. He decides that it would have: Adam and Eve would have copulated without lust, commanding their members by will: "The man, then, would have sown the seed, and the woman received it, as need required, the generative organs being moved by the will, not excited by lust . . ." rather as we move our hands. *The City of God*, Book XIV, ch. 18-24, transl. by Marcus Dods (Modern Library ed., 1950), 466-72.

with Western license, acts the part of the serpent. Diderot, then, wryly accepts the Fall. He only transfers the burden of responsibility: it is Christianity that is guilty of introducing sin into the world—the sin against nature. Diderot relates that after Bougainville's landing, the ship's chaplain is invited to stay in one of the natives' huts. Orou and his family make their guest comfortable, and feed him a "wholesome though frugal meal." When the chaplain is about to go to sleep, his host appears by his bed with his wife and three daughters, "all naked as Eve," and makes him a little speech: "You are young and healthy and you have just had a good supper. He who sleeps alone, sleeps badly; at night a man needs a woman at his side. Here is my wife and here are my daughters. Choose whichever one pleases you most, but if you would like to do me a favor, you will give your preference to my youngest girl, who has not yet had any children."

The chaplain declines, pleading "his religion, his holy orders, his moral standards, and his sense of decency," a refusal that sends Orou into a lyrical defense of nature: "I don't know what this thing is that you call 'religion,' but I can only have a low opinion of it because it forbids you to partake of an innocent pleasure to which Nature, the sovereign mistress of us all, invites everybody." The refusal is impolite, it offends hospitality as well as the need for offspring. The only excuse Orou will accept is physiological: "I cannot ask you to do anything that might harm your health; if you are too tired, you should by all means go to sleep at once." The conflict between unnatural discipline and natural desire ends as it must end—exclaiming over and over, "But there is my religion! My holy orders!" the chaplain spends the night with the girl.[8]

[8] *Supplement*, 223.

This manly act of gratitude emboldens Orou to question his guest about Christianity and to unmask its unnaturalness. Their dialogue goes beyond the usual *philosophe* diatribe: it juxtaposes a natural morality that accepts human urges and shapes them to their finest expression, and an unnatural morality that seeks to suppress or denigrate these urges. The Christian God appears to insist that sexual intercourse be practiced only after certain rites have been observed, and only within certain limitations: one man is restricted, for life, to one woman. These precepts Orou finds "contrary to nature, and contrary to reason." They are "admirably calculated to increase the number of crimes and to give endless annoyance" to the God of Christianity. The laws regulating morality in the West appear to Orou "contrary to the general order of things. For in truth is there anything so senseless as a precept that forbids us to heed the changing impulses that are inherent in our being . . . ?"[9] Mere verbal injunctions, the orders or incantations of priests, do not change what is good in nature to evil: "Would you like to know what is good and what is bad in all times and places? Pay close attention to the nature of things and actions, to your relations with your fellow-creatures, to the effect of your behavior on your own well-being and on the general welfare. You are mad if you believe that there is anything in the universe, high or low, that can add or subtract from the laws of nature." Indeed, and this is the heart of Diderot's indictment of Christianity and his most revolutionary insight—by decreeing unnatural restrictions, Christianity makes people miserable and criminal: "People will no longer know what they ought or ought not to do. They will feel guilty when they are doing nothing wrong. . . ."[1]

[9] Ibid. 207.

[1] Ibid. 209.

Tahitians live according to nature; Europeans try to live against it and fail. It is easy for Orou to get the chaplain to admit that in Europe the precepts of Christian morality are constantly violated and rarely punished. Diderot's point is not that there ought to be no restrictions on sexual behavior, but that the restrictions ought to grow only from certain limits which are themselves pointed out by nature. Bigamy, fornication, incest, adultery—these are all imaginary crimes. In Tahiti, both love affairs and marriages may be dissolved after a month but not sooner, and there are strict taboos on sexual intercourse before full sexual maturity has been reached: "That's the main object of our children's education within the family circle, and it's the most important point in our code of public morality."[2]

It should not be imagined that the debate between Orou and the chaplain is wholly one-sided. The chaplain makes one shrewd hit which Diderot had vision enough to invent but not vision enough to exploit fully: the chaplain objects that loose family ties in Tahiti reduce "tenderness between husband and wife, and maternal love," and Orou can only feebly admit that this is so and contend—even more feebly—that the loss is more than made up for by the gratification of the impulse of self-interest. Diderot has succeeded in breaking the antithesis of virtue and gratification, of passion and goodness, but he has not yet discovered (at least not in the *Supplément*) the possibility of relating passion to love, to affection, to constancy. He has not yet made the jump from involvement to attachment; to the extent that he seems unwilling to subject love to the voluntary bonds of affection, he has failed to reach full maturity.

[2] Ibid. 213.

Or would it be better to say that his Tahitians have not yet reached full maturity? In his passion to criticize the *ancien régime*, Diderot frequently becomes didactic; he is too interested in showing the social utility of a relaxed sexual code to follow through the consequences of his own description or to dwell sufficiently on the sheer physical joy of sexual relations. There are moments when his description breathes a kind of carefree, good-humored rapture—the chaplain in bed with the girl, the initiation rites—but all too often Diderot is selling a program, and the propaganda interferes with the purity of his perception.

That Diderot himself could think—and feel—beyond the Tahitian view of love, he demonstrates in some of his other works. In the article "*Jouissance*" in the *Encyclopédie*, Diderot rises from the joy of purely physical union to the union of souls, from simple satisfaction of an urge to a careful choice of mate, from momentary gratification to that soberer but more worthwhile happiness of a permanent union crowned by children.

If we take, then, Diderot's *Supplément*, and round it out with other works, we find that his view toward sexual passion is dialectically related to Rousseau and Laclos: it represents the complete and positive repudiation of Christian morality. I have said that in Rousseau the characters win through losing, and that in Laclos the characters lose through winning. In Diderot, finally, they win through winning: gratification creates further gratification, the reward of passion is happiness. With all its limitations, the prevailing emotion of *Supplément au Voyage de Bougainville* is love.

6

RHETORIC AND POLITICS IN THE FRENCH REVOLUTION

THE professional historian is an amateur psychologist, whether he knows it or not. The obscure links between thought and action, ideology and policy, engage his closest attention and elicit his boldest guesses. As historical personages parade before him, he can see their acts but he must infer their motives. Consciously or unconsciously, he finds himself operating with a theory of human nature. He operates, too, with a set of tastes, which make him into a part-time literary critic and with a private scale of values, which make him (a little furtively) into a Monday morning moralist. Judge, critic, psychiatrist—the historian is a busy man.

The French Revolution brings his varied talents into full play. Here is an event that was stirring, complicated, far-reaching, suitably portentous, and superlatively vocal. The protagonists of the Revolution, Mirabeau, Vergniaud, Danton, and Robespierre, not only acted, they talked. Indeed, their very talk was action. Their speeches, and the reception of those speeches, were something new. It was not the rabble alone that was being roused.

It is not surprising, then, that the rhetoric of the French Revolution has long excited the interest of historians and that the interpretation of the words has usually served as a step toward an interpretation of the acts.

Before our century, this did not have any startling consequences: historical opinion followed a predictable party line. Historians who hated the works of the Revolution hated its speeches; historians who admired the one admired the other. Burke, who set the fashion in this as in so many other notions about the Revolution, spoke for the prosecution as early as December 1791, when he condemned a belligerent speech of Brissot's as "full of false philosophy and false rhetoric, both . . . calculated to captivate and influence the vulgar mind. . . ."[1] Through Carlyle's indigestible pages, the revolutionary orators wander, filled with abstract theories, spouting the unrealistic gospel of Jean-Jacques, orating dully, but exercising a fascination that no self-respecting man could understand, let alone share. Of the Jacobin Club, central arena for rhetoricians, Carlyle exclaims: "Its style of eloquence? Rejoice, Reader, that thou knowest it not, that thou canst never perfectly know. . . . impassioned, dull-droning Patriotic-eloquence; implacable, unfertile—save for Destruction, which was indeed its work: most wearisome, though most deadly."[2]

In different language, but with the same aversion, Taine stigmatized the Jacobins as hypocritical and murderous orators, who concealed, or rather revealed, their maniacal lust

[1] Edmund Burke: *Thoughts on French Affairs*, *Works*, 12 vols. (1866), IV, 374.

[2] Thomas Carlyle: *The French Revolution* (Modern Library ed.), 254.

for power with false eloquence: "Whatever the charlatan can do with his labels, sign-boards, shouting and lies for the next six months, will be done to disguise the new nostrum," that is, the Jacobin Constitution of 1793. "All is mere show and pretence. Some of the workmen are shrewd politicians whose sole object is to furnish the public with words instead of things; others, ordinary scribblers of abstractions, or even ignoramuses, and unable to distinguish words from things, imagine that they are framing laws by stringing together a lot of phrases.—It is not a difficult job; the phrases are ready-made to hand."[3]

For the defense, Michelet singled out the National Assembly for its wealth of orators and praised Robespierre for embodying the true principles of the Revolution and the true desires of the French people.[4] H. Morse Stephens, who published a valuable collection of revolutionary speeches over half a century ago, begins his general introduction with the observation that "The French people have as much cause to be proud of their orators as of their actors,"[5] and sprinkles his commentary with approving epithets. And Aulard, good republican and historian of revolutionary oratory, thought that revolutionary eloquence filled "a glorious page in our literature,"[6] and sought to awaken his contemporaries to the more admirable points in the speeches of the modern French heirs of Demosthenes and Cicero.

But all this changed a few generations ago, with the invasion

[3] Hippolyte Taine: *The French Revolution*, transl. by John Durand, 3 vols., (1931), III, 5.

[4] See Jules Michelet: *Histoire de la révolution française*, 9 vols. (1883–1887), I, *passim.*

[5] *The Principal Speeches of the Statesmen and Orators of the French Revolution, 1789-1795*, ed. H. Morse Stephens, 2 vols. (1892), I, 1.

[6] F.-A. Aulard: *Les Orateurs de l'assemblée constituante* (1885), 3-4.

of the historical discipline by the social sciences. The spectrum of opinion has narrowed. Apart from a handful of stubborn exceptions like Georges Lefebvre, liberal historians have joined nostalgic royalists in condemning revolutionary rhetoric in tones of condescending amusement or unrelieved horror.[7]

In challenging this prevailing view, I do not mean to offer still another defense of the French Revolution. The Revolution has its defenders, and not all of them live in East Germany. I want, instead, to raise a question of method. The last generation looked hopefully to "the new history"; this generation is being confronted by what William Langer called, in his presidential address to the American Historical Association, "the next assignment": to use the techniques and insights of allied disciplines to illuminate our own, and to illuminate without blinding it.[8] I want to argue that this has not yet been done in studying the impact of the French Enlightenment on the French Revolution.

The current view of the relation of rhetoric to action in the Revolution may be summarized, that is, caricatured, as follows: Robespierre lost his Christian faith early and substituted destructive revolutionary enthusiasm for it. In his youth he read Rousseau who had read Plutarch in *his* youth; this reading created in Robespierre's mind the picture of a supremely desirable commonwealth, where Spartan youths

[7] Thus Lefebvre could write about Robespierre's violent denunciation of a representative on mission, made in an improvised harangue to the Convention on September 25, 1793: "I cannot reread that page without a shudder"—presumably of delight. "A la mémoire de Maximilien Robespierre," in *Maximilien Robespierre, 1758-1794: Beiträge zu seinem 200. Geburtstag*, ed. Walter Markov (1958), 13-14.

[8] William L. Langer: "The Next Assignment," *American Historical Review*, LXIII (Jan. 1958), 283-304.

allow foxes to eat out their insides with no sound of complaint. Laboring on the Committee of Public Safety to create a utopia in France, he found that there were many foxes, but only one true Spartan—himself. Driven mad by this discovery he set about to convert Frenchmen into Spartans, even if he had to kill them all in the process.

When we examine this construction closely, we find that it consists of three charges: revolutionary rhetoric displays the secular religion of the reign of virtue; it is burdened with the nightmarish weight of the cult of antiquity; and it is disfigured by an ugly, self-satisfied bombast, the sign of bloodthirsty fanaticism. These charges, it is worth noting, have no necessary logical connection, but historians treat them as if they do and cite them all to justify a single verdict. Revolutionary rhetoric, they tell us, condemns the revolutionaries for acting unpolitically, at best as utopians, at worst as early totalitarians.

In substantiating the first charge, historians have fondly reread Burke and Tocqueville. Burke first denounced "political theologians" in his *Reflections on the French Revolution* and later compared events in France to the Reformation. "*It is a revolution of doctrine and theoretic dogma*," he wrote. "It has a much greater resemblance to those changes which have been made upon religious grounds in which a spirit of proselytism makes an essential part."[9] Tocqueville gracefully elaborated Burke's observation in his book on *The Old Regime*, whose incisive formulations still haunt us. "The French Revolution," said Tocqueville, "though ostensibly political in origin, functioned on the lines, and assumed many of the aspects, of a religious revolution." It was abstract,

[9] Burke: *Thoughts on French Affairs*, *Works*, IV, 319.

missionary, carrying the good news to all mankind and promising "regeneration of the whole human race."[1]

This religious analogy was so persuasive that even Michelet, Aulard, and Mathiez could not escape its magic. In this country it was wittily naturalized by Crane Brinton in his book which dissected the Jacobins and in his later books on the revolutionary period. Offering a bouquet of nauseating appeals to virtue, stilted oratory, misplaced classical allusions, and reminiscences of Christian ritual, doctrine, and turns of phrase, Brinton concluded that Jacobin "emotions must be accepted as a variety of religious experience."[2] His conclusion has set the tone for American scholarship. Many historians have imitated Brinton's skeptical and tolerant sociology.

For all its plausibility, the notion of secular religion raises questions. It is one of those happy, evocative phrases that writers like to use to produce a shock of recognition. But what does it mean?

That there are activities not ostensibly religious that elicit behavior commonly associated with religious convictions is admittedly a suggestive idea. Men, we say, are "devoted" to their cause, "enthusiastically" support a program, and "faithfully" attend meetings, but the gains achieved by this phraseology, real as they are, have by now been assimilated into our store of historical knowledge; it is time to count up the losses. "Secular religion" carries too much weight, much of it contraband.

[1] Alexis de Tocqueville: *The Old Regime and the French Revolution*, transl. by Stuart Gilbert (1955), 11, 13.

[2] Crane Brinton: *The Jacobins: An Essay in the New History* (1930), 205. See also his *A Decade of Revolution, 1789-1799* (1934), ch. IV, "The Republic of Virtue"; and *The Anatomy of Revolution* (1957), ch. VII, "Reigns of Terror and Virtue."

To begin with, its use of "religion" is special and restricted. It is taken to mean enthusiasm, intolerance, visionary optimism. But there are forms of religious behavior that do not fit this definition, and conversely, there are forms of behavior quite obviously nonreligious that do fit it—the conduct of organized mobs, of crowds in a panic, of adolescents, and of a variety of psychological cripples from compulsive neurotics to paranoiacs. The evidence offered to prove the existence of a secular religion, moreover, is far from conclusive. Revolutionaries (to borrow Brinton's dry summary) may intone "a republican invocation beginning 'Chaste daughter of the heavens, O Liberty'; a republican salutation, 'I salute you, *Sans culottides*, revered name'; a republican credo, 'I believe in a Supreme Being, who has made men free and equal'; and 'republican Ten Commandments'. . . . A 'patriotic sign of the cross' in the name of Marat, Lepeletier, Liberty, or Death appears in several provinces. . . . The list of such practices is endless, reaching its height perhaps at the 'miracles' achieved by the 'Holy Guillotine.' "[3]

There is no mystery about these doings. Some are avowedly religious acts of revolutionaries who are far from being atheists and who seek to celebrate the Supreme Being in an august manner. But other activities reflect no more than the depths of poor taste reached by obscure and half-educated men suddenly propelled into positions of public responsibility—or at least audibility. All too many republican gestures were clumsy farces, revealing the unprepossess-

[3] Brinton: *A Decade of Revolution,* 157. I am indebted to Henry L. Roberts for first arousing my suspicion of the notion of "secular religion." See his report to the Council on Foreign Relations, *Russia and America* (1956), 19: "It must be admitted that a 'secular religion' is not an altogether obvious entity."

ing visage of long-repressed hatred; while the widespread use of phrases with religious connotations proves no more than the ease with which the revolutionaries used familiar metaphors, the poverty of their linguistic treasure house, and the dehydration of religious terminology. There is no irony, except a verbal one, in saying that a Parisian Jacobin "religiously" attended dechristianization meetings. It may be that this Jacobin had been a Christian in his youth and that his new activity is a surrogate for the old, but we minimize, or we obscure, the significance of his conversion when we call him "really religious."

But, one may insist, if Jacques Hébert proclaims his atheism, but paints, in the same oration, a dazzling picture of man's total and immediate regeneration, should we not call his views "messianic," his expectations "apocalyptic," his ideals, in a word, "religious"? Is not politics the art of the possible?

It is, but it is harder to define the possible than the cliché suggests. Usually, it is success which defines the bounds of realism. When on September 2, 1792, Danton exhorted the faltering Legislative Assembly to stay in Paris and face the allied invaders—"We need boldness, more boldness, still more boldness"—all the realists were against him, and yet events proved Danton right. Ever since Robespierre argued in February 1794 that the state was a school for character, realists have shuddered at his utopianism. Yet events did not wholly belie Robespierre's call to virtue. The France of Thermidor, as R. R. Palmer observes, could have used a little more virtue.[4] It is hard to know whether an orator is a utopian, charlatan, or statesman. The utopian treats the im-

[4] See R. R. Palmer: *Twelve Who Ruled: The Committee of Public Safety during the Terror* (1941), 279.

possible as possible, the charlatan creates the illusion that the impossible is possible, and the statesman converts the impossible into the possible. The notion of a "secular religion" does not help us to decide where to place the revolutionaries in this spectrum, for it prejudges the issue. It suggests a psychological paternity that either does not exist or, when it does exist, is not very important. All we can safely conclude from their fervent language and their fervent hopes is that the revolutionary generation were groping for new forms of address, of celebration, of social control, with a limited fund of ideas and with an unslakable thirst for sociability.

The second charge, like the first, is not new. As Harold T. Parker shows in his valuable monograph, the notion that the revolutionaries paid rhetorical tributes to a "cult of antiquity" was first advanced in the Revolution itself.[5] But it is only recently that it has been included among the accepted generalities of historians. Revolutionary orators, we are told, were prevented from seeing their world steadily and clearly because they adored antiquity and submitted without murmur to a tyranny of Rome over France, of Sparta over Paris. Historian after historian has depicted dreamy orators, steeped in Plutarch, seeking to impose ideals that had never existed on a society that could not use them.

The theory that idealized images or reference groups shape political action is a valuable contribution of sociology to history. But Parker's statistical information about allusions to antiquity suggests that the only flaw of his study is its title. He should have called it "The Neglect of Antiquity by the French Revolutionaries." For it reveals a sur-

[5] Harold T. Parker: *The Cult of Antiquity and the French Revolutionaries: A Study in the Development of the Revolutionary Spirit* (1937).

prising paucity of allusions to ancient philosophers or rhetoricians. Here are hundreds of revolutionaries, most of them with solid classical educations, giving thousands of speeches and writing thousands of articles. Yet Parker could discover only eighty-three references to Cicero, everyone's favorite. Horace (hardly a fanatic) and Plutarch were second with thirty-six references each. Rousseau, often considered the favorite transmitter of the classical cult, was cited only nine times.[6]

It might be argued that counting is so crude a sieve that the impact of the imaginary past would slip through the meshes. But qualitative tests are as unimpressive as quantitative ones. Not all the men who admired the ancients became revolutionaries; not all the revolutionaries admired the ancients. Some despised the imperfect primitive institutions of antiquity as not worth imitating; some adored it as a lost Garden of Eden impossible to imitate; some, like the notorious cultist Madame Roland, lost interest in antiquity before the Revolution. Only a few of the revolutionaries truly qualify as members of the cult.[7]

And it was, to use religious language, a Protestant rather than a Catholic cult. There was no authoritative doctrine; private judgment ran wild. Each believer found support in antiquity for his own position. Camille Desmoulins used Tacitus to discredit the Terror, and Saint-Just used Lycurgus to support it.[8] Madame Roland and Robespierre, implacable enemies, both greatly admired Rousseau, one of the few tastes they had in common.

Still, pagan antiquity flavored revolutionary rhetoric and in a few instances, as with Robespierre, may have influenced

[6] Ibid. 18-19.
[7] Ibid. 1-2.
[8] Ibid. 148-9.

policy. But I suspect that the relation of antiquity to the revolutionaries runs counter to the accepted view. Far from imposing itself on docile disciples, far from dictating impractical goals to impractical orators in search of a blueprint, antiquity served as a kind of attic, to be pillaged at will. It was accessible because classical education was widespread among the leaders and some of their audience; it contained stuff worth appropriating because the revolutionaries were deliberately rejecting their Christian heritage and their traditional institutions and creating new institutions which needed impressive names and high-flown justifications. Far from being dominated by the past, the revolutionaries dominated it.

From the worship of Plutarch to bombast is only one step, and that a short one. Proof for one is often taken as proof for the other: when Brinton cites Madame Roland's calling herself "Cato's wife" and Brissot, to whom she is writing, "Brutus," he may be stigmatizing the cult of antiquity, revolutionary pretentiousness, or both.[9]

Much of the rhetoric is admittedly appalling. To say nothing of Marat's bloodthirsty demagogy, many of the speeches were choked by grandiose sentiment, cheap fervor, and complacent moralizing. A Jacobin from Le Havre, rescued from deserved obscurity by Brinton, exhorts his fellow club members to carry on the war "until the children of the Mountain have flown the flag of liberty on the walls of London, Madrid and Berlin." Another orator apostrophizes equality: "It is thou, O holy Revolution, who hast brought us happiness; it is thou whom I should love with all my strength, whom I should defend with my life-blood, that

[9] Brinton: *A Decade of Revolution*, 155n.

thou mayest triumph over the tyrants banded against thee!'"[1]

The more prominent revolutionaries rarely reach higher levels of taste than this, and only a few of them, like Mirabeau, spoke with an eloquence that reflected good taste. Listen to Vergniaud's irresponsible warmongering: "Gentlemen, above all you may be sure that the kings are not without uneasiness; they know that there are no Pyrenees for the philosophic spirit which has given us liberty; they would shudder to send their soldiers to a land still burning with that sacred fire; they would tremble lest a single day of battle turn two hostile armies into a people of brothers [applause]."[2]

Or the terrifying, laconic cruelty of Saint-Just denouncing the proscribed Girondin deputies: "All the prisoners are not guilty; the largest number of them are only misguided; but as in a conspiracy the safety of the country is the supreme law, you were compelled to sacrifice the freedom of a few to the salvation of all; the prisoners, like the Court, made war on the laws through the laws. Nothing resembles virtue so much as a great crime . . ."[3]

Or the pedantic self-satisfaction of Robespierre: "I too was Pétion's friend; when he unmasked himself I abandoned him. I too was acquainted with Roland; he committed treachery and I denounced him. Danton wanted to take their place, and he is no more in my eyes than an enemy of the country [applause]."[4]

Granted that this is uncongenial rhetoric. But what does it prove? Does it unmask the orators as impractical or un-

[1] Brinton: *The Jacobins*, 151, 155.

[2] To the Legislative Assembly, October 25, 1791, on the *émigrés*. *Principal Speeches*, ed. Stephens, I, 257-8.

[3] To the Convention, July 9, 1793, ibid. II, 476.

[4] To the Convention, March 31, 1794, on the arrest of Danton and the Dantonists, ibid. II, 388.

political? Some reservations suggest themselves at once. The purple prose I have quoted (and which is always quoted) was not the only style used by the revolutionaries. J. M. Thompson observed that in the weeks preceding the expulsion of the Girondin deputies from the Convention, invective reached unprecedented heights. But after June 2, 1793, "suddenly, oratory was put aside, and the debates became cold and businesslike."[5]

There is amusing evidence, moreover, that bombast bored almost as many as it aroused. Brinton cites example after example of good sense among Jacobins, of clemency, good nature, moderation, and even humor, which is usually the first casualty in heated controversy. The Jacobin Club of Montignac deserves to be remembered for an entry in its minutes. As Brinton records, "The order of the day brings next the reading of the report of M. Robespierre on the connection between religious and moral ideas and republican principles; and hardly has the reader reached the middle of the report when, the room being quite deserted, the president adjourns the meeting."[6]

We might remember, too, that while the revolutionaries probably produced more bombast per cubic inch than other mortals, their love of the high style was not unique. The most eloquent of the *émigrés* used the same colorful images and made the same hyperbolic threats as their bitterest persecutors; and well-rounded periods had magical powers over the public in other countries. The rhetorical talents that made for success in revolutionary France made for success in counterrevolutionary England; the oratory that moved Parisians moved Philadelphians.

[5] J. M. Thompson: *The French Revolution* (1945), 414.

[6] Adapted from Brinton: *The Jacobins*, 226.

Clearly, then, the metaphor of a secular religion, evidence of a classical cult, or repellent phrases do not, singly or together, constitute an adequate interpretation of revolutionary rhetoric. We must begin again.

When we look at revolutionary oratory without these preconceptions, it appears as the confluence of four streams: the tradition of eloquence, which did not depend on revolutionary events; ideology, which helped to shape revolutionary events; mental predispositions among the leaders, which refracted and distorted revolutionary events; and the revolutionary events themselves.

I have already said something about the tradition of eloquence. Let me add that the rhetoric of the French Revolution built on a long and glorious history, and the orators of the Revolution were, for the most part, trained in its shadow. We can detect in their speeches the three traditional branches of rhetoric: pulpit, legal, and academic oratory. The orators had in their bones the great models whose most celebrated speeches they had practiced and admired in school. An orator standing before the Convention faced several exacting audiences: his fellow revolutionaries on the floor; the public in the gallery; an impressive network of Parisian and provincial clubs which looked for polished performances and demanded orations that did not stray too far from the familiar patterns; and an invisible audience, not posterity of which too much has been made, but the past—a powerful group of French rhetoricians, l'Hôpital, Massillon, Bourdaloue, and Bossuet. The Revolution offered hundreds of lawyers, petty officials, and former priests, large, influential, and half-captive audiences, brilliant occasions for talk, and exciting opportunities to approach, if not surpass, these great orators. It is no wonder that most revolutionary orations were meticulously composed, written to be published, and delivered with loving care. They certainly sound that way.

The second stream, ideology, demands more exhaustive analysis than is possible here, or than it has ever been given. The prevailing view is expressed in its most emphatic form by J. L. Talmon, who holds that the speeches of Saint-Just and Robespierre reflect the pernicious ideas of the *philosophes* and foreshadow the pernicious actions of the Terror, as well as later terrorists like Stalin or Mussolini. Even moderate historians who reject the parallels to the twentieth century see an unfortunate influence of the *philosophes* on the orators.

This view is unconvincing because it does an injustice to the *philosophes* and oversimplifies their effect on revolutionary ideology. The *philosophes*' hope for transforming the world was modest indeed. A radical like Holbach was a pessimist; even the dangerous Rousseau professed a Platonic theory of degeneration. If Rousseau's proposals for Corsica were what Talmon calls a "totalitarian blueprint," those for Geneva were moderate, and those for Poland, conservative.[7] To learn utopian optimism from the *philosophes*, the revolutionaries would have had to misread them completely.

But evidence is accumulating that they did not so misread them. The ideas of Voltaire, of the Encyclopedists, and of Rousseau played a relatively minor part in revolutionary speeches and thought. Nor were the *philosophes* the property of one wing. Robespierre had no monopoly on Rousseau. Even the *émigrés*, Alfred Cobban reports, found many of

[7] J. L. Talmon: *The Rise of Totalitarian Democracy* (1952), *passim.* Talmon fully accepts the "cult of antiquity." For a brief critique of his thesis, see pp. 278–83.

Rousseau's ideas appealing.[8] The relation of ideology to oratory offers a fruitful field for further research.[9]

The third stream, the psychology of the leaders, offers equally exciting opportunities. Something has been done in the best biographies; and Georges Lefebvre took the first step to a theory of revolutionary mentality with his famous observation that "defensive reaction" is always followed by the "desire to punish." But most of the work remains to be done because historians have been as amateurish in their psychology as they have been dogmatic. They have usually subscribed to a psychology of simple realism, positing a clear-cut stimulus from the "real world" without, setting up a clear-cut response within. Such a psychology implies a judgment. When the historian finds an orator using language or proposing action that appears to be incongruous with the "true" situation, he accounts for the incongruity by a simple condemnation—the speaker must be a madman, a fanatic.

More sophisticated historians, of course, have been ready to build more complicated models. I have no intention of ridiculing them. Our sober profession can afford to be much more adventurous than it is. But the trouble with practically all the suggestions that I have seen is that they leave untapped

[8] See Alfred Cobban: *In Search of Humanity: The Role of the Enlightenment in Modern History* (1960), 168. See also his remarkable analysis of Rousseau's influence on a "royalist, who ended as an *émigré* of a most reactionary type," the comte d'Antraigues, in his *Rousseau and the Modern State* (1934), 187-91, 255-85.

[9] A beginning, but only a beginning, has been made by such books as Daniel Mornet's *Origines intellectuelles de la révolution française* (1933), which studies the diffusion of philosophic ideas through French society in the second half of the eighteenth century with admirable diligence. But the book confirms, inadvertently, that an understanding of the relations of the Enlightenment to the Revolution must be based firmly on an understanding of the former.

the great resources of psychoanalysis. Let me, speculatively, tap them here.

Action results from a complex internal collaboration. Robespierre is advocating the harsh law of 22 Prairial. What forces work on him? The objective situation of plot and attempted assassination; the situation interpreted by his conscious mind; the conscious mind influenced by certain long-range political goals, certain short-range political pressures, and by unconscious needs and wishes. What is unconscious is hard to reach, but fortunately it leaves its telltale marks on expression. All the historian needs in order to understand those marks is sensitivity and an adequate psychological theory. It is the spring of 1794, the invaders are gone, and the Vendée is pacified. Why is Robespierre nervous and suspicious? He is beset by frustration and the rage it builds, frustration stemming from long-endured disappointments, and the need for long-postponed revenge. He is beset by exhaustion, a physiological phenomenon with psychological consequences. When on 8 Thermidor Robespierre rose to make his last speech to the Convention, how deeply did he suffer from the depression that often follows superhuman exertions? How much sleep had he had for a year?

These questions suggest others, still more frankly speculative. What was the impact of Louis XVI's flight to Varennes? Here was a king who had preached, and whose forefathers had preached, that the monarch is the father of his country, fleeing that country in undignified disguise. Did the revolutionaries, far from resenting, cherish the grievance against the treacherous father? Certainly it allowed them to embark on a year of unexampled disobedience and justified parricide. And what was the impact of that parricide? The ever more frantic demand for unanimity, the ever-growing imputation of evil motives to dissenters suggests an obsessive need to share guilt by associating all with the parricide, or better yet, to purify oneself by projecting guilt on others.

It is only an apparent paradox to say that the answers to such psychological questions cannot be found in psychology alone. They must be sought in politics, in day-to-day events.

The brilliant investigators who have undermined the grandiose syntheses of nineteenth-century historians have been, on the whole, patient empiricists. Their minute examinations of the incidence of the Terror, of the political pressures of Parisian extremists, of the behavior of the revolutionary crowds have not dealt with psychology, but they have illuminated it. And they have not dealt with rhetoric, but they have illuminated *it* by substituting a living world where human beings address other human beings, for a cardboard stage where heroes and villains posture and declaim.

Revolutionary rhetoric took place in, and was meant to influence, a rapidly changing political situation. We know, but we need to be reminded, that the orators were under persistent and conflicting pressures. There were the crowds, anxious over the price of bread, filled with irrational hatred for "hoarders." They had to be gratified, kept under control, and enlisted to support the war effort. There were the professional revolutionaries, seeking to decentralize and intensify the Terror, often for shady reasons. They had to be exposed, and anticipated by a centralized Terror which, terrible as it was, was clemency compared with the persecuting zeal of the agitators. There was the war, which needed troops, supplies, trustworthy generals, and a cause to fight for. There was the counterrevolution, which showed its hand in the occupied territories of the north, where it undertook to wipe out all revolutionary legislation. There was, finally, the young republic with new courts, new schools, new priests, a new calendar. Institutions had to be invented, administered, and staffed. The Revolution had to be explained and defended; therefore rhetoric was an indispensable governmental activity.

It was a heady time, and one did not need to be a Wordsworth to be dizzy. The revolutionaries governed, on the whole, with astonishing success. They did make some grievous mistakes. They drifted into a war which they won, but which they might have avoided or at least postponed. They unavoidably alienated the peasants, but they might have managed this more adroitly. They failed to keep repression within sensible bounds. Their fanaticism was not, however, quasi-religious or pseudo-Spartan. It was less a permanent policy than a sporadic failure, a failure to act sensibly in the political situation.

And this failure must be understood through that situation itself. Politics is a late acquisition, a mature fruit of civilization, requiring renunciation of instinctual gratification. It runs counter to man's deepest need to strike out against identifiable enemies. Politics, indeed, is a demanding activity. It requires suppleness, the ability to compromise, to fit means to ends (that is, to propound ends for which means are available), to temper principles for the sake of reaching agreement, to turn burning moral issues into administrative questions, to convert mortal enemies into amiable opponents, the duel into a debate. But such behavior, being the last hired, is also the first to be fired. The very situation that most demands coolness of judgment and moderation of oratory is least likely to give politics room to breathe. From

1789 on, the situation in France was a permanent crisis: these were the times that tried men's nerves.

To make things worse, politics labors under a built-in irrationality. It feeds on issues and opponents, on unsolved questions. If they do not exist, they are manufactured. In a settled system with spoils, prestige, power for the victors, and hope for the vanquished, this irrationality is not fatal. But in the French Revolution, where institutions were delicate, untried, and under relentless attack, regression to more primitive modes of behavior was inescapable. We should be surprised not at the regression but at its mildness.

I have tried to recall the world in which revolutionary rhetoric had its place. It is all too easy to forget it, in our time of concentration camps, mass manipulation of audiences, "double-think," and nihilistic fanaticism; it is all too easy to draw plausible analogies, to see Danton in Mussolini or Robespierre in Lenin. But such analogies, persuasive as they sound, are obstacles rather than ways to historical understanding. Caution without daring may be pedestrian, but daring without caution is irresponsible. We must speculate, but such speculation must grow organically from the material at hand, from the concerns of the time, not from the concerns of our time. I am pleading, I suppose, for the higher naïveté. After all, as Sigmund Freud once said, there are times when a man craves a cigar simply because he wants a good smoke.

PART THREE

Unfinished Business

INTRODUCTION

THE ENLIGHTENMENT began with controversy, thrived in controversy, and has remained a subject of controversy for two centuries. Almost inescapably, then, the historian of the Enlightenment finds himself enmeshed in polemics, and in a decade of writing about the eighteenth century I have had my share of arguments. This section represents some of these arguments.

Controversies about the Enlightenment are generally both historical and political. The historian, as historian, must first establish what he conceives the movement to have been. It is only after this that he is ready to argue, as a political being, that it was something valuable. It would be naïve to deny the political passions that underlie the arguments over historical facts: the historian who undertakes to clear the Enlightenment of what he regards as misinterpretations is usually an admirer of the Enlightenment.

At the same time, not all polemics about the Enlightenment follow strict party lines. In these three essays, I have taken issue with writers whose sympathies certainly lie with the Enlightenment. Liberals all of them, their criticisms are criticisms from within. I have criticized these critics not because I consider the Enlightenment beyond criticism, but because I consider their particular criticisms to have been misdirected.

The first of the essays, "Carl Becker's Heavenly City," was first read to a historians' meeting devoted to discussing Becker's book twenty-five years after its appearance. It has been the subject of a certain amount of discussion,[1] but I am willing to let the essay stand with only one methodological remark. When I was asked to address myself to the meaning of *The Heavenly City*, I decided to steep myself in the book, disregard all biographical and historical details that might have influenced its argument, and concentrate on answering a single question: What does the book say? I am aware, and was aware, that this is not all that may be said about *The Heavenly City:* it was written at a difficult time in Becker's life, in the midst of a Depression in the United States and a dismal political situation abroad. Obviously, these circumstances shaped the book, and my method, borrowed from the new criticism, in no way exhausts all its dimensions. But since *The Heavenly City* had become a most influential classic, I decided to attempt to determine its real message, and to assess that message.

"Reading About Rousseau" is less polemical than the essay that precedes and the essay that follows it. For all the per-

[1] See Raymond O. Rockwood, ed., *Carl Becker's Heavenly City Revisited* (1958), which contains my essay, other talks delivered on the same occasion, and a large number of criticisms of my views.

sistent misreadings of Rousseau, and for all the popular nonsense about the "noble savage," the recent literature on Rousseau has been admirable. My essay reflects that admiration. I have put it under "Unfinished Business" because it points to a task that needs to be done: we still need a good biography of Rousseau in English, and my essay sets down some guidelines for such a biography.

My concluding piece, "The Party of Humanity," summarizes the polemics I have carried on since 1954, usually in reviews. Its title, which I thought appropriate for the book as a whole, records my conviction that we have as much to learn from the philosophical thought of the Enlightenment as from any other philosophical movement—perhaps more. To be sure, the *philosophes*' specific formulations have been outmoded, partly by the passage of time, partly by their very success. Some of the *philosophes*' hopes have been disappointed, some of their enemies have faded, and some of their problems have been solved. For all the complexity of the *philosophes*' philosophy, the life of men and of societies has turned out to be even more complex than they imagined. And yet, in an age of timid return to dependence on the supernatural, to tradition and authority, this philosophy—the commitment to criticism, to humanity, to passion; the respect for the classical past coupled with a healthy self-confidence; stoic courage in the face of suffering; and irreverent humor—remains refreshing and relevant. But to say all this is merely to record my convictions as a political being. As a historian I trust that even those who reject my politics will accept my analysis.

7

CARL BECKER'S HEAVENLY CITY

> This certainly isn't history. I hope it's philosophy, because if it's not it's probably moonshine: —or would you say the distinction is over subtle?
>
> —CARL BECKER, on the flyleaf of *The Heavenly City*, presented to T. V. Smith[1]

CARL BECKER'S *The Heavenly City of the Eighteenth-Century Philosophers* was published more than a quarter of a century ago.[2] Its urbane examination of the *philosophes* has had great and lasting influence; few recent books on European intellectual history have been as widely read and as generously received. It is that rare thing, a work of scholarship that is also a work of literature—a masterpiece of persuasion that has done more to shape the current image

[1] Quoted by Charlotte Watkins Smith: *Carl Becker: On History and the Climate of Opinion* (1956), 212.

[2] Becker delivered his lectures in 1931, and his book was first published in 1932. The symposium at which this essay was delivered was held in 1956.

of the Enlightenment than any other book. Despite the skepticism of some professional historians, its witty formulations have been accepted by a generation of students and borrowed in textbook after textbook.[3]

When Becker delivered his lectures at the Yale Law School in 1931 and when he slightly revised them for publication, he seems to have thought of them as a *jeu d'esprit*, a collection of aphorisms and paradoxes meant to stimulate and (I suspect) to shock his audience.[4] But, as Terence warned long ago, the fate of books depends upon the capacities of the reader. And the worldly fate of *The Heavenly City* has been success—unexcelled, uninterrupted, and, I believe, unwarranted success. When it was first published, Charles Beard greeted it as a classic[5]; today *The Heavenly City* is in its tenth printing, it appears prominently in bibliographies on the eighteenth century, and many a student reads no other book on the *philosophes*. It is indeed time that the book be subjected to a careful analysis.

"Before estimating a book it is well to read its title with

[3] The reviews of *The Heavenly City* were almost unanimous in their praise. One notable exception was the perceptive review by Ira O. Wade in the *Journal of Modern History*, vol. V, No. 2 (June 1933), 233-5. One amusing exception was "J.A.L." in *America*, who complained that "There is a great deal about atmosphere and climate in this little book. After reading it, one feels that the professor is living in a fog." *America*, vol. XLVIII, No. 15 (January 14, 1933), 365. I am grateful to Professor Raymond O. Rockwood for pointing out that there were a few other critical reviews as well. See his remarks in the book he edited, *Carl Becker's Heavenly City Revisited*, vii-x.

[4] I have heard *The Heavenly City* defended on the ground that Becker had only wanted to stimulate his auditors, to make them think and to re-examine their presuppositions. This amounts to the view that because the contents did not matter, the book could not have been misleading.

[5] In the *American Historical Review*, vol. XXXVIII (April 1933), 591. In estimating the influence

care," Becker suggests, and the title of this book briefly states its central theme: the *philosophes* destroyed less well than they knew.[6] They were believers in their most skeptical moods, Christians in their most anti-Christian diatribes: "In spite of their rationalism and their humane sympathies, in spite of their aversion to hocus-pocus and enthusiasm and dim perspectives, in spite of their eager skepticism, their engaging cynicism, their brave youthful blasphemies and talk of hanging the last king in the entrails of the last priest —in spite of all of it, there is more of Christian philosophy in the writings of the *Philosophes* than has yet been dreamt of in our histories. . . . I shall attempt to show that the *Philosophes* demolished the Heavenly City of St. Augustine only to rebuild it with more up-to-date materials."[7]

Before launching upon this theme, Becker expounds a general assumption about the relation of change to permanence in history. There is change in history: Thomas Aquinas

---

of *The Heavenly City*, we must remember: first, the abundance of favorable reviews; secondly, the almost complete absence of published criticism; thirdly, the favorable comments in such distinguished and popular textbooks as Leo Gershoy's *From Despotism to Revolution, 1763-1789* (1944), in which *The Heavenly City* is recommended for being "penetrating and subtle" (329), and Mr. Gershoy's *French Revolution and Napoleon* (1941), in which Becker's book is called "four brilliant essays on the *philosophes;* a penetrating analysis of their ideas and ideals" (539). In the widely used text by Crane Brinton, John B. Christopher, and Robert Lee Wolff, *A History of Civilization*, 2 vols. (1955), *The Heavenly City* is described as "a charming series of essays, stressing the similarities between the eighteenth-century Age of Reason and the medieval Age of Faith" (II, 92).

[6] For Becker's remark, see *The Heavenly City*, 115. It has been said, and Becker himself said it jokingly, that *The Heavenly City* is not history at all but a moral tract. If it is not history at all, it should certainly not be recommended as good history.

[7] Ibid. 31.

and David Hume both used the word "reason" but meant very different things by it, so that to compare their philosophies by investigating simply what they said about "reason" would do injustice to both. Words persist, but their meanings change. But also there is permanence in history: no era wholly liberates itself from its antecedents, although its spokesmen may proudly (or perhaps anxiously) proclaim that they have made a complete break. Rhetoric may change while ideas persist. Becker suggests that intellectual historians must reckon with this dialectic of permanence and change and must be misled neither by what I might call spurious novelty nor by spurious persistence.

This historiographical warning is the most valuable idea in *The Heavenly City;* unfortunately, Becker fails to heed it when he elaborates his thesis. He argues that despite the great change in the climate of opinion between the thirteenth and eighteenth centuries the two centuries were far more closely related than would immediately appear or would be admitted by the *philosophes.* The *philosophes*' claim to be modern must therefore be discounted: "I know it is the custom to call the thirteenth century an age of faith, and to contrast it with the eighteenth century, which is thought to be preëminently an age of reason. . . . In a very real sense it may be said of the eighteenth century that it was an age of faith as well as of reason, and of the thirteenth century that it was an age of reason as well as of faith."[8] The overriding fault of the *philosophes* was their naïveté: they

[8] *The Heavenly City*, 8. Becker's use of the term "Climates of Opinion" as the heading of his first chapter suggests, correctly, that he relied heavily on Whitehead's *Science and the Modern World* (1925). Indeed, Becker repeatedly quotes or paraphrases Whitehead's book without indicating his source—a sign not of unwillingness to give credit, of course, but of Becker's conviction that

"exhibited a naïve faith in the authority of nature and reason."[9]

This is to fall into what I have called the trap of spurious persistence. It is true that the medieval Catholic rationalists, of whom Thomas Aquinas was the most prominent, assigned to reason an important place in their epistemologies. It is also true—and Becker's reminders are valuable—that the *philosophes* depended upon some unexamined premises which, to the extent that they were unexamined, may be called "faith."

But Becker infers far too much from this. Aquinas's rationalism was by no means as characteristic of the thirteenth century as Voltaire's empiricism was of the eighteenth century. Moreover, Becker forgets his own caution that words may be used in many different ways when he argues that "there were, certainly, many differences between Voltaire and St. Thomas, but the two men had much in common for all that. What they had in common was the profound conviction that their beliefs could be reasonably demonstrated."[1] But the point is precisely that the two philosophers differed over what constitutes reasonable demonstration. For Aquinas reasonable demonstration was deductive and definitional[2];

Whitehead's views were generally known and accepted. Whitehead describes the eighteenth century as the "age of reason, based upon faith" (83) and asserts that "*les philosophes* were not philosophers" (86). They were men who hated "dim perspectives" (ibid.). Whitehead, like Becker, appreciated the *philosophes:* he admired their humaneness, their hatred of cruelty and cant. But like Becker he thought them not quite first-rate: "If men cannot live on bread alone," he remarks with reference to Voltaire, "still less can they do so on disinfectants." (87). All these formulations reappear in *The Heavenly City*.

[9] *The Heavenly City*, 30. Becker does say that "Voltaire was an optimist, although not a naïve one" (ibid. 37).

[1] Ibid. 8.

[2] Becker himself quotes a characteristic specimen of Aquinas's

Voltaire derided such demonstrations as "metaphysics," as examples of the despised *esprit de système.*

Aquinas and Voltaire both believed that the powers of reason are limited, but they drew sharply different conclusions from this: for Aquinas, that which is inaccessible to human reason concerns the foundations of Christian theology. Where the light of reason does not shine, the lamp of faith supplies illumination. For Voltaire, on the contrary, that which is inaccessible to reason is chimerical. What can never be found ought not to be sought; it is the realm not of the most sacred, but of the most nonsensical—that is, of "metaphysical" speculation. Where the light of reason does not shine, man must console himself with that philosophical modesty so characteristic of Voltaire's heroes, Newton and Locke. While Aquinas could make categorical statements about the nature of the soul, Voltaire proudly proclaimed his ignorance in such matters. In seeking to show that "the underlying preconceptions of eighteenth-century thought were still, allowance made for certain important alterations in the bias, essentially the same as those of the thirteenth century,"[3] Becker thus unjustifiably plays with the word *reason.*

Becker plays the same verbal game in his assertion that both centuries were centuries of faith. The word *faith* usually serves to describe two rather different psychological processes. Thirteenth-century faith (if I may simplify a complex matter) was submission, not necessarily to what was absurd, but to what was beyond proof and, after a certain point, beyond argument. Failure to have faith (as Voltaire put it

---

deductive method of arguing (ibid. 3). Here as in many other places in his book Becker provides material for the refutation of his case.

[3] Ibid. 31.

facetiously) led to burning in this world and in the next. Eighteenth-century faith in reason, while perhaps often naïve, should be designated by the more neutral term *confidence*. Its affirmations were public, open to examination and refutation. "Faith in reason" meant simply that for the *philosophes* the method of reason (strictly speaking the scientific method of such natural philosophers as Newton) was superior to other methods of gaining knowledge; it was superior to revelation, authority, tradition, because it was more reliable.[4] In Diderot's pornographic novel, *Les Bijoux indiscrets*, there is a charming dream: the dreamer sees himself transported into a building that has no foundations and whose columns rise into the mists. The crowds walking in and around the building are crippled and deformed old men. It is the land of hypotheses, and the cripples are the makers of systems. But there is a vigorous small child, growing into a giant as the dream progresses, who draws near the fantastic building and destroys it with one blow. That giant is Experiment—no dweller of the heavenly city.[5] Did not the *philosophes*, in their reveries, see themselves as that giant? And did they not include thinkers like Aquinas among the lame makers of systems? To denounce the *philosophes* for having faith in reason may be witty, but the paradox solves no problems in intellectual history.

Near the end of the first chapter, Becker adduces evidence

[4] I do not want to assert that the *philosophes* were always consistent or thorough-going empiricists. Rousseau, who showed his respect for factual knowledge in books III and IV of his *Contrat social* could also urge in the *Discours sur l'inégalité*, "Let us begin by setting all the facts aside, since they don't affect the question." But he was seeking to elucidate the foundations of morality, and if he did not ask a factual question he was not, after all, seeking a factual answer.

[5] *Œuvres complètes*, ed. Assézat and Tourneux, IV, 255-9.

to buttress his thesis. But the evidence is unsatisfactory. It is embodied in a dozen-odd generalizations designed to contrast the anti-Christian ideology of the *philosophes* with their real beliefs and premises, which were Christian or at least greatly indebted to Christianity: "If we examine the foundations of their faith, we find that at every turn the *Philosophes* betray their debt to medieval thought without being aware of it." Becker's generalizations are indefensible not because they are too general—most generalizations are—but because some of them are inadequately explored, some are misleading, and others are simply wrong.

"They denounced Christian philosophy," Becker begins, "but rather too much, after the manner of those who are but half emancipated from the 'superstitions' they scorn." This sentence contains an important truth: the *philosophes* were venturing into territory that was largely unexplored, or had not been explored for many centuries, and they were often appalled at their own daring. However, the recurring discussions of the need for a social religion for the masses suggests not that the *philosophes* were "but half emancipated from the 'superstitions' they scorn" but, rather, that they were afraid sometimes of the social consequences of their emancipation. It is the substance of their opposition to Christianity, not the shrillness of their attacks upon it, that matters: much of the *philosophes*' vehemence can be explained by what they considered to be their mission. They were determined to expose *l'infâme* loudly, repeatedly, insistently, unsparingly, until that large public which was tepidly Christian had been won over to the new ideas.

"They ridiculed the idea that the universe had been created in six days, but still believed it to be a beautifully articulated machine designed by the Supreme Being according to a rational plan as an abiding place for mankind." True, but why "but"? There is nothing essentially Christian about this idea of "cosmos"—it had been the foundation of Stoic philosophy. There is nothing essentially Christian about this idea of God as architect—the watchmaker argument for the existence of God, a favorite with the *philosophes*, appears prominently in the discourses of Epictetus. The beautifully articulated machine of the *philosophes* is not a Christian but a pagan machine. What is remarkable is not the supposed resemblance of this machine to Christianity but its always implicit and often explicit repudiation of miracles: God acts through general and uniform laws alone. Here as elsewhere Becker exploits parallels or similarities or correspondences between Christian and *philosophe* thought to claim that the two are identical or that, at the least, the latter is the direct descendant of the former. This has as much logical merit as the assertion that, since Calvin was a determinist and Holbach was a determinist, Holbach was a Calvinist.

"The Garden of Eden was for them a myth, no doubt, but they looked enviously back to the golden age of Roman virtue, or across the waters to the unspoiled innocence of an Arcadian civilization that flourished in Pennsylvania." Becker is doubtless right—a mood of nostalgia for the past or for an unspoiled civilization pervaded Enlightenment thought. But this nostalgia is not merely a substitute for the Christian state of innocence: Roman virtue, Tahitian simplicity, Chinese wisdom, and Quaker pacifism provide worldly standards. They are standards, moreover, which helped the *philosophes* to evade the censorship in the *ancien régime*. Voltaire's England, Diderot's Tahiti, Montesquieu's Persia are not simply utopias; they are indirect indictments of France.

"They scorned metaphysics, but were proud to be called

philosophers." True again, but it is hard to see what this sentence proves. A philosopher is a man who loves knowledge, and when he rejects authority, revelation, system making, he may argue that in his empiricism he is the only *true* philosopher, while his forerunners were idle dreamers. This may be a justified or an unjustified claim, but it does not make the *philosophes* Christians.

"They dismantled heaven, somewhat prematurely it seems, since they retained their faith in the immortality of the soul." Damaging if true, but it is largely false. Montesquieu did not believe in the immortality of the soul, nor did Diderot, nor Hume, nor Helvétius, nor Holbach. Voltaire was far from unequivocal about immortality. Rousseau "retained his faith," or rather claimed that he must believe in order to survive: his was a desperate personal need, by no means representative of the *philosophes.*

"They discussed atheism, but not before the servants."[6] This remark is patently derived from an anecdote told about Voltaire: one evening at supper (runs this story of doubtful authenticity) Voltaire interrupted his guests Condorcet and d'Alembert, who were voicing doubts of the existence of God, and sent the servants out of the room. "Continue your attack, gentlemen," Voltaire said after the three *philosophes* were alone. "I do not want my throat cut or my money stolen tonight." Two comments may be made on this anecdote: most of the *philosophes* of the early generation were not atheists, never claimed to be atheists, and only "discussed atheism" in order to refute it. This did not make them Christians, since their deism was a philosophical doctrine more

[6] Becker's statements about the *philosophes* in this and the six preceding paragraphs are in *The Heavenly City,* 30-1.

than once removed from Christianity. Moreover, this anecdote does not concern religion as religion but religion as a social policeman. Whether the uneducated masses needed a supernatural religion to keep them under control was much debated in the Enlightenment, but surely this was a most utilitarian, a most un-Christian debate.

In the second chapter of *The Heavenly City*, "The Laws of Nature and of Nature's God," Becker seeks to show that the *philosophes* belonged to the natural law tradition, that natural law is a significant link between the Christian and Enlightenment climates of opinion, but that the *philosophes* failed to recognize this link.

Becker rightly reminds us that the *philosophes* were not cynics; that their negations were far less important than their affirmations; that they were enthusiastic projectors, reformers, moralists; that their confidence in their ability to penetrate into the mysteries of the universe and to prescribe effective remedies for social ills was often exaggerated and sometimes naïve. The *philosophes* might not admit it, but their "childlike faith" was fundamentally Christian: the *philosophes* were the "secular bearers of the Protestant and Jansenist tradition"; their programs for peace and brotherhood were inspired by "the Christian ideal of service"; the words they coined—*bienfaisance*, *humanité*—were meant to "express in secular terms the Christian ideal of service." And this "childlike faith" was shared by nearly all the *philosophes:* "In the eighteenth century the words without which no enlightened person could reach a restful conclusion were nature, natural law, first cause, reason. . . ." And again: "Nature and natural law—what magic these words held for the philosophic century." This was the *philosophes*' true faith in reason: that they could read God's purposes in the book of nature and that natural law expressed those purposes. "This is the new revelation, and thus at last we enter the secret door to knowledge."[7]

It is difficult to sort out what is true and what is false in this plausible account. I have suggested that the *philosophes* were not free from naïveté, but that is all, I think, that should be conceded. Historians and political theorists know that the natural law tradition is infinitely complex; to draw a map of its growth, its multiple ingredients, its changing modes and varied influence, would be like drawing a map of the Nile Delta. Becker does nothing to clarify and a great deal to confuse the matter by lumping together, in the same paragraph and sometimes even in the same ironic exclamation, natural law and the appeal to nature. The appeal to nature, as Becker himself tells us with engaging candor, has been employed by most schools of thought. He mentions a most miscellaneous crew of thinkers, from Aristotle and Marcus Aurelius to Calvin, Montaigne, and Pascal. He might have added Burke, the great adversary of the *philosophes*. To say, then, that the *philosophes* appealed to nature is to say that they used this word to embody the standard by which they could judge existing institutions, morals, and forms of government. They were doing what most of their predecessors had done, and what most of their successors would do. What is notable about the Enlightenment, as Ernst Cassirer reminds us, is that "it returns again and again to the persistent problems of philosophy."[8]

The natural law tradition is much narrower than this appeal

[7] Ibid. 46, 42, 41, 39, 47, 51.

[8] *The Philosophy of the Enlightenment* (1951), 234. Even if we admit for the sake of argument that the *philosophes* had taken the materials of their philosophy from Christianity alone, what would matter for the historian is

to nature. Becker's rather superficial discussion of natural law is based on two assumptions, neither of which is tenable. He suggests that natural law is essentially Christian. But natural law had originated with the Stoics and, in a less systematic form, with the Greeks. With the writings of Justus Lipsius and Grotius in the early seventeenth century, natural law was beginning to strip off its Christian associations—witness Grotius's celebrated assertion that nature would be orderly even if God did not exist. Christian natural law, even at its most rationalist in Aquinas's systematic theology, is part of a complex of laws (eternal, divine, natural, and human) all of which depend upon the wisdom of God. Modern natural law is secular, "profane," autonomous.

Moreover, Becker neglects the fact that many *philosophes* were reaching beyond even this secular natural law. Diderot still employed the conception of *droit naturel*, Vattel still carried on the seventeenth-century tradition of the natural lawyers, but other *philosophes*, following out the implications of British empiricism, were rejecting the natural law arguments in favor of utilitarianism. Inevitably, there was much ambivalence and uncertainty concerning natural law in this time of transition.[9] But far from being disciples of any natural law doctrine, the *philosophes* were providing a bridge to

---

that they transformed these Christian ideas. "Grace was translated into virtue," writes Becker in *The Heavenly City*, 49. Is that not a significant translation? The *philosophes* "had only given another form and a new name to the object of worship: having denatured God, they deified nature" (ibid. 63). Only? But the fact is that the sources of Enlightenment thought must not be sought in Christianity alone. Where Becker writes, "A distinction between good and bad! Not a novel idea, certainly; on the contrary, a very old, a most Christian idea" (ibid. 86), he might well have substituted the word "Stoic" for "Christian."

[9] Voltaire is perhaps the best example of this ambivalence. He continues to affirm the existence of natural law but is uneasy with it. As an empiricist, as a disciple of Locke's philosophic "modesty,"

nineteenth-century utilitarianism and historicism. Bentham and Hegel are the philosophical heirs of Hume and Turgot: it is this real continuity between the eighteenth and nineteenth centuries that Becker neglects in favor of a fancied continuity between the Enlightenment and Christianity.[1]

Finally, Becker fails to distinguish between natural law as rhetoric and natural law as conviction; while most of the time he does not take the *philosophes* seriously enough, he takes their rhapsodic paeans to natural law too seriously. The *philosophes* were, above all, practical social reformers, and through their rhetoric we can sense their impatience to get to work. When Voltaire affirms that some moral rules are universally accepted and that this proves the existence of natural law, when Voltaire says briskly that "a day suffices for a sage to know the duties of man," he seems to be saying to his reader: "You and I know what is wrong in this society; you and I know what evils must be rooted out and what institutions must be changed; to split hairs about the fundamentals of morals is to escape responsibility, to substitute talk for action."[2] Social reform in the first half of the eighteenth century rested on philosophic positions no longer fully convincing even to its most fiery proponents. In overlooking this gap between talk and action, in taking the rhetoric of the *philo-*

---

as a caricaturist of the *esprit de systême*, he is driven to doubt the existence of a law in which he would like to believe. He solves the dilemma (unsatisfactorily) by arguing that there is empirical proof for the existence of a universal, uniform law of nature.

[1] Once again Becker can be quoted on the other side of his own argument. He describes eighteenth-century natural law: "Instead of being a construction of deductive logic [it] is the observed harmonious behavior of material objects." "This," he adds truly, "was a new kind of 'law of nature' " (ibid. 57). But he fails to draw the necessary inferences from these observations.

[2] For some details on this question, see my *Voltaire's Politics*, Appendix I, "Voltaire and Natural Law."

sophes as a literal transcription of their deepest convictions, Becker, while claiming to penetrate to fundamentals, only too often confines his analysis to the surface.

What then has become of Becker's thesis that the *philosophes* did not know what they were doing and were rebuilding the old heavenly city, only with new materials? Without wishing to be paradoxical for the sake of paradox, let me suggest that Becker's formulation turns the truth upside down: the *philosophes* knew exactly what they were doing; they were building a new, earthly city. And in building it they used, along with much new material, some of the old Christian bricks. Far from being less modern than they knew, they were even more modern than they claimed.

Becker's analysis of natural law is unphilosophical; his analysis of the relation of the *philosophes* to history is unhistorical. That does not make it any the less delightful: in the last two chapters Becker catches, with superb wit, a certain mood of the *philosophes*. His deft characterization of Madame Roland weeping that she was not born a Roman, of Robespierre apostrophizing posterity; his apt quotation from Diderot, "*La postérité pour le philosophe, c'est l'autre monde de l'homme religieux*"—all these almost convince us that this antienthusiastic century was crowded with enthusiasts. As Becker says, the *philosophes*' aversion to enthusiasm was itself an enthusiasm.[3]

But—like Voltaire's Zadig (and, for that matter, like Becker himself) we are compelled to say "but" once again—while Becker's insights into the character of the *philosophes* are valuable, they are marginal rather than central, and Becker places too heavy a load upon his evidence.

Let me summarize his case: the sensationalism of the *philo-*

[3] *The Heavenly City*, 37.

sophes, first explored by Locke and extended by his disciples, was at first a heady and later a frightening prospect for them. If Locke was right, there was no total depravity. But if nature was good, whence evil? "How then could Philosophers say that all was somehow good in God's sight unless they could also say that there was no evil to be observed in the world of nature and man?" Pure reason confronted the *philosophes* with "an ugly dilemma, emerging from the beautiful promises of the new philosophy," and in order to escape this dilemma they turned from reason to history. "They found . . . that reason is amenable to treatment. They therefore tempered reason with sentiment, reasons of the heart that reason knows not of; or held in leash by experience, the universal judgment of mankind. . . ." Becker professes to observe a change of temper and ascribes it to fear. "The Philosophers *began to* cold-shoulder abstract reason. . . ." "The age of reason had scarcely run half its course before the Philosophers *were admitting* the feebleness of reason, *putting the ban on* flippancy, and *turning to* the study of useful, that is to say, factual, subjects." And Becker claims to see this historical development in the works of some of the leading *philosophes*, above all in Hume: "Hume's *turning away from* speculation to the study of history, economics, and politics was symptomatic of a certain change in the climate of opinion. . . ."[4]

It is doubtless fruitful to divide the Enlightenment into two

[4] Ibid. 67, 69, 69-70, 83, 84, my italics. Becker qualifies his case at one point: "I would not leave the impression that the philosophers began to cold-shoulder abstract reason merely, or chiefly, because they found a logical dilemma in the path; still less that they embraced the cause of virtue with greater emotional warmth because they could find no ultimate reason for embracing it at all. There may be something in all that—I am inclined to think that there is; but I do not wish to make too much of it" (ibid. 83). But having said that he does not wish to make too much of it, he proceeds to make too much of it.

periods. In the first half of the century the *philosophes* were an embattled and socially inferior group; in the second half of the century they were confident that they were winning the contest for public opinion and social prestige. In the first half of the century the rhetoric of natural law had still been prevalent; in the second half it was largely supplanted by utilitarianism. But for Becker's division—the shift from pure reason to reason softened by sentiment, from nonhistorical reason to historical reason—there is little convincing evidence. Diderot, in many respects the most representative of the *philosophes*, celebrated the passions in his earliest writings; Vauvenargues, one of Voltaire's favorite writers, warned against separating the intellect from the sentiments; Hume, developing his epistemology in the 1730's, gave the sentiments the precedence over reason.

Similarly, it cannot be shown that the *philosophes* "turned to" history because they were afraid of the implications of their godless rationalism. They wrote history as they wrote everything else: as men of letters they thought of history as a branch of literature. Voltaire wrote history—and very good history—as early as 1727–1728, when he began his *Histoire de Charles XII*, and his other historical masterpieces were conceived and probably begun in the 1730's. Nor is there the slightest evidence that the *philosophes* became more, rather than less, cautious: indeed, their daring grew with their successes. Deism was characteristic of the first half of the eighteenth century; a far bolder atheism was, if not characteristic, prevalent in the second half.[5]

[5] Becker's sketch of the *philosophe* as frightened by his own temerity and afraid to undermine morality is incorrect in many respects. Becker makes much of Hume's refusal to publish his masterly and radical *Dialogues Concerning Natural Religion* and attributes this refusal chiefly to the fact that Hume "took no pleas-

Why should Becker have discovered a shift in the Enlightenment that did not exist? I suspect that he needed the shift to account for the *philosophes*' solution of their moral dilemma—how to explain evil in the face of an all-good nature. But the dilemma is as imaginary as its solution. Becker does well to remind us that the *philosophes*' contribution to theodicy was unimpressive. Perhaps, if God becomes unimportant, it becomes equally unimportant to justify him. The *philosophes* viewed nature as good but not as omnipotent: Rousseau was not the only one who held that human institutions could deprave man, that goodness could be thwarted, and that the original intentions of God could be perverted.[6] The *philosophes*' affirmation that man is by nature good does not mean that they could not account for the existence of evil, and Becker's case (that to the Enlightenment writers history provided a standard which philosophy had destroyed) falls to the ground.

---

ure in being regarded as the cold and finished skeptic, a destroyer of illusions. He was much more ambitious 'to be esteemed a man of virtue than a writer of taste'; and the fact that his history won for him the popularity he craved naturally confirmed him in his belief that it was useless to search into 'those corners of nature that spread a nuisance all around.'" (*The Heavenly City*, 77-8). But the fact is that Hume was extremely eager to publish the *Dialogues* and had to be firmly dissuaded by his friends, notably Adam Smith. And Adam Smith was not afraid that Hume would destroy morality but that he would get into trouble. In the last year of his life Hume revised the *Dialogues* once again and changed his will several times to make sure that they would be published after his death (since he was too ill to see them through the press himself) and published without being emasculated. See Norman Kemp Smith: "Introduction," Appendix C, *Hume's Dialogues Concerning Natural Religion* (ed. 1947), 87-96. Becker's account of the development of Voltaire's philosophy is equally unconvincing.

[6] See Voltaire's little known story, *Songe de Platon*, in which he portrays the world as created by a

While Becker rightly rejects the nineteenth-century charge that the Enlightenment was unhistorical, he accepts the charge that Enlightenment history was not "real" history but ideology. The Enlightenment historians "start out, under the banner of objectivity and with a flourish of scholarly trumpets, as if on a voyage of discovery in unknown lands. They start out, but in a very real sense they never pass the frontiers of the eighteenth century, never really enter the country of the past or of distant lands. They cannot afford to leave the battlefield of the present where they are so fully engaged in a life-and-death struggle with Christian philosophy and the infamous things that support it—superstition, intolerance, tyranny."[7]

Becker is equally harsh on nineteenth-century historians. The *philosophes*, he argues, wrote history in order to change society; the nineteenth-century historians wrote history in order to keep society as it was.[8] His criticism of historians is therefore not one-sided. But it implies either that to write "objective" history is impossible or that the *philosophes* fell short of writing good history. It was surely the first of these implications that Becker intended to stress, but it is the second that others have stressed in their disparagement of the *philosophes*.

I do not want to enter into the debate on the possibility of

---

minor angel who made it as good as he could—which is far from perfect. In their moral and religious writings the *philosophes* sought to discredit the Christian doctrine of the fall of man, and their use of nature did not deprive them of a standard by which actions and institutions could be judged. It is only in the marquis de Sade's version of naturalism that we find the notion that nature speaks only in one voice and that everything possible or even imaginable is "natural." This is an interpretation of "natural" that the *philosophes* would never have accepted.

[7] *The Heavenly City*, 105.

[8] Ibid. 95-7.

objective history here. I only want to point out that the criticism of Enlightenment historians can be overdone. Montesquieu, Voltaire, Hume, Robertson, Gibbon, wrote better histories than their present-day reputations would indicate. Becker quotes two juicy morsels: "Mankind are so much the same, in all times and places, that history informs us of nothing new or strange in this particular. Its chief use is only to discover the constant and universal principles of human nature." Thus David Hume. "History is only a pack of tricks we play on the dead." Thus Voltaire, and it is easy to see why this should have been one of Carl Becker's favorite quotations. But if we look at Hume's history of England instead of this pronouncement on history, if we look at Voltaire's masterpieces instead of this *bon mot* about history, we are impressed by their scrupulous concern for truth, their careful sifting of evidence, their intelligent selection of what is important, their keen sense of drama, their grasp of the fact that a whole civilization is a unit of study. What if Becker had quoted from the opening pages of Voltaire's *Siècle de Louis XIV*, or from some of Voltaire's and Hume's correspondence about their historical works? These quotations might not have been so amusing or so telling as the words Becker actually quoted, but they might have been far more revealing about eighteenth-century historiography.

It is perhaps a reflection of how intent Becker was to debunk Enlightenment historians that he makes a significant mistake. "The Philosophers felt that Montesquieu was too much enamored of facts as such to treat certain facts as harshly as they deserved, and it shocked them to see him dallying lightly with episodes that were no better than they should be. Voltaire (Voltaire of all people!) criticized Montesquieu for his *levity*." The *Esprit des lois* "left a bad taste in the mouths of the Philosophers because Montesquieu insisted that the 'constant and universal principles of human nature' were after all 'relative.' "[9] The opposite is true: Voltaire and other *philosophes* admired Montesquieu but criticized him because he was a proponent of the *thèse nobiliaire*, a defender of the privileged *parlements*. They criticized him because he was a conservative, and not because he was a relativist. Voltaire criticized Montesquieu, too, for being slipshod in his research, for accepting improbable travelers' tales—not for being "too much enamored of facts as such" but for being too little enamored of facts as such. When Voltaire (and why not Voltaire of all people?) accused Montesquieu of levity, he was referring to Montesquieu's gullibility.[1]

But it is not mistakes such as these that really disappoint the reader in this charming book; the disappointment is, I think, more profound. *The Heavenly City*, as I have said, begins with a significant truth: history is concerned with the dialectical struggle between persistence and change. The eighteenth century is a century in which this struggle becomes peculiarly dramatic and complex, and the opportunities for fruitful research are great. Becker rightly urges the reader to ask searching questions, but he continually suggests the wrong answers. He argues for persistence where there was change, and he argues for one kind of persistence when there was really another.

The *philosophes* lived in an epoch in which the vitality of Christianity was waning and in which natural science,

[9] Ibid. 100-1.

[1] For Voltaire's appreciation (inadequate) and criticisms (excessive) of Montesquieu, see especially his *Commentaire sur l'Esprit des lois; Questions sur l'Encyclopédie*, article "Loix, esprit des"; *Pensées sur le gouvernement* and "*L'A,B,C.*"

the centralized state, the development of industrial capitalism, imposed the need for a new world view. In building their earthly city, the *philosophes* fashioned their materials from the most varied sources: Christianity, a revived Stoicism and Epicureanism, and a pragmatic recognition of the needs of the new state and the new economy. In their battle for liberation from the old standards and in their search for new standards they experienced the difficulties that any individual struggling for autonomy must face. They contradicted themselves; they failed to see all the implications of their ideas; they sometimes used old words to describe new things; they sometimes used rhetoric that was inappropriate to their ideas. All these problems *The Heavenly City* resolves—wrongly, I believe—with the too simple formula of its title.

The failure of the book is all the more paradoxical in view of Becker's own position. His criticisms of the *philosophes* were from the inside; as Leo Gershoy has said, Carl Becker "had always remained a believer at heart. . . . He had rejoined Voltaire and Condorcet and Wells and all the goodly company who wished humanity well."[2] But in his impatience with his intellectual forebears—an impatience which is always so much greater with those whom you admire than with those you detest—he portrayed the *philosophes* as naïve and as a little fraudulent. Becker was no conservative, but the conservative implications of *The Heavenly City* are plain.

And *The Heavenly City* failed in another, and even more paradoxical, way—through its success. Carl Becker dedicated *Everyman His Own Historian* to those who had assisted him in clarifying his ideas, "chiefly by avoiding the error of Hway, a pupil of Confucius. Hway, said Confucius, is of no assistance to me; there is nothing that I say in which he does not delight."

[2] "Introduction," to Carl Becker, *Progress and Power* (1949), xxxvii.

In the quarter century that the book has been before the public, the error of Hway has not been avoided. It is time we admitted, borrowing from Lytton Strachey, that Carl Becker's critique of the *philosophes*, like Samuel Johnson's critique of Shakespeare, had every virtue save one, the virtue of being right.

8

READING ABOUT ROUSSEAU

Il faut étudier la société par les hommes, et les hommes par la société: ceux qui voudront traiter séparément la politique et la morale n'entendront jamais rien à aucune des deux.
—JEAN-JACQUES ROUSSEAU, *Émile*

1 · A Survey of the Literature

THE FIRST and for a long time the least consulted interpreter of Rousseau's thought was Jean-Jacques Rousseau himself. Throughout his life he insisted that his work embodied a coherent rational philosophy, and that the discrepancies in his writings were purely superficial—the echo of extraneous influences.[1] "All that is daring in the *Contrat social*," he wrote in his *Confessions*, "had previously appeared

[1] In his *Confessions*, Book IX, Rousseau attributed the "satirical and cutting" tone of his earlier works to Diderot's baleful influence. *O.C.*, I, 405n. In this essay, I shall cite from two collected editions of Rousseau's works, the standard *Œuvres com-*

in the *Discours sur l'inégalité;* all that is daring in *Émile* had previously appeared in Julie."[2] Defending his *Émile* against the condemnation pronounced by the Archbishop of Paris, he said firmly: "I have written on diverse subjects, but always on the same principles, always the same morals, the same belief, the same maxims, and, if you wish, the same opinions."[3] As he came to reflect on his work once more near the end of his life, he reiterated his claim to consistency. All his writings, he said again, were constructed on "one great principle."[4]

For over a century, hardly anyone took this appraisal seriously. Disciples and critics alike treated him as a sort of elemental force rather than as a thinker, and claimed to find the "message of Rousseau" in his adventures instead of his ideas, or in his epigrams instead of his chains of argument. To Voltaire belongs the dubious distinction of launching this sort of interpretation by taking a posture for a philosophical position. Acknowledging Rousseau's *Discours sur l'inégalité*, Voltaire thanked him for his "new book against the human race," and added that reading the work made him want to walk on all fours. "Still, since I lost that habit more than sixty years ago, I feel that it's unfortunately impossible for me to resume it."[5]

---

plètes, Hachette, 13 vols. (1871-1877 and often reprinted), and the fine *Œuvres complètes* now in progress in a Pléiade edition, ed. Bernard Gagnebin, Bernard Guyon, et al., of which two volumes have so far appeared (1959, 1961). Volume I of this edition contains the autobiographical writings, Volume II the *Nouvelle Héloïse* and other literary works. I shall cite the Hachette edition as *Œuvres*, and the Pléiade edition as O.C. For a thorough, well-organized survey of the literature on Rousseau down to 1940, the reader should consult Albert Schinz's judicious *État présent des travaux sur J.-J. Rousseau* (1941).

[2] Book IX, *O.C.*, I, 407.

[3] *Lettre à Monsieur de Beaumont*, *Œuvres*, III, 59.

[4] *Rousseau Juge de Jean-Jacques*, "Third Dialogue," *O.C.*, I, 934.

[5] (August 30, 1755), *Correspondence*, ed. Besterman, XXVII, 230.

Later critics, who shared Voltaire's malice and were, in addition, hostile to the Enlightenment, saw Rousseau as the incarnation of aimless modernity. To Burke, he was the supreme representative of the godless Age of Reason, while Bonald condemned him as the advocate of ruinous disorder. On the other hand, nineteenth-century readers like Sir Henry Maine attacked him for setting up a "collective despot" and for reintroducing, in the *Contrat social*, "the old divine right of kings in a new dress."[6]

While his opponents rejected Rousseau's teachings for the widest variety of reasons, his admirers were just as catholic in their praise. The Jacobins defended the Terror in his name; the German Romantics hailed him as a liberator; and Schiller portrayed him as a martyr to wisdom:

> As Socrates by sophists was brought low,
> So Christians tortured, Christians felled Rousseau—
> Rousseau, who called on Christians to be men.[7]

Edmund Burke was surely right when he observed that, "were Rousseau alive, and in one of his lucid intervals, he would be shocked at the practical frenzy of his scholars."[8] There is nothing surprising in seeing a thinker maltreated by commentators, but few have had to endure so much as Rousseau. Conflicting interpretations, pronounced with equal dogmatism, long obscured the integrity of his thought on which he had insisted so often.

The conflict of interpretations in no way diminished after

[6] *Popular Government* (1886), 157, 160.

[7] Schiller, "Rousseau":
Sokrates ging unter durch Sophisten,
Rousseau leidet, Rousseau fällt durch Christen,
Rousseau—der aus Christen Menschen wirbt.
(English translation by J. Christopher Herold.)

[8] *Reflections on the Revolution in France*, in *Orations and Essays* (1900), 529.

the smoke of revolution and reaction had cleared away. Rousseau never ceased to be a symbol in the political struggle, especially in France, and he continued to be loved or hated with vehemence and in confusion. His economic ideas were described as the foundations of socialism or cited in support of the sanctity of private property; his religious ideas were shown to be "fundamentally" deist, Calvinist, or even Catholic; his moral teachings were alternately seen as rigid and Puritan or emotional and relaxed; his thought as a whole was sometimes considered rationalist and more often irrationalist in tendency.

While Rousseau's commentators did not confine their disputes to his political theory, most of them treated Rousseau as a political theorist, or judged his ideas in the light of his political philosophy. In this arena of interpretation, four Rousseaus were set to battle against one another: the individualist, the collectivist, the confused, self-contradictory enthusiast, and curiously combining these three, the individualist who shifted in mid-career to collectivism.

The conception of Rousseau the individualist was the first in the field. The radicals of the *Sturm und Drang* acclaimed him as the prophet of the coming age of freedom, and Hölderlin, who called him a demi-god, translated Rousseau's purported defiance of law into extravagant verse.[9] Not long after, such counterrevolutionaries as de Maistre accused Rousseau of a destructive individualism, of irresponsible impiety toward established tradition. More recently, French interpreters like

[9] See especially Hölderlin's "Hymne an die Freiheit," "Hymne an die Menschheit," "Rousseau," and "Der Rhein." In the last poem Rousseau's message to man is seen as a revelation which the demigod transmits to humanity and which Hölderlin characteristically sees as *gesetzlos*—lawless.

Émile Faguet argued that "all of Rousseau can be found in the *Discours sur l'inégalité*. That is a commonplace . . . but I think it is true."[1] This "novel of humanity" has one central theme: man is good and becomes evil by embracing society. Faguet felt constrained to admit that the *Contrat social* is "antiliberal" and contains "not an atom of liberty or security."[2] But he explained this difficulty away: the *Contrat social* "seems an isolated part of Rousseau's work" and "contradicts his general ideas," while the individualism of the *Discours sur l'inégalité*, "the antisocial idea," is central—it pervades nearly all his writings and appears with particular power in *Émile*.[3]

A quarter of a century later, Henri Sée reached a similar conclusion by a different logical path. "The *Discours sur l'inégalité*," he wrote, in agreement with Faguet, "is inspired by an individualist, indeed almost anarchist, conception." But —and here he departs from Faguet—"in the *Contrat social* Rousseau remains an individualist, despite appearances to the contrary."[4] Rousseau's political thought is an attempt to "assure the individual the full development of his liberty"; hence Rousseau is "an individualist and a liberal. It is not true to say that he wants the state to have absolute and aggressive authority."[5] Thus it is hardly surprising to read in C. E. Vaughan's famous edition of Rousseau's political writings, published in 1915, that "the work of Rousseau is little known in this country and less understood. The title of the *Contrat social* is familiar. But to most men it suggests an extreme form of individualism."[6]

[1] *Dix-huitième siècle* (n.d.), 345.
[2] Ibid. 401, 403.
[3] Ibid. 360-77, 399, 400.
[4] *L'évolution de la pensée politique en France au XVIIIe Siècle* (1925), 426.
[5] Ibid. 146, 161.
[6] C. E. Vaughan: *The Political Writings of Jean Jacques Rousseau*, 2 vols. (1915), I, 1.

Probably the most influential voice for the opposite view, that Rousseau is a collectivist, was Taine. His bulky and bitter history of eighteenth-century France was animated by the conviction that the French Revolution had been the work of salon-intellectuals whose knowledge of the world had been slight, and who had been guided by an abstract Cartesian conception of life: "brutal force placed itself at the disposal of radical dogma, and . . . radical dogma placed itself at the disposal of brutal force."[7] Irresponsible *philosophes*, with Rousseau as their prototype, had infected the eighteenth-century French mind with the sickness of revolutionary ideas. Taine introduced a new notion into Rousseau-criticism—the unintended consequence. Rousseau's political thought, he argued, had been designed as the supreme assault on law and order and had resulted, paradoxically but inevitably, in tyranny: "The doctrine of popular sovereignty, interpreted by the masses, will produce perfect anarchy until the moment when, interpreted by the rulers, it produces perfect despotism."[8] Rousseau's state is a "layman's monastery," and "in this democratic monastery which Rousseau establishes on the model of Sparta and Rome, the individual is nothing and the state everything."[9]

To quote Taine is to quote the view that has become fashionable in our age. We hear echoes of it in Karl Popper's dismissal of Rousseau's thought as "romantic collectivism,"[1] or in Sir Ernest Barker's tart observation: "In effect, and in the last resort, Rousseau is a totalitarian. . . . Imagine Rousseau

[7] *Les Origines de la France contemporaine*, vol. I, *L'Ancien régime*, (1896), 521.

[8] Taine: *L'Ancien régime*, 319.

[9] Ibid. 323, 321. Alfred Cobban says that "practically all the modern literary criticism of Rousseau is derived" from Taine. *Rousseau and the Modern State* (1934), 40.

[1] K. R. Popper: *The Open Society and Its Enemies*, 2 vols. (1945), II, 50.

a perfect democrat: his perfect democracy is still a multiple autocracy."[2] Rousseau has come a long way from the days of Schiller's *Räuber*, when he was a romantic outlaw battling against all authority. Many of Rousseau's present-day readers, remembering the supremacy of the general will, the forcing of men to be free, the civil religion, and forgetting the rest of his writings, are in agreement with Taine and Barker. The modish Rousseau is a totalitarian—a "democratic totalitarian" perhaps, but a totalitarian nevertheless.[3]

Most partisans of these two irreconcilable schools of interpretation sacrificed the complexities of Rousseau's thought to the simplicity of their categories; but some of them hinted at a third method of solving the "Rousseau Problem" by explaining away inconvenient Rousseauian ideas as aberrations or, better yet, as signs of a deep inner confusion. Faguet saved his view of Rousseau the individualist by treating the *Contrat social* as an irrational lapse into collectivism. Barker on the other side saved his view of Rousseau the collectivist by treating most aspects of Rousseau's thought as a haphazard collection of vague notions: "You can find your own dogmas in Rousseau, whether you belong to the Left (and especially to the left of the Left) or whether you belong to the Right (and especially to the right of the Right.)"[4]

The same line of argument had been adopted earlier in John Morley's vigorous and persuasive biography. Morley accused Rousseau of continuous, incurable, and deliberate confusion. Rousseau, he argued, had neglected both history and experience—the only evidence on which a sound social theory could

[2] "Introduction," *The Social Contract* (1948), xxxviii.

[3] For an intelligent statement of this position, see Michael Polanyi: "Beyond Nihilism," *Encounter*, XIV (March 1960), 34-43.

[4] "Introduction," *The Social Contract*, xxxix.

be based. He derided what he called Rousseau's "narrow, symmetrical, impatient humor" and the "desperate absurdity of the assumptions of the Social Contract."[5] Following Burke, he described Rousseau as the "typical schoolman" who "assumes that analysis of terms is the right way of acquiring new knowledge about things" and who "mistakes the multiplication of propositions for the discovery of fresh truth."[6] In fact, Morley concluded, "many pages of the Social Contract are mere logical deductions from verbal definitions, which the slightest attempt to confront with actual fact would have shown to be not only valueless but wholly meaningless."[7]

This is strong talk, but it gained wide currency. It seemed appropriate somehow to an enthusiast who himself confessed that he had discovered his "one great principle" while lying under a tree half-conscious, his coat bathed in tears. The critics who took this line seemed undisturbed by their inability to agree whether Rousseau's thought was worthless because it was a product of abstract reasoning or irresponsible emotionalism.

This third group seems more a symptom than a school, but it at least pointed to the richness of Rousseau's ideas. With the work of C. E. Vaughan, to whom all students of Rousseau are deeply indebted, this profusion was ordered by being plotted on the curve of time. In his sympathetic introduction to Rousseau's political writings he acknowledged that individualism and collectivism lay side by side in Rousseau, "not so much reconciled, as in ill-veiled hostility, to each other,"[8] but

[5] Morley: *Rousseau,* 2 vols. (1873), II, 126, 134.

[6] Ibid. II, 135. Morley would not even grant that Rousseau practiced his scholastic method skillfully. "Rousseau was always apt to think in a slipshod manner." Ibid. I, 192.

[7] Ibid. II, 135.

[8] *The Political Writings of Jean-Jacques Rousseau,* I, 5.

he insisted that the interpreter of Rousseau must account for this conflict, and if possible solve it. Vaughan himself accounted for it by distributing the dominant elements of Rousseau's thought over his career as a thinker. As a young man, in the two first famous discourses, Rousseau had written as a moralist, criticizing the vices of his time through extreme statements. In this period, leaning on Locke and Plato, he had enunciated abstract principles. Later, in his maturity, he had come under the influence of Montesquieu, learning that life is never clear-cut and that principles are modified by circumstances. Hence, concrete illustrations and political science began to take the upper hand; they dominate the last sections of the *Contrat social* and his later political writings, such as the *Lettres écrites de la montagne* and the *Considérations sur le Gouvernement de Pologne*. This double evolution, from moralist to political scientist and from abstract to concrete thinker, is accompanied by his growth from individualism to collectivism. "The political work of Rousseau, when taken as a whole, presents an unbroken movement from one position almost to its opposite. He starts as the prophet of freedom, in the most abstract sense conceivable. His ideal, in the second *Discourse*, is a state of things in which each individual is absolutely independent of the rest." The first few sentences of the *Contrat social* belong in the same camp, but except for them, "the *Contrat social* represents a very different—and assuredly a less abstract, as well as a less individualist—idea. Here freedom is no longer conceived as the independence of the individual. It is rather to be sought in his total surrender to the service of the State." This metamorphosis is unannounced, but "silent though it is, the change of abstract individualism of the second *Discourse*, the abstract collectivism of the *Contrat social*, are alike forgotten." What we have at the end is a kind of concrete collectivism. "The long journey is at last ended. And Rousseau now stands at the opposite point of the compass from that at which he started."[9]

Vaughan's interpretation is the most refined interpretation possible for a reader who concentrates on Rousseau's political writings to the exclusion of his other work. It abounds in prescient hints; its portrait of Rousseau the moralist, of Rousseau's thought as a living, evolving organism, and of Rousseau's conception of the state as an idealized entity that does not yet exist—all these were explored further by later commentators. But while Rousseau was a political theorist, and a great one, his political theory can be understood only in the context of his whole work, in conjunction with *Émile*, the *Nouvelle Héloïse*, and the *Confessions*. Vaughan's interpretation, by its very virtues, demands to be superseded by a larger view.

In the very years that C. E. Vaughan was collecting manuscripts for his great edition, a small band of scholars began to examine Rousseau's work in its entirety and extracted from it the unity of his philosophy. These scholars had not lost interest in the question of Rousseau's individualism or collectivism, but such political categories no longer held a central place in their attention. They did not deny the paradoxical character of many of Rousseau's pronouncements, but they agreed with Rousseau that these paradoxes do not impair his fundamental consistency. By 1912, the bicentennial of Rousseau's birth, a new age of interpretation had begun.

The birth of the new did not cause the death of the old; for decades several sets of interpretations persisted side by side.

[9] Ibid. I, 80-1.

With a writer as rich and as problematical as Rousseau, this is only natural. But some views of Rousseau lay well outside the range of rational discussion; they illustrate the persistence of the kind of irresponsible reading first practiced by Voltaire on the *Discours sur l'inégalité*. It may be that Rousseau invited misunderstanding, but it is certain that all too many critics were ready to accept the invitation.

They had some provocation. Rousseau was, unhappily, the coiner of memorable epigrams. David Hume had observed in 1766 that Rousseau's "Writings are so full of Extravagance, that I cannot believe their Eloquence alone will be able to support them,"[1] but as it happened, it was his eloquence more than his extravagance that caused Rousseau trouble. Thus, "The man who thinks is a depraved animal," has been quoted over and over again as proof that Rousseau despised thought and rationality.[2] "Man is born free and everywhere he is in chains," the ringing sentence that opens the first chapter of the *Contrat social*, has usually been cited as the beginning of a hymn to extreme individualism; no wonder that the readers who took this statement literally felt cheated by the rest of the book. "Let us begin then by setting all the facts aside, since they do not affect the question," has been offered as a conclusive demonstration that Rousseau cared little for empirical evidence, and had a passion for abstract propositions spun out in indifference, or even hostility to truth.[3]

Taken out of context, the rhetorical power of such phrases gave them an importance far beyond their significance to Rousseau's line of argument, and a meaning quite contrary to Rousseau's intentions. Rousseau himself was aware that his

[1] J.Y.T. Greig, ed.: *The Letters of David Hume*, 2 vols. (1932), II, 103.

[2] *Discours sur l'inégalité, Œuvres,* I, 87.

[3] Ibid. I, 83.

intensely personal style might cause his readers difficulties. He warned Madame d'Épinay about his use of words in his letters: "Learn my vocabulary better, my good friend, if you would have us understand each other. Believe me, my terms rarely have the common meaning; it is always my heart that converses with you, and perhaps you will learn some day that it speaks not as others do."[4] It might have been useful if Rousseau had issued a similar warning about his published writings. "In lapidary inscriptions a man is not upon oath," Samuel Johnson once said about epitaphs, but Rousseau found few readers sensible enough to keep such a caution in mind. Significantly enough, the critics who revolutionized the interpretation of Rousseau were also the readers who read him generously. "We must weigh the meaning and import of the texts seriously," wrote Gustave Lanson in 1912, "and consider the spirit more than the letter."[5]

This was hard to do, partly (one might say) because the letter was so spirited. Rousseau's style exercised such an irresistible fascination on his critics because it mirrored, in its passion, a strange and stormy life. For many interpreters, Rousseau always remained Byron's

> self-torturing sophist, wild Rousseau,
> The apostle of affliction, he who threw
> Enchantment over passion, and from woe
> Wrung overwhelming eloquence.[6]

[4] March 1756. Theophile Dufour and Pierre Paul Plan, eds.: *Correspondance générale de J.-J. Rousseau,* 20 vols. (1924–1934), II, 266.

[5] "L'Unité de la pensée de Jean-Jacques Rousseau," *Annales de la société Jean-Jacques Rousseau,* VIII (1912), 6. (Henceforth cited as *Annales.*)

[6] *Childe Harold's Pilgrimage,* Canto the Third, stanza lxxvii.

Nothing was easier than to reduce the ideas of the "apostle of affliction" to a mere reflection of his experiences—or rather, a reflection of the twisted interpretations which he gave to these experiences. And nothing is easier than to find examples of this sort of criticism. Thus F. J. C. Hearnshaw argues, "So intimately . . . were Rousseau's writings associated with his life that it is impossible to comprehend them without a detailed knowledge of his curious and remarkable career."[7] Fortified by this statement, in itself innocent enough, Hearnshaw divides Rousseau's life into five periods: the undisciplined boy, the supertramp, the would-be man of the world, the inspired maniac, the hunted fugitive.[8] Thus spared the necessity of grappling seriously with Rousseau's meaning, Hearnshaw can sum up one of the greatest of political theorists with these words: "He was an unsystematic thinker, untrained in formal logic. He was an omnivorous reader with undeveloped powers of assimilation. He was an emotional enthusiast who spoke without due reflection. He was an irresponsible writer with a fatal gift for epigram."[9] All true, to be sure, but can Rousseau be captured by epigrams such as these?

The lengths to which this sort of interpretation can be pushed was illustrated in Irving Babbitt's influential *Rousseau and Romanticism.* This book, laden with ill-tempered denunciations of Rousseau, shows that to concentrate on sordid detail is not the proper method for an intellectual historian. Babbitt dismisses Rousseau's trenchant critique of eighteenth-century polite society: "Rousseau's spite against

[7] "Rousseau," in F. J. C. Hearnshaw, ed.: *The Social and Political Ideas of Some Great French Thinkers of the Age of Reason* (1930), 172.

[8] Ibid. 173-83, *passim.* See also Taine's lurid character sketch, *L'Ancien régime*, 289.

[9] Hearnshaw: "Rousseau," 185-6.

eighteenth-century Paris was largely due to the fact that he had not acquired young enough the habits that would have made it possible for him to conform to its conventions." He demolishes Rousseau's solution of the theodicy problem: "The faith in one's natural goodness is a constant encouragement to evade moral responsibility." He disdainfully contrasts Rousseau's statements on love, which remind him of "the cult of the medieval knight for his lady," with his practice: "So much for the ideal; the real was Thérèse Levasseur." Again, as with Hearnshaw, all true, but not the whole truth. In fact, Babbitt succeeds in misunderstanding Rousseau's ideas with impressive consistency and vigor: Rousseau looks "upon every constraint whether from within or from without as incompatible with liberty." "His programme amounts in practice to the indulgence of infinite indeterminate desire." "One may learn from Rousseau the art of sinking to the region of instinct that is below the rational level instead of struggling forward to the region of insight that is above it."[1]

Now no one, least of all the interpreters who revolutionized our understanding of Rousseau, would deny the value of biography to the study of ideas. But—it is almost too obvious to need saying—the genesis of an idea neither exhausts its meaning nor affects its value. Like other great and difficult men, Rousseau lived a life that was all too often a pathetic caricature of his thought, and to reduce his philosophical views to personal anecdotes only results in distortion and vulgarization. Rousseau's confession that he abandoned his five illegitimate children at a foundling home does not discredit his educational program in *Émile*. His admissions that his pose of bearish independence sprang in large part from his inability

[1] *Rousseau and Romanticism* (1919), 174, 155, 221, 220.

to learn the manners of Parisian society, or that his refusal to accept a pension from Louis XV was based not on principled dignity but on fear of losing control of his bladder in the Royal Presence, do not invalidate his critique of eighteenth-century civilization. These are elementary canons of criticism, but they were persistently violated by interpreters overwhelmed by the drama of Rousseau's life: "There are familiar writings in the Rousseau literature," wrote Ernst Cassirer, explicitly addressing himself to Irving Babbitt, "which give us in place of the work almost the man alone, and which describe him only in his dissensions and divisions, his inner contradictions. The history of ideas threatens here to disappear into biography, and this in turn appears as a pure case history."[2]

This was a mistake the new interpreters of Rousseau intended to avoid. They understood, and they made it explicit, that Rousseau's life and Rousseau's ideas were inextricably intertwined, but they insisted, as Cassirer put it, that his "fundamental thought, although it had its immediate origin in his nature and individuality, was neither circumscribed by nor bound to that individual personality."[3] They went further: they discovered that Rousseau's work had a certain rationality and coherence—they rediscovered, in short, Rousseau's estimate of himself.

A pioneer of this new school of thought, determined to see Rousseau's work as a whole, reduce his epigrams to their contexts, and use his life to clarify rather than muddy his ideas,

[2] *Rousseau, Kant, Goethe* (1947), 58.

[3] *The Question of Jean-Jacques Rousseau*, transl. by Peter Gay (1954), 39-40. Pierre Burgelin, whose *La Philosophie de l'existence de Jean-Jacques Rousseau* (1952) is a substantial reinterpretation of Rousseau's thought, quotes this passage, and more, from Cassirer. See "Introduction," 12-13.

was Gustave Lanson. In mid-career, already the author of a distinguished history of French literature, Lanson had an instructive conversion: he came to understand the unity and appreciate the value of Rousseau's thought by the simple expedient of reading him through with care. As a result, he accepted Rousseau's reiterated claim that his philosophy was the elucidation of "one great principle," a principle enunciated in the first sentence of *Émile*, implied in all his writings, and finally restated in *Rousseau juge de Jean-Jacques:* "Nature has created man happy and good, but society depraves him and makes him miserable."[4] Using this pronouncement as a key, Lanson then expounds the canon of Rousseau's work: the *Discours sur l'inégalité* describes the way in which society depraves men, by setting up inequalities of wealth, inequalities not ordained by nature. The *Contrat social* demonstrates man's goodness overwhelmed by evil social institutions; but the book also shows the way out by means of another principle on which Rousseau also insisted: "Human nature does not turn back."[5] The natural man cannot escape society, but must re-create it to re-create himself. The educational program of *Émile* follows logically: it outlines the growth of the natural man, "with all the advantages and without any of the vices of civilized man."[6] The *Nouvelle Héloïse* furnishes further illustrations of the same theme: it establishes the moral values of personal relations which alone make both the individual and society truly good. Finally, Rousseau includes God

[4] "Third Dialogue," *O.C.*, I, 934. See Gustave Lanson: *Histoire de la littérature française*, 8th ed. (1903), 769. Among others who argued for the unity of Rousseau's thought early were Harald Höffding: *Rousseau und seine Philosophie* (1897); and G. D. H. Cole: "Introduction," *The Social Contract and Discourses* (1913).

[5] Lanson: *Histoire de la littérature française*, 771.

[6] Ibid. 773.

in his system in the *Profession de foi du vicaire savoyard:* God has made man good and has implanted in him the moral energy to overcome the evils of a society not built on natural principles. Thus, Lanson argues, all parts of Rousseau's thought hold together, supplement one another, and express the central doctrine from which issues all the power of Rousseau's vision —the belief that man, good by nature, can transform himself into the good citizen in the good society.[7]

Lanson admitted that we can discover contradictions in Rousseau's work, and that we may point, if we like, to the gap between doctrine and life. But the general direction of his thought is constant and clear. Rousseau's writings are all attempts to resolve a single problem: "How can civilized man recover the benefits of the natural man, so innocent and happy, without returning to the state of nature, without renouncing the advantages of the social state?"[8] The early *Discours* protest against all hitherto existing societies, but not against society as such; *Émile* and the *Nouvelle Héloïse* point the way to the reform of the individual in the spheres of personal morality, family relations, and education; the later political writings outline the kind of society in which the good man can properly live. Lanson's interpretation is both intellectually convincing and aesthetically satisfying. It goes back to the author himself, to his announced intentions and the complete body of his work, treating each of his creations as a commentary on the others. Best of all, by asserting the unity of Rousseau's thought, Lanson pays Rousseau the supreme compliment of taking him seriously as a philosopher. Rousseau the man of feeling, the tearful vagabond and pathetic masochist, was no longer permitted to engross the

[7] See ibid. 774-5.
[8] "L'Unité de la pensée de Jean-Jacques Rousseau," *Annales*, VIII, 16.

center of the stage, and his assault on culture was integrated into a total, rational vision of man in society.

Lanson was a pioneer, but he was not alone. Others after him professed to discover a center to Rousseau's thought, although the location of that center remained a matter of controversy. Albert Schinz found it in Rousseau's "pragmatism,"[9] while René Hubert, a specialist on the *Encyclopédie* and the Encyclopedists, found it in Rousseau's political ideas as brought to mature perfection in the *Contrat social*.[1] Then, in 1928, E. H. Wright imported this type of interpretation into English-speaking countries. Wright undertook to elucidate Rousseau's thought, he wrote, because he could find "no document in English, and but few in any language," that attempted to discover simply what Rousseau meant to say.[2] Significantly, Wright's method was precisely Lanson's: "In the effort to find out his doctrine, I have tried to ponder all his work together. If I am in error, I would ask to have it shown by an appeal to all his utterance rather than to an occasional flash of paradox."[3]

Wright's book was an important event in the history of Rousseau criticism because it concentrated on Rousseau's conception of nature. It was precisely at this point that Rousseau's influence had been most potent and his interpreters most superficial: Rousseau had been treated as the supreme sentimentalist of the pastoral—the man who, as it were, thought outdoors. Wright saw that Rousseau had used the word nature at once more broadly and more deeply. "The idea that man must be perfected by his reason in accordance

[9] See Albert Schinz: *La Pensée de Jean-Jacques Rousseau* (1929).

[1] See René Hubert: *Rousseau et l'Encyclopédie: Essai sur la formation des idées politiques de Rousseau* (1928).

[2] E. H. Wright: *The Meaning of Rousseau* (1929), v.

[3] Ibid. vi.

with his nature runs through all of Rousseau's work and gives it an essential unity." The natural man recognizes that "nature is right." But this does not mean that he must retrogress into an animal or a savage condition, since reason and conscience are part of man's nature, too—and, indeed, his better part. Nor does it mean that he should reject art and civilization: "All art is right which simply enlarges us, but none is right if it distorts us." The task of reason is to show man what is natural to him at a given stage of his development; the task of freedom is to enable him to act as he ought. Freedom is meaningful only if we obey law, but only the law to which we assent freely because we recognize its rationality: "When our will becomes autonomously one with principle we shall know the ultimate freedom."[4] It follows that for Rousseau natural education prevents the formation of a little tyrant or a little slave. We must let the child find the bounds of his own capacities for himself; we must reason with him only when he is old enough to reason—that is the only way to create the natural man. Rousseau's political theory carries the theme of nature—the natural society—into a new dimension of experience. Men, such as they are now, are not fit for liberty. They must be made fit, and they must create for themselves a state that will make them so: "If the citizens must make the state, the state in turn must make true citizens."[5] Wright's view of Rousseau may be summarized in one sentence: Rousseau is opposed to treating children as adults or adults as children. Natural religion, finally, is the logical outgrowth of Rousseau's thought. Its object is to know God not through disputation or ritual but by the natural employment of reason in full concord with sentiment. "The natural religion . . . is the latest of

[4] Ibid. 32, 7, 24, 29.

[5] Ibid. 112.

religions to develop and the heir of all the others . . . the natural man is not our first brute forebear, but the last man whom we are travelling on to be."[6] To see this much coherence and depth in Rousseau was to see not more than is there, but more than had been seen before. With Wright's little volume, Rousseau criticism had reached maturity.

It now became possible to discover new dimensions in Rousseau. Lanson had still found it useful to defend Rousseau's individualism against imputations of collectivism, but Wright discarded the old categories. The *Contrat social*, he wrote, "is meant for neither individualist nor absolutist."[7] The road was open to consider Rousseau's thought in all its problematic depths. It was explored, with signal brilliance, by Ernst Cassirer in 1932. Both a philosopher and a historian of ideas, Cassirer was superbly equipped to catch the reverberations of Rousseau's writings and to set them in the context of his times: he read them as an attempt to deal with the supreme question of eighteenth-century moral thought—how to justify the universe without recourse to the traditional Christian explanation. As a Neo-Kantian, Cassirer had a kind of privileged access to Rousseau's mental world: as Cassirer was fond of pointing out, Kant had been almost the only eighteenth-century reader of Rousseau to appreciate his real, rather than his alleged, virtues, and Cassirer now took Kant's reading of Rousseau as his own starting point.[8] In the tradition of Dil-

[6] Ibid. 164.
[7] Ibid. 103.
[8] *The Question of Jean-Jacques Rousseau.* This essay first appeared as a series of two articles under the title "Das Problem Jean-Jacques Rousseau," in the *Archiv für Geschichte der Philosophie*, XLI (1932), 177-213, 479-513. On February 27, 1932, in an address on "L'Unité dans l'œuvre de Jean-Jacques Rousseau" before the Société Française de Philosophie, Cassirer presented the substance of this essay in French. See *Bulletin de la Société Française de Philosophie*, 32nd year, No. 2 (April-June 1932), 46-66.

they, Cassirer sought to understand Rousseau by searching for the dynamic center of his thought, by sympathetically entering and imaginatively re-creating his world of ideas. In Cassirer's hands, history, biography, and philosophy, retaining their distinct methods and stores of information, collaborated to draw an impressive portrait of Rousseau, the man and thinker.

Cassirer's essay is an achievement of the first order. It seizes—as it set out to do—both the complexity and the unity of Rousseau's work and world. It takes account of conflicting interpretations; does justice to critical moments in his life; appreciates the tense relation of the man to his friends, critics, and enemies; and explores the dramatic interaction of reason and sentiment, happiness and duty, in Rousseau's major works. Cassirer's Rousseau is a rationalist with deep roots in feeling, and a moralist who rises beyond the positivism and hedonism of the Encyclopedists to a grand conception of freedom under self-imposed law. For Cassirer, as for Kant before him, the heart of Rousseau's thought lies in his concern for man's dignity. This concern dissolves the contradictions between Rousseau's youthful assault on culture and his mature respect for law, his enthusiasm for sentiment and his praise of rationality, the individualism of his educational program and the sociability of the general will. Cassirer treats Rousseau as a tormented *philosophe* who translates his shattering personal experiences into a philosophical whole that retains its power today.

Cassirer's essay is, in the full sense of the word, beautiful; it soon found its admiring readers.[9] Yet, as Cassirer would have been the first to agree, it did not close discussion, but

[9] See C. W. Hendel's important study, *Jean-Jacques Rousseau Moralist*, 2 vols. (1934), which explicitly expresses the "very closest agreement" with Cassirer's "excellent discussions" (I, ix), and Robert Derathé, *Le Rationalisme de Jean-Jacques Rousseau* (1948).

lifted it to a new plane, and raised two tantalizing questions. As an Idealist, Cassirer gave an account of Rousseau's thought that appeared at once too orderly and too rationalistic. Was the "history of reason" in Rousseau's philosophy really so neatly structured? And what were the irrational, unconscious origins of Rousseau's ideas? In recent years, years of intense and productive concentration on Rousseau, several scholars have addressed themselves to both of these questions. Here I shall mention only the two most notable contributions to the literature: Robert Derathé's *Rationalisme de Jean-Jacques Rousseau,*[1] which undertakes to answer the first, and Jean Starobinski's *Jean-Jacques Rousseau: la transparence et l'obstacle,*[2] which undertakes to answer the second of these questions.

In itself, Derathé's thesis is not new; readers of Lanson, Wright, or Cassirer are prepared for it: Rousseau, Derathé argues, belongs in spirit with the rationalist individualists whom he is supposed to have denied and overcome. The "enemy of reason" is restored to his true place as the theorist of reason; the "pre-Romantic" once again becomes the true son of the Enlightenment. But while the thesis is not new, it

[1] See previous note. In addition, Derathé has written an authoritative analysis of *Jean-Jacques Rousseau et la science politique de son temps* (1950). His work has been appreciated in the United States by Alfred Cobban in an extensive review, "New Light on the Political Thought of Rousseau," *Political Science Quarterly*, LXVI, No. 2 (June 1951), 272-84. Cobban himself has published a thoughtful study of Rousseau's political theory which belongs in the tradition set by Lanson, Cassirer, and Wright: *Rousseau and the Modern State* (1934).

[2] (1958). Ronald Grimsley, *Jean-Jacques Rousseau: A Study in Self-Awareness* (1961) arrives at conclusions similar to Starobinski's with a different method. Unfortunately, it came to my notice too late to receive the attention in this essay that it obviously deserves.

retains its freshness, and it is more persuasively argued here than elsewhere. It remains fresh, because no cliché is hardier than the cliché of Rousseau the sentimentalist. And it is most persuasively argued because Derathé is willing to read Rousseau's treatment of reason as a complicated problem rather than as a settled doctrine. Rousseau anticipated Kant, but he was not a Kantian *avant la lettre*.[3] Derathé insists that Rousseau sees reason as an evolving faculty: the *Discours sur l'inégalité* and the fragmentary *Essai sur l'origine des langues* show the growth of reason in the human species, while *Émile* shows its growth in the individual. Rousseau's supposed hostility to reason is thus dissolved into hostility against a false rationalism or an untimely rationality. Reason is a sound and healthy faculty (an idea which his eighteenth-century pious critics rightly saw as a denial of original sin), but it is hard to use soundly. It has its limits: passions, prejudices, bad institutions, or the unlimited pride of speculative philosophy all lead it astray. But it has its guide: the sentiment of conscience; and its arena: freedom. Derathé quotes, as a decisive declaration, Rousseau's observation that God has endowed man "with conscience to love the good, reason to know it, and liberty to choose it."[4] For Derathé, therefore, Rousseau is a "rationalist aware of the limits of reason,"[5] a *philosophe* wary of metaphysics, resolutely opposed to blind faith, dogmatism, and dependence on authority.

In Derathé's book, a severe exercise in the history of ideas, the tensions underlying Rousseau's thought hover beneath the surface; in Starobinski's, one of the most sensitive and elegant books on Rousseau ever written, these tensions are made

[3] *Le Rationalisme de Jean-Jacques Rousseau*, 188.

[4] Ibid. 112. The quotation is from Rousseau's "Profession de foi du vicaire savoyard."

[5] Ibid. 176.

explicit. They become, in fact, the center of the analysis. Starobinski portrays Rousseau as wrestling all his life with one problem—how to close the gap between appearance and reality. Rousseau's first systematic statement of this problem appears in his *Discours sur les sciences et les arts*, but it derives its energy from an archetypal private experience: when young Jean-Jacques is unjustly accused of breaking a comb, he confronts the world in all its obtuseness and cruelty. The boy knows he has not committed this little act of vandalism; his conscience is clear and transparent, but it is thwarted by the pitiless obstacle of unfavorable appearances.

In this incident Rousseau experiences in full force, for the first time, the pain of being separated from others; his first *Discours* then dramatizes this separation in its account of man's fall from innocence. The *Discours* does more than to describe man's fate: it sets man's task. For all of his nostalgia, Rousseau knows that man can never return to his original state; he must overcome separation and restore transparence by moving forward into a new society. This is the common theme of all of Rousseau's writings: "their *unity of intention*, which aims at the safeguarding or the restitution of transparence."[6] Rousseau sets himself as a model for the world: his heart is "as transparent as crystal,"[7] and society must become so. But this is a hard, perhaps an impossible task: The social structure is a persistent lie, politeness a veil, private life a negation of nature. Yet one must try: in 1756, Rousseau sheds his fancy attire and seeks complete independence. His protests against inauthenticity is complete: he renounces society and denounces the half-hearted radicalism of the *philosophes*. Thus Rousseau

[6] *Jean-Jacques Rousseau: la transparence et l'obstacle*, 14.

[7] Ibid. 317, and elsewhere: Starobinski shows that this is one of Rousseau's favorite images.

seeks to achieve transparency in his own life by living his conviction, and by expressing, in his lonely existence, universal human values.

But here, as Starobinski shows, is only the first of many agonizing paradoxes in Rousseau's enterprise: he is solitary, but he must explain himself to others; his estrangement makes reconciliation all the more precious. Hence there is only one step from solitude to autobiography; he wants to be silent, but he must tell all, and this, as Rousseau is the first to recognize, involves the dangerous weapon of words: "Rousseau, the marvelous writer, protests ceaselessly against the art of writing"; he needs "the mediation of language to say that he does not want this mediation."[8] That is why Rousseau turns to gestures, to facial expressions, even to illness, to make himself understood, and tells his correspondents to judge his writings by his character, rather than his character by his writings: "Everything is said by the emotion itself, and the word is only its accidental echo."[9] That is why Émile grows up among things.

Yet even signs are deceptive, as Rousseau's life tragically shows. Especially toward the end, Rousseau finds that signs only confirm what he already knew: that people are hostile, in league against him, even though he is and has always been innocent.

Starobinski demonstrates that this despairing search for transparence is the central theme of Rousseau's autobiographical writings. At first, Rousseau appears optimistic: in the *Confessions* he confidently proclaims his uniqueness, since he alone has dared to reveal himself fully. Yet, as his later autobiographies testify, his goal escapes him: "He undertakes the

[8] Ibid. 174, 177.

[9] Ibid. 170.

Dialogues as though he had not already painted himself in the *Confessions*, where he claims to have 'said everything.' Then come the *Rêveries*, where all is to be begun again."[1] One reason for this growing pessimism is his growing recognition that while he is as transparent as crystal, others persist in misjudging him; his is a "transparence without spectators."[2] His earthly judges are hanging judges; hence his autobiographies are not evidence introduced in a first trial, they are appeals. Nothing, not even his resolution to eschew all artificiality, all style, to tell everything in obsessive completeness, secures him against his enemies. That is why he increasingly turns to delusions of helplessness, which allow him to disclaim all responsibility before the world, and to God, who will absolve him—paradoxically, God can be controlled more easily in Rousseau's imagination than Diderot.

This portrait raises a disturbing question, which Starobinski does not try to shirk: If Rousseau was mad, are not his ideas invalidated or at least gravely compromised? Starobinski admits that Rousseau's most magnificent constructions and maddest reveries have a common source, and offers some instances of the close affinity between Rousseau's rational positions and his irrational fantasies: in the major writings, Rousseau depicts reflection as an ambivalent gift of nature to man, indispensable but dangerous; in the late *Dialogues*, he considers it a pure evil, the supreme enemy of transparence. Similarly, Rousseau in his earlier writings treats the obstacles nature puts in man's way as a largely beneficent force; they are a stimulus to the kind of effort that makes man truly man. Toward the end of

[1] Ibid. 225. Starobinski, like Cassirer before him, pays equal attention to all of Rousseau's autobiographical writings, instead of concentrating on the *Confessions*.

[2] Ibid. 229.

his life, however, Rousseau can see any effort, any obstacle to immediate gratification, only as the result of a plot, and he moves uncertainly between feelings of omnipotence and feelings of impotence. Yet, Starobinski insists that while the sane balance of Rousseau's thought is upset in his paranoia, even his paranoid fantasies are recognizable, if distorted versions of his true philosophy. Rousseau's madness thus caricatures his thought, but does not destroy it.

In his essay Starobinski only glances briefly at the relation of that thought to the character he is exploring, but what he says opens the way to further explorations. Rousseau's search for transparence, he writes, involves the criticism of myths, the attempt to disenchant credulous and misguided men by rending the veil of error. Similarly, for Rousseau to write his autobiography is a political act: he is neither a bishop, like St. Augustine, nor a gentleman, like Montaigne: "Jean-Jacques wishes to be recognized; not merely as an exceptional soul, not merely as a victim pure in heart, but as a simple man and a stranger without quarterings of nobility, who for all that will all the more be able to offer an image of man that has universal validity."[3] The institutional radicalism of the *Contrat social* is thus echoed and reinforced by the personal radicalism of the *Confessions*. Finally, Starobinski shows what his analysis of Rousseau's character can do for our understanding of Rousseau's novel. The *Nouvelle Héloïse*, he writes, is a "prolonged reverie on the theme of transparence and the veil."[4] Nature, beautifully and repeatedly evoked, is limpid, an enemy to secrecy; the main characters mirror that nature: they are open with one another. The plot deals with the reconquest of transparence after its loss through sensual passion, and the

[3] Ibid. 232.

[4] Ibid. 99.

small ideal society in which the novel's personages live has something of the happy unanimity of the general will: "All is linked at Clarens. Economic self-sufficiency presupposes the unanimity of the social group; this unanimity presupposes open hearts, a reciprocal confidence, transparent consciences."[5] In such perceptions, life illuminates ideas and is, in turn, illuminated by them. Starobinski has not written the biography of Rousseau, but he has made that biography possible.

2 · *A Blueprint for a Biography*

The high quality of Rousseau scholarship in the last fifty years raises the prospect of an authoritative intellectual biography which would finally comprehend Rousseau the man, the writer, and the thinker, and integrate the disturbing aspects of his ideas and behavior into his total achievement. In English, at least, there is no biography that even remotely resembles this desideratum. Morley's well-known, hostile *Rousseau* (1873) is thoroughly dated in all respects; Matthew Josephson's *Jean-Jacques Rousseau* (1931) is racy, well-informed, and sympathetic, but it lacks interpretative depth. In recent years, there have been two biographies, both failures in very different but equally revealing ways. F. C. Green's *Jean-Jacques Rousseau: A Critical Study of His Life and Writings*, published in 1955, is clear in its narration, and has sensitive pages on Rousseau's literary works and on his sufferings. It is a serious and attractive book. But Green sees Rousseau's ideas through the dim lenses of outmoded scholarship; he writes as though the analysis of Rousseau's political and religious ideas had stopped around half a century ago, with Vaughan and Masson. Frances Winwar's recent *Jean-Jacques Rousseau:*

[5] Ibid. 136.

Conscience of an Era, on the other hand, is an unhappy example of the sort of popularization that has dogged Rousseau for so long. It turns his life into a bedroom comedy, regales the reader with Rousseau's sentimental effusions, and manages to overlook practically all his thought. Green fails to move from life to ideas, and Winwar degrades life to melodrama.

That there should be no satisfactory Rousseau biography is less surprising than appears at first glance: it should by now be obvious that such a biography would impose heavy demands. Since each of Rousseau's books, indeed each of his ideas, is a single entity and, at the same time, the sum of many forces converging on a single moment of expression, the biographer must both dissect and synthesize. If such a biography is to be written, it is likely to be built up of layers which somehow, at the end, will amount to a coherent portrait. It might, I suggest, contain the following ingredients.

The Lifelong Adolescent. Emotionally, Rousseau never grew up, and relived, all his life, the experiences of his childhood. His arrested development caused him much pain, and finally drove him into paranoid delusions of persecution. But it also opened vistas hidden to other men: when ordinary men seek self-knowledge, their search has moral importance, but only for themselves. With Rousseau, this search achieved historical importance.

While we cannot remain with Rousseau's childhood, we must therefore begin there. His early life was dominated by incidents detrimental to psychological stability: his father was adventurous, sentimental, and irresponsible—far less attractive a man than the parent Rousseau drew in the *Confessions.*[6] Evi-

[6] For Rousseau's early life and his family, see the work of Eugène Ritter, especially his "Jean-Jacques Rousseau, notes et recherches," *Annales,* XI (1916-1917), 1-235; and "La Famille et la jeunesse de Jean-Jacques Rousseau," first printed in 1896 and reprinted in *Annales,* XVI (1924-1925).

dently, Isaac Rousseau never really forgave Jean-Jacques for "killing his mother": Suzanne Rousseau had died in bearing him, and the father never ceased suggesting that his son had been responsible for her untimely death. Thus, for Jean-Jacques Rousseau the trauma of birth was attended not merely with the usual anxiety of separation, but with the added burden of inexpiable guilt. It is doubtless here, in his motherless existence embittered by his father's veiled reproaches, that Rousseau first experienced the sense of loss coupled with his yearning for an earthly paradise—a paradise of transparence—that is so persistent a motif in his writings.

His early sexual life is another unfortunate legacy from his childhood: Rousseau's all-too-candid confessions testify to the infantile fixations of a wounded being. His need for love was enormous, and, with its narcissism, insatiable: consummation brought him not satisfaction but guilt. In some celebrated passages of the *Confessions* Rousseau reports his dawning, and lasting, sexual enjoyment in being beaten, either in actuality or symbolically, through humiliations; he describes his lifelong habit of masturbating and of populating his erotic imagination with delicious fulfillments that no real woman could provide; he confesses to acts of exhibitionism accompanied by marked tendencies toward a feminine passivity. With all his frantic search for authenticity, for frankness and intimacy, Rousseau appears morbidly afraid of his passions, as though full indulgence might kill him. Hence his interminable constructions of *ménages à trois,* in fiction as in real life; his repeated wish to be considered a child, only exacerbated at being treated as one; his infantile desire for a "pure voluptuousness" combining gratification and innocence. True happiness in love, he insisted, lay not in conquest or possession, but in desire, and in refusal to "dishonor" the beloved by carnal knowledge: "I loved her too much," he writes about Madame d'Houdetot, the passion of his middle years, "I loved her too much to want to possess her."[7]

If this were all, we should have a classic case of the sensitive neurotic in desperate inner tension—a man at once passionate and fearful, incapable of frank dependence or genuine independence, yearning at the same time for friendship or solitude, crippled by the feeling of unworthiness and projecting this feeling upon the outside world by making such extravagant demands upon it that the rejection he had at once hoped and feared to incur becomes inevitable. Yet, of course, this is not all: thousands of neurotics have suffered like Rousseau and displayed similar symptoms without writing a line worth remembering. Rousseau does not remain in his tension; he seeks to discover objective correlatives, and objective cures, for his personal situation in the state, the fam-

[7] *Confessions, O.C.*, I, 444. Rousseau's psychological development has received some well-informed attention. See (1) the voluminous notes on the *Confessions, Rêveries*, and *Dialogues* in volume I of *O.C.*; (2) the sensitive biography by Jean Guéhenno, *Jean-Jacques, en marge des Confessions*, 3 vols. (1948-1952), which tries to reconstruct Rousseau's life almost day by day, eschewing all hindsight; (3) Bernard Groethuysen's brilliant essay, posthumously published, *Jean-Jacques Rousseau* (1949), which concentrates on his "duality," his inner tension; (4) several articles in the *Annales:* Robert Osmond, "Contribution à l'étude psychologique des *Rêveries du Promeneur Solitaire*," XXIII (1934), 7-135; Marcel Raymond, "Jean-Jacques Rousseau, Deux aspects de sa vie intérieure (intermittences et permanence du 'moi,')," XXIX (1941-1942), 7-57; Henri Guillemin, "Les Affaires de l'ermitage (1756-1757), Examen critique des documents," XXIX (1941-1942), 59-258; Basil Munteano, "La Solitude de Jean-Jacques Rousseau," XXXI (1946-1949), 79-168; Jean Wahl, "La Bipolarité de Rousseau," XXXIII (1953-1955), 49-55; (5) psychoanalytical studies by René Laforgue, especially his *Psychopathologie de l'échec* (1944), ch. ix, "Jean-Jacques Rousseau," and "Étude sur Jean-Jacques Rousseau," *Revue française de psychanalyse* (1927), 370-402.

ily, and in education, or he anchors himself in the universal human situation by an almost voluptuous self-examination. Rousseau's life becomes a heroic spectacle, a supreme effort at self-analysis that failed, but which produced, even in failure, the masterpieces that continue to move his readers and perplex his interpreters.

The Modern Ancient. Plutarch, wrote Rousseau late in life, "was the first reading of my childhood; it will be the last reading of my old age."[8] The ancients were another early experience that accompanied Rousseau through his life. They were intensely useful to him; a writer as given to dramatic poses as he inevitably looked for idealized environments that would fit his predispositions and furnish him with models. Classical antiquity, at once intimate and remote, was the first of these models. This, in itself, was not unusual in the Enlightenment. The other *philosophes*, who had received an excellent classical education in Jesuit and Jansenist *collèges*, discovered they had an exhilarating affinity with the critical philosophies of ancients like Cicero or Lucretius, and with the severe practicality of Epictetus or Seneca. Rousseau was self-educated, and came to some of his classical reading late, but the ancients pervasively affected his ideology. When he found it necessary

[8] *Les Rêveries du promeneur solitaire, O.C.*, I, 1024. Early in Book I of his *Confessions*, Rousseau makes this famous observation on his childhood: "Ceaselessly occupied with Rome and Athens; living, so to speak, with their great men, myself born Citizen of a Republic, and son of a father whose patriotism was his strongest passion, I took fire from his example; I thought myself Greek or Roman; I became the personage whose life I was reading: the recital of constancy or intrepidity which struck me made my eyes sparkle and my voice strong. One day when I was recounting Scaevola's adventure at table, they were frightened to see me come forward and put my hand on a chafing dish to represent his action." *O.C.*, I, 9.

to justify the abandoning of his five illegitimate children, he argued that he had acted as a citizen of Plato's Republic—a feeble, and even rather unpleasant excuse, but a revealing piece of testimony to his imaginative use of antiquity.[9] Similarly, his tireless advocacy of a life rich in civic duties in a small state reflects his immersion in Plato[1]; while his critique of artificial society and delineation of a new cultural ideal—man's return to morality, to nature, to his best inner self—is the reward of his study of Seneca.[2] Diderot, who often liked to identify himself with one of Seneca's Stoic heroes, or with Diogenes, visualized Rousseau as a Roman. When he saw La Tour's cheerful portrait of Rousseau, exhibited in 1753 when he was still Rousseau's friend, Diderot was gravely disappointed. "I seek in it the censor of literature, the Cato and Brutus of our age; I expected to see Epictetus in careless garb, in disordered wig, frightening the men of letters, the magnates, and the men of the world with his severe look; and I see nothing but the author of the *Devin du village*, well dressed, well combed, well powdered. . . ."[3]

[9] There has been much dispute over these five children—it has even been suggested that Rousseau was impotent and invented his "crime" of abandoning five imaginary children just to have something to confess. Recent scholarship, however, tends to support Rousseau's account of the affair. The literature on this issue is summarized in *O.C.*, I, 1416-22.

[1] See especially Hendel's *Jean-Jacques Rousseau Moralist.* His interpretation has been disputed by Albert Schinz, *Annales*, XXIII (1934), 201-6.

[2] See L. Thomas: "Sénèque et J.-J. Rousseau," *Académie Royale de Belgique. Bulletin de la classe des lettres et des sciences morales et politiques et de la classe des Beaux Arts* (1900), 391-421; Léon Herrmann: "Jean-Jacques Rousseau traducteur de Sénèque," *Annales*, XIII (1920-1921), 215-24; K. S. Tchang: *Les Sources antiques des théories de J.-J. Rousseau sur l'éducation* (1919); and above all, G. Pire: "De l'influence de Sénèque sur les théories pédagogiques de Jean-Jacques Rousseau," *Annales*, XXXIII (1953-1955), 51-92, and *Stoïcisme et pédagogie: De Zénon à Marc-*

At the same time, Rousseau's boyish enthusiasms, and his extravagant adulation of Plutarch, did not make him into a victim of what has been called the "cult of antiquity."[4] Like the other *philosophes*, he glorified Spartan simplicity, Roman dignity, Stoic courage and independence, but he did not adopt them uncritically. The phrase current among the *philosophes* —that the ancients had been great because they had had no ancients of their own—was in his own mind as well. Ancient ideals, therefore, were transformed into ingredients in a modern philosophy.

The Cosmopolitan Genevan. In Rousseau's patriotic imagination, antiquity and Geneva were two sides of one reality. It was in his childhood, in Geneva, that he had first read Plutarch on the ancients' love of country, self-denial, and superhuman valor, and he had long believed that his native city embodied all these ancient virtues. It was only after his disillusionment that he came to see the vast gulf between Geneva and Sparta.[5]

While two Genevas, real and ideal, alternated in Rousseau's

Aurèle, De Sénèque à Montaigne et à J.-J. Rousseau (1958).

[3] *Essai sur la peinture, Œuvres,* eds. Assézat and Tourneux, 20 vols (1875-1877), X, 483. Quoted in *O.C.*, I, 1484.

[4] An example of this popular interpretation (which moves from the fact that Plutarch was Rousseau's favorite author to the false inference that Rousseau's thought is merely an idealization of Sparta) is André Oltramare's "Plutarque dans Rousseau," *Mélanges d'histoire littéraire et philosophique offerts à M. Bernard Bouvier* (1920). Oltramare's thesis is curtly but reasonably refuted in F. C. Green's *Jean-Jacques Rousseau*, 5. On the notion of the "cult of antiquity" in general, see above, pp. 170-2.

[5] As the Genevan physician Théodore Tronchin, who belonged to one of the most powerful ruling families, put it in a letter to Rousseau on November 13, 1758: "This country, my good friend, is not what you imagine it to be. . . . Geneva does not resemble . . . Sparta." Quoted in *O.C.*, I, 1517.

mind, both had an enduring influence on his style of thought. As a masterpiece in the history of political theory, his *Contrat social* has many dimensions, but one of the most significant of these is also the most neglected. When the Genevan Council of Twenty-Five condemned the *Contrat social* in June 1762, it did so on grounds involving domestic politics. In his condemnation of the book, Jean-Robert Tronchin, the attorney-general of the republic, singled out numerous ideas in the *Contrat social* that reflected the doctrines of the rebellious bourgeois party, and that had been current in Geneva for half a century. In 1763, Voltaire, who could never read the book in any other way, told d'Alembert that the *Contrat social* had "taken the part of the people against the magistrates. . . ."[6]

To be sure, Geneva was not merely a political reality for Rousseau. Its very way of life—the small commercial city without any hereditary aristocracy, the Calvinist theocracy gradually relaxing the most rigorous proscriptions of hedonist enjoyments, the sheer sense of intimacy (at once of fraternity and social snobbery)—formed his social, political, and religious categories.[7] Yet, while he never ceased to be *citoyen de Genève* in spirit, he also moved away into the great world of literature and society. It is true that his commerce with it was always uneasy: Rousseau arguing with Voltaire, accepting the patronage of the maréchal de Luxembourg, or visiting Hume in England was always the frightened Genevan bourgeois.

[6] September 28, 1763, *Correspondence*, LIII, 46.

[7] For Rousseau's Genevan experience, see John Stephenson Spink, *Jean-Jacques Rousseau et Genève* (1934), and Gaspard Vallette, *Jean-Jacques Rousseau Genevois* (1911), both excellent; Guglielmo Ferrero, "Genève et le *Contrat social*," *Annales*, XXIII (1934), 137-52; R. R. Palmer's refreshingly original chapter, "A Clash with Democracy: Geneva and Jean-Jacques Rousseau," in *The Age of the Democratic Revolution* (1959). See also Peter Gay, *Voltaire's Politics* (1959), ch. 4.

Still, he became more than that: the world of his imagination opened vistas inaccessible to the average Genevan, his mastery of French style made him into a European figure in a continent in which French literature set the tone, and, besides, his ideas seemed applicable elsewhere—indeed, everywhere. Rousseau the Genevan and the European are a single figure, with the particular and the general in perpetual tension.

This same tension pervades the most ambiguous legacy that Geneva left to Rousseau: his Calvinism. Geneva and Calvinism were practically synonymous, but since with Rousseau nothing was simple, neither the objective history nor the subjective meaning of his religious loyalties can be characterized without inviting contradiction. Rousseau had briefly converted to Catholicism, had long remained under the influence of Madame de Warens's Pietism, and had expressed his affinity for the deist wing of the Enlightenment during his most productive years—it is significant that his most extensive work on religion, the *Profession de foi du vicaire savoyard*, was the only one of his writings that Voltaire read with any delight. The correspondence of Calvinism to certain classical philosophical teachings further complicates an already complicated matter, but Voltaire was largely right—Rousseau was a deist touched by reminiscences of Calvinist doctrine.[8]

But there is more to Calvinism than doctrine. There is also a Calvinist style of life, and this style was a central ingredi-

[8] The most thorough treatment of Rousseau's religious views is the exhaustive study by P. M. Masson, *La Religion de Rousseau*, 3 vols. (1916), which should, however, be read in conjunction with the works of such critics as Cassirer and Derathé. On his Calvinism, see especially Leopold Cordier, *Jean-Jacques Rousseau und der Calvinismus* (1915); the relevant chapters (15-18) in Burgelin, *La Philosophie de l'existence de Jean-Jacques Rousseau;* and the brilliant chapter devoted to Rousseau in Karl Barth, *From Rousseau to Ritschl*, transl. by Brian Cozens (1959).

ent in Rousseau's make-up. To be sure, this Calvinist style has too often been caricatured rather than captured by the picture of the dour, erect censor who pries, with prurient self-righteousness, into the private pleasures of others. Calvinism, both in Calvin's writings and later in his Geneva, was a theology of energy, preaching the sanctification of daily activities, legalistic perfectionism, and strenuous civic living that would turn society into a holy community. As readers of Troeltsch and Weber remember, Calvin's asceticism was worldly.

The effects of this style of life were generally predictable, but by the eighteenth century, when it had been seriously compromised by its long-standing success in Geneva, by the growing wealth and social isolation of the Genevan patriciate, and by the impact of the relaxed, neo-Classical, Catholic culture of France, Calvinist living took many forms. There can be little doubt that Rousseau responded warmly to certain aspects of Calvin's message. Its moral energy appealed to him, especially since he was, as a petty bourgeois, in opposition to the Genevan patriciate which was markedly influenced by the French. He was similarly touched by its claim that it provided inner certainty of salvation. The obsessive rigidity of conviction, the transcendent significance of all activity, the need to justify each casual act as useful to a pure community—all this Rousseau needed, and expressed. His version of Calvinism was a private one, complicated by his vision of a Platonic community, his Stoic insistence on philosophical discipline, his frustrations as a reformer translated into rage, his ambivalent fearful longings for social approval and sexual encounters. It is therefore impossible to be categorical: when Rousseau rejects play for its own sake and insists on a powerful, centralized community which allows the individual only a narrow private sector, he may be speaking as a Stoic, a

Platonist, a petty bourgeois, or as a neurotic. But the particular form of his moral absolutism is within a tradition that he himself always recognized: Genevan Calvinism. I submit that it is here, in this tradition, that the unpalatable aspects of Rousseau's moral and political theory originate.

This tradition also explains a curious failure. The *philosophes* were in search of a secular philosophy of life, and Rousseau seemed uniquely equipped to formulate that philosophy. As the discoverer of the lonely walk, of green nature, as the celebrant of simple feeling, unfeigned affection, transparent honesty, Rousseau was, in the best sense of the word, a sentimentalist. As the educational reformer and historian of culture tracing the growth and inveighing against the abuse of reason, he was a rationalist. Yet he never fused these elements into the passionate rationalism that seemed within his grasp. His *Nouvelle Héloïse* treats sex with timid disdain: the protagonists are made to pay for their scanty nights of passion with endless renunciations and endless moral preachments. And in Rousseau's *Lettre à d'Alembert sur les spectacles* (a document of cardinal importance for an understanding of his limitations) the fear of pleasure for its own sake emerges with dramatic, indeed frightening intensity. D'Alembert, after a visit to Voltaire near Geneva, had suggested that the republic would do well to permit establishment of a theater in its territory; Rousseau's passionate rejection of this advice was written in three weeks, at a high pitch of moral fervor. "In writing it, what delicious tears did I shed!"[9] In writing it, Rousseau thought he had really rediscovered himself.

The controversy over the theater was a curious one for Rousseau to get into. Rousseau knew, and said, that behind

[9] *Confessions, O.C.*, I, 496. There is a useful critical edition of this *Lettre* by M. Fuchs (1948).

d'Alembert's suave advice to the Genevan city fathers stood Voltaire, who had settled in the neighborhood and was performing his own plays in his own little theater, much to the annoyance of those Genevans who were not invited. To speak out against the theater was thus to challenge Voltaire. In addition, it was an old controversy in which Rousseau had at least implicitly taken the side of hedonism, by his writings for the stage. As Grimm and other *philosophes* did not neglect to point out, Rousseau was denouncing the very craft in which he had displayed some talent and had won a certain acclaim. Rousseau's attack on the theater must therefore be seen as a deliberate defiance of powerful *philosophes*, and an open break with his own past, a part of his personal "reform."

There is a less dramatic explanation for Rousseau's *Lettre à d'Alembert* than this: the question of the theater had begun as a moral issue, but had ended as a political one. In the political troubles that divided Geneva in the first half of the eighteenth century, the patriciate (French in its training, sympathies, and tastes) had favored the theater, while the bourgeoisie had opposed it. In writing against *spectacles*, Rousseau was taking the side of the bourgeoisie at a time when political controversies were reviving, and he was aware of these controversies. But as he wrote, he was swept away by a wave of self-righteous conviction. The *Lettre à d'Alembert* was more than political, it was personal.

In the course of his diatribe, Rousseau displays all the philistine hostility to cultivated refinement of which he is capable. The stage does not teach morality: if it seeks to inculcate virtue, it only confirms what people already know. It is far more likely that it teaches immorality, both on the stage, with its literary message, and off the stage, by the scandalous behavior of actors and actresses. The theater is an amusement, replacing other activities. For Rousseau this is a conclusive condemnation, since going to the theater leads the individual to forget his most sacred obligations, his country, his family, his public duties. Entertainments should be functional: they should be civic festivals rewarding good actions, inculcating respect for the old, and serving as sanitary meeting places for the young.

This moralistic, utilitarian view of culture, whatever its precise origins, is Rousseau at his most unpleasant. In the course of a long and wrong-headed attack on Molière's *Misanthrope*, Rousseau says nothing of the spectator's enjoyment of wit, or the cultivation of his sensibilities in the presence of great theater. Everything is reduced to a lesson, and the *Misanthrope* teaches a pernicious lesson by "ridiculing" Alceste and thus blackening virtue. Here, in the *Lettre à d'Alembert sur les spectacles*, is Rousseau the advocate of the strenuous life, the pitiless critic of "artificial" culture, the stern Spartan who insists that every activity must be a school for character, the relentless moralist who sees play as a civic instrument. Nor is this an isolated vision: it reappears in the *Contrat social*, with its civic religion, its expulsion of the unbeliever, and its sentence of death for the perjurer; it reappears in the *Gouvernement de Pologne*, with its prescription for public festivals; and it reappears, most significantly, in the *Nouvelle Héloïse*, with its idealized picture of a rustic *fête* as the model for all public gatherings. Thus nostalgia for a Geneva that never existed drove Rousseau into a social vision that ought never to be realized. It is not necessary to drag Rousseau out of his century, to make him into an ancestor, no matter how remote, of modern totalitarian systems, to regret this aspect of his thought. It is unpalatable enough in itself.

The Practical Utopian. These are the main ingredients of

Rousseau's personality and early experience. It is out of them that he creates his first works: the *Discours sur les sciences et les arts* and the *Discours sur l'inégalité*, rather oddly supported by the *Lettre à d'Alembert sur les spectacles*, are products of personal alienation raised to the level of cultural criticism. They were all written in the 1750's—the letter to d'Alembert was published in 1758. They were followed by a string of masterpieces, recognizably by the same man, and yet so cogent, so revolutionary, and so universal, that even admirers of the early works could not have foreseen them. *Julie, ou la Nouvelle Héloïse*, which had an immediate, enormous, and lasting success, was published late in 1760; *Émile* and the *Contrat social*, which soon achieved their own notoriety, came out early in 1762. With this magnificent trio, Rousseau had risen from his subjectivity to philosophical objectivity on a grand scale.

These works confront the biographer with a sensitive assignment. They must be read in and for themselves, in the light of one another, in relation to the books that preceded and followed them, and with an eye to the times from which they came and the times they helped to make. Each of them has several faces—the multiplicity in unity that is the mark of all masterpieces. Even the *Nouvelle Héloïse*, which appears as nothing more than a sentimental novel following the pattern set by Richardson, has intellectual depths and philosophical implications that are only now beginning to be explored.[1] In the same way, *Émile* is more than a didactic educational Utopia. Its first readers followed its recommendations but

[1] The novel is coming into its own among the critics. See the voluminous notes appended to it in *O.C.*, II; the relevant pages in Starobinski, *Jean-Jacques Rousseau;* Daniel Mornet's critical edition (1925); René Hubert, "L'Amour, la Nature et la société

called it a novel; and the *Profession de foi du vicaire savoyard*, which makes up a substantial segment of *Émile*, is not an inorganic intrusion but a fitting component of the book: religion and education are two paths of man's road to maturity. The *Contrat social*, of course, is complex on its face. As one of a dozen or so major writings in the history of political theory, it calls for internal criticism of its logic and the coherence of its ideas; as part of the tradition of political theorizing in the seventeenth and eighteenth century, it must be studied in conjunction with Hobbes, Locke, and the writings of the natural lawyers; as a Genevan document, it must be placed within its historical context; and as a prophecy, its revolutionary implications must be developed with scrupulous care for its meaning to Rousseau himself.

In addition, these books mirror one another, and may each be understood as a developing part of a total program. Here the writings of Lanson, Wright, Cassirer, and Derathé serve us splendidly, for they have insisted on the mutual relevance of the three masterpieces. Each book deals with man as he may become, in the family, in the educational process, and in the larger society. This is why Vaughan was ill-advised to concentrate on the political texts: to read the *Contrat social* without reading *Émile* is to understand neither, and to read both in conjunction with the *Nouvelle Héloïse* is to understand all three better.

There is another dimension of these works, for which the reader of this essay is well prepared. While none of them can be explained by, or reduced to Rousseau's biography, his

chez Jean-Jacques Rousseau: *La Nouvelle Héloïse*, roman à thèse," *Revue d'histoire de la philosophie* (July-Dec. 1939), 193-214; and the dissertation by M. B. Ellis, *Julie, or La Nouvelle Héloïse: A Synthesis of Rousseau's Thought* (1949).

biography enters into them all. From his need for transparency to his conception of negative education in *Émile*, from his overwhelming desire for friendship to his definition of equality in the *Contrat social*, from his refreshing love of landscape to his exposition of the ideology of nature in the *Nouvelle Héloïse*, there is only one step.

One further question remains. These three books, as I have said, are statements of a great program. They are, in a large sense, Utopian. But Rousseau's Utopianism is not the inevitable result of his inability to think practically, it is rather his readiness to confront the problems of society with a decisive, uncompromising vision of its total regeneration. But while there was a time to set the facts aside, there was also a time to heed the facts: Rousseau's Utopianism is happily supplemented by his thoroughly practical writings. The *Émile* and the *Contrat social*, therefore, should also be read in conjunction with the *Lettres écrites de la montagne* of 1764, which show Rousseau the Genevan politician at work, and with his *Considérations sur le Gouvernement de Pologne* of 1772, which show him as a cautious reformer. The pupil of Plato was also the pupil of Montesquieu.

The Isolated Philosophe. While the recent literature on Rousseau has narrowed the spectrum of sensible interpretations of his work, the controversy over his true place in the Enlightenment goes on. It is generally assumed that Rousseau was sharply divided from the *philosophes* in character as well as in ideas, and in recent years it has become fashionable to call him a "pre-Romantic," the harbinger of a new movement and a new mood desperately out of place in the eighteenth century. But the facts are not quite so simple, and I, for one, object to what I have called definition by larceny: it is all too easy to remove Rousseau—and Diderot—from the Enlightenment by definition and then complain about the coldness of the movement.[2]

It is true that Rousseau broke with the *philosophes:* he quarreled with Diderot, with Voltaire, with Hume. And it is equally true that the *philosophes* regarded these quarrels as more than personal: Voltaire, to be sure, called him a madman, but the other *philosophes* sensed something else, some uncanny, solitary philosophical search that accorded ill with their own confident sociability. But there are other facts demanding explanation: Rousseau broke with the *philosophes* as he broke with others, and in the late 1740's and early 1750's, in the midst of his critique of civilization, Rousseau liked the persons and admired the ideas of the men of the Enlightenment.[3] He consulted Diderot on his first famous book, the *Discours sur les sciences et les arts.*[4] He was deeply influenced by the sensationalist psychology of Condillac, and by Buffon's writings on style and on natural history.[5] It is revealing that

[2] The relation of Rousseau to romanticism has called forth some specialized studies, especially on Rousseau and the Germans, but the question requires a great deal more work. The notion of pre-Romanticism, which I consider confusing rather than helpful, has been given wide circulation in the writings of Paul van Tieghem, *Le romantisme dans la littérature Européenne* (1948), Book I, and *Le Pré-romantisme,* 2 vols. (1924–1930). Essential correctives are to be found in Ernst Cassirer, *The Philosophy of the Enlightenment,* transl. by Fritz C. A. Koelln and James P. Pettegrove (1951); and in Arthur O. Lovejoy, "The Supposed Primitivism of Rousseau's *Discourse on Inequality,*" and "On The Discrimination of Romanticisms," both reprinted in his *Essays in the History of Ideas* (1948).

[3] See his celebrated letter of August 18, 1756, to Voltaire, *Correspondance générale,* II, 303-24.

[4] The argument over Diderot's supposed claim that he inspired Rousseau's rejection of civilization in the *Discours* has been carefully examined by George R. Havens in his critical edition of the first *Discours* (1946).

[5] For these influences, see the notes in *O.C.,* I, 1333, 1351, 1372, 1383.

Rousseau admired the thinkers whom the *philosophes* admired: both Locke and Newton, with their empiricism and their rules of philosophical modesty, were significant models for him.[6] Finally (and this, in my opinion, is decisive) Rousseau's whole conception of philosophy was the conception of the Enlightenment. He objected to system-building, visualized himself as a modern Cicero philosophizing for the sake of action, demanded that criticism be permitted to penetrate all areas of human activity, including politics and religion. If I am right in defining the Enlightenment as an age of criticism which was also an age of philosophy, Rousseau fits into this age with ease, and in fact becomes one of its representative thinkers.

Not even Rousseau's feeling for nature and for sentiment makes him a stranger among the *philosophes*. He always insisted that his solitude was a personal preference, designed to permit him to criticize false, and to found true sociability. In his analysis of sentiment he was in the same camp with Hume or Vauvenargues or, later, Kant, while his advocacy of sensibility was, if anything, more timid than Diderot's.

At the same time, there was something about Rousseau that made him unique. His vision was at once very general and very specific, and he did the supreme thing a thinker can do: he invented new areas of inquiry and discovered new material for study. Few *philosophes* could even approach his speculative boldness: it required vast intellectual imagination to rethink the educational process by making Émile grow up in experimental isolation or to attempt to solve the supreme problem of political theory—the reconciliation of freedom with authority—by visualizing a contract in which each

[6] See Starobinski, *Jean-Jacques Rousseau*, 41-56.

participant was at once ruler and ruled, the sovereign giver and the obedient servant of the laws.

Similarly, Rousseau's gift for specificity allowed him to make penetrating observations that reached hitherto neglected depths of experience. In raising his psychological history to the level of universal importance Rousseau moved beyond the accepted subject matter of classicism. And as he battled against the classical rules, he tried to move beyond literature as well—without success. "He writes so well," one perceptive Genevan observed to another, "that one always reads him with pleasure. Voltaire says that Rousseau's pen burns the paper."[7] Such heat, as Rousseau himself said, was not the style of his time. Yet for all his efforts to make language simply expressive of feeling by removing the intervening veils of stylistic conventions, the form, the logic, and the balance, of classicism distinguish the best of his work.

What is one to make of so mercurial a creature? The question becomes a problem only if the Enlightenment itself is misread as a cold, heartless rationalism. In fact, the *philosophes* laid the theoretical foundations for romanticism, and cultivated the aesthetic expression of feeling: Diderot's admiration of Richardson is characteristic of a new mood, just as Hume's denial of any valid principle of proportion in the arts is characteristic of a new inner freedom. On the other hand, the admiration of a Byron for a Voltaire suggests the wide range of the Enlightenment, in the field of the arts as much as in social criticism. Rousseau the preacher of autonomy, the advocate of unsparing criticism, the ally of Diderot and the

[7] Quoted in *O.C.*, I, 1540.

teacher of Kant, belongs not to Romanticism but to the Enlightenment.[8]

The Innocent Penitent. At the same time, the biographer cannot avoid the uncomfortable fact that the Romantics claimed Rousseau while the *philosophes* repudiated him. One might suggest, a little maliciously, that it was Rousseau in his sane moments, with his moderation, his rationalism, his critical penetration, who was the *philosophe*, while Rousseau the sick enthusiast inspired the Romantics—it is tempting to suggest this especially when we remember Goethe's famous remark that the classical is healthy and the romantic is sick.[9] But as always with Rousseau, the facts are complicated. The sick Rousseau was never so sick as to lose control of his pen: in the lowering darkness of his last years, crowded with enemies real and imagined, and with his lonely search for absolution from fictitious crimes, he produced autobiographical works that were pioneers in clarity of observation, honesty of purpose, and sheer commitment to truth. That they inspired much nonsense, much needless effusion, and vague sentimental posturing, no one can doubt. But then, even the most severely rational of Rousseau's works, like the *Contrat social*, had unintended consequences among hasty or prejudiced readers. At their best, the autobiographical writings of Rousseau's late years belong in the history of European literature as well as in the history of European self-awareness. Rousseau's voyage of self-discovery was remarkable because of what he found when he reached his destination.

For the biographer, the *Confessions*, *Dialogues*, and *Rêv-*

[8] See Karl Barth, *From Rousseau to Ritschl.*

[9] *Gespräche mit Eckermann,* April 2, 1829. *Gedenkausgabe,* XXIV, 332.

eries are at once indispensable and dangerous. They must be constantly checked against his correspondence and the testimony of others, for Rousseau is at once creating an image and telling his story, and he introduces some serious distortions of facts and feelings.[1] His frustrations and failures are rationalized in devious and ingenious ways. Yet even the Rousseau of the autobiographies is in some sense the true Rousseau, since a lapse of memory or transposition of an event is as much a biographical fact as the bald truth, and may be even more revealing than that truth. The Rousseau of the last works is the innocent penitent: the world persists in thinking him guilty of a variety of crimes, yet he is innocent, and must convince all that he is innocent. Yet he is penitent as well, for there are moments when the charges of his enemies ring true and must be refuted over and over again. To turn from his masterpieces of the early 1760's to the autobiographies of the seventies—grandiose and awful, like a crumbling ruin—is to enter the pathetic world of the sickroom. Still, this world is part of the whole Rousseau.

The Nostalgic Prophet. At this point the biographer might well consider his task complete. Yet Rousseau remains so controversial, so alive, that his meaning for us remains a subject of fruitful speculation. "Unswervingly fixed and, as it

[1] Here Guéhenno's biography is of the greatest assistance. In addition consult the careful analysis of the various manuscripts of Rousseau's *Confessions* offered by Hermine de Saussure, *Rousseau et les manuscrits des Confessions* (1958). The debate over the "persecution" of Rousseau continues. It is certain that Diderot, Madame d'Épinay, and Grimm tampered with Madame d'Épinay's so-called "mémoires" to create an unfavorable impression of Rousseau. See G. Roth, ed.: *Histoire de Madame de Montbrillant: Les pseudo-mémoires de Madame d'Épinay*, 3 vols. (1951). See also Albert Schinz: "La Querelle Rousseau-Hume," *Annales*, XVII (1926), 13-52.

were, submerged within himself," thus Ernst Cassirer concludes his essay on Rousseau, "he nevertheless advanced to treating problems of absolutely universal significance—problems which even today have lost nothing of their force and intensity and which will long survive the accidental form, limited by his individuality and his time, that Rousseau gave them."[2] Beyond the obvious intrinsic interest of his writings, and their equally obvious historical importance, there remains a permanent legacy.

This legacy, I think, is ambiguous. His political speculations, and the candor of his cultural and political criticism, retain their value: we could do with some of his capacity to look upon culture from a distance, with his earnest if unsuccessful attempts to integrate reason and passion, and with his preoccupation with freedom in society. His conclusions are another matter. As criticism Rousseau's ideas are superb; as a constructive program, they are at best unrealistic and at worst pernicious.

Rousseau's thought has this double character because it springs from a longing to turn the impossible into the possible: Rousseau the prophet looks back with nostalgia upon a purity and innocence and intimacy that had never existed, either in his own childhood or in the childhood of the race. When such nostalgic Utopianism is coupled with rigorous logic and realistic observation—as it was with Rousseau—its uses become obvious. Rousseau's "one great principle"—that man is good, that society makes him bad, but that only society, the

[2] *The Question of Jean-Jacques Rousseau*, 128. Rousseau's influence on the French Revolution has not yet been fully investigated. Two interesting contributions to the subject have been made by Alfred Cobban in his *Rousseau and the Modern State*, and by Gordon H. McNeil: "The Anti-Revolutionary Rousseau," *American Historical Review*, LVIII (July 1953), 808-23.

agent of perdition, can be the agent of salvation—affirms not merely that reform is desirable, but that it is possible, and it offers suggestions for the way this salvation can be accomplished. In his general plan, then, as in his specific recommendations, Rousseau is the philosopher of the democratic movement: he tells us that freedom and equality, far from being incompatible, are indispensable to each other; that the political public must be absolutely general; and that institutional forms are less important than the moral and social foundations of citizenship.

But Rousseau is not the philosopher of the democratic state, which rests on the very tensions that Rousseau wants to abolish.[3] For Rousseau, the contradictions between freedom and authority can be resolved in a society of Émiles who want for themselves only the things that are good for society as a whole. Against this assertion there stands the liberal view—which I share—that authority and liberty are forever in conflict, and that it is the task of the free society to reduce their tensions, define their jurisdictions, and make them live together in peace even if not in amity.

But of course, Rousseau was not purely a political theorist: he was a moral philosopher. The state was merely one agent designed to create an autonomous human being—the kind of being that does not yet exist. His work, therefore, does not fit into the political categories of individualism or collectivism into which it has so often been forced. That is precisely why the recent scholarship on Rousseau is so impressive; it has discarded time-worn clichés and traditional labels to send us back to what really matters: the whole Rousseau. We can now

[3] My teacher, the late Franz Neumann, was the first to suggest to me that Rousseau could be understood as the theorist of the democratic movement but not of the democratic state.

know him as he really was—an eccentric who was more than an eccentric, a gadfly who for all his sentimentality and self-pity was more perceptive than the *philosophes* who rejected him, a critic and a visionary as pertinent to our century as he was to his own, an antique censor in modern dress—and it is out of this knowledge that his biography will be written.

9

THE PARTY OF HUMANITY

IN ITS CAREER as the target of polemical attack, the Enlightenment has been assailed for ideas it did not hold, and for consequences it did not intend and did not produce. Over the years, it has acquired a reputation that covers its mobile face like a rigid mask. Yet the accepted view of the Enlightenment does not reflect the work of the specialists: I can think of no area of historical study in which the gap between the scholar and the general public is as wide, and as fateful, as it is with the Enlightenment. And in speaking of the "general public" I am speaking of the consumers of textbooks, and, I am afraid, all too often their producers as well. We have at our command a rich supply of authoritative monographs which demonstrate in detail that the *philosophes* were often pessimists, usually empiricists, generally responsible hard-headed political men, with sensible programs, limited expectations, and a firm grasp of history. Yet everybody seems to be sure that the men of the Enlightenment were naïve optimists, cold rationalists, abstract literary men, with a Utopian vision of the world and (worst of all) no sense of ambiguity or tragedy whatever. The *Shorter Oxford English Dictionary*, presumably a serious and objective authority, defines the Enlightenment as "shallow and pretentious intellectualism, unreasonable contempt for authority and tradition," thus collecting most current prejudices in one convenient spot.

The origins of such stubborn misreadings are not hard to discover. Many of the criticisms later leveled against the Enlightenment were first leveled by the *philosophes* themselves: as I have suggested elsewhere, they were a quarrelsome family who liked criticizing each other almost as much (but not quite) as the Church. Some of the most persistent clichés about the *philosophes* can be traced back to the Enlightenment: Voltaire was among the first to spread the canard about Rousseau's primitivism,[1] a canard echoed by other *philosophes* and later given its final vulgar form by Napoleon: "I am especially disgusted with Rousseau," he said in 1803, "since I have seen the Orient. Savage man is a dog."[2] No amount of documented refutation has ever been able to destroy the supposed ideal of Rousseau, the "noble savage." In return, by an act of poetical injustice, the reputation of Voltaire the irresponsible, flighty poet was, if not established, at least propagated by such *philosophes* as David Hume. The game of criticism was enlivened by caustic British visitors like Horace Walpole, who shared many of the Enlightenment's ideas while disliking its most articulate spokesmen. "The *philosophes*," wrote Walpole in 1765, "are insupportable, superficial, overbearing, and fanatic: they preach incessantly."[3] And at the same time in the German states, *Aufklärer* like

[1] See above, p. 212.

[2] Conversation in 1803, quoted in J. Christopher Herold, *The Mind of Napoleon* (1955), 156.

[3] Horace Walpole to Thomas Gray, November 19, 1765, *Letters*, ed. Mrs. Paget Toynbee, 16 vols. (1904), VI, 352.

Lessing established their identity as German literary men by noisily freeing themselves from their French models.

All this mutual denunciation was the vigorous rough and tumble of a healthy family. In the face of a threat from church or state the squabbling brethren united in a solid and formidable army. The really damaging criticism came from other sources. In the 1770's the enthusiasts of the *Sturm und Drang* vehemently objected to what they called the deadly materialism of the Enlightenment: in a famous passage of his autobiography, Goethe pictures himself and his youthful friends shuddering at Holbach's *Système de la nature:* "it seemed to us so grey, so Cimmerian, so deathlike, that it was hard for us to stand its presence."[4] But the *Sturm und Drang* faded, and Goethe developed a sympathetic understanding of the Enlightenment as a whole. He translated Voltaire and Diderot, studied Rousseau and Kant. It was, of course, the so-called French Revolution—a world-wide revolution that took its most spectacular form in France—that made criticism of the Enlightenment into a really serious business. A king decapitated, thousands executed, a whole army of aristocrats driven into exile, church property secularized, Jews and actors enfranchised, schools and hospitals put under public secular authority, an irresistible army officered by commoners and manned by conscripts—this was the fruit of a century of philosophic criticism!

As usual, to be sure, the critics did not agree just which aspects of the Enlightenment had been most lethal: some of the German Romantics separated Rousseau from the rest of the *philosophes*, and exalted him as the prophet of true feeling, while French counterrevolutionaries treated Rousseau as the

[4] *Dichtung und Wahrheit*, Book XI, *Gedenkausgabe*, X, 537.

most extreme, and hence most despicable product of the Age of Reason. Voltaire, too, was sometimes pictured as a malicious wrecker, and sometimes as a brilliant writer, the pride of French letters despite it all, who had merely gone too far and been too clever. But these divergences mattered little: uncertain allies though they were, the critics created an image of the Enlightenment which still haunts us today. In fact, we do not see the Enlightenment directly but through the eyes of the Romantic period.

The ingredients of the Romantic interpretation of the Enlightenment, whether favorable or unfavorable, are few but powerful: the Enlightenment was not serious, it was abstract and literary, impious and superficial. Even Byron, a *philosophe* out of his time, saw his much-admired Voltaire as a Protean talent, as

> fire and fickleness, a child
> Most mutable in wishes;[5]

while Blake, who had much sympathy for radical humanitarian ideas, fiercely repudiated the form they had taken in the Enlightenment:

> Mock on, mock on, Voltaire, Rousseau;
> Mock on, mock on, 'tis all in vain!
> You throw the sand against the wind,
> And the wind blows it back again.

The scholar who knows the history of the Enlightenment's reputation reads these lines with a shock of recognition: they anticipate more than a century of conservative French criticism, from Chateaubriand to Taine, from Taine to Faguet and

[5] *Childe Harold's Pilgrimage,* Canto III, verse cvi.

Brunetière, and from Faguet and Brunetière to most of the textbooks now in use. Nor do these lines anticipate merely the conterrevolutionary views of Frenchmen who hated the Third Republic as the irreligious offspring of the First. Friendly critics, too, were captured by the Romantic vision: Alfred North Whitehead, who had high regard for the *philosophes*' clarity of intellect and humanity of purpose summed up the case against them in 1925, in a celebrated phrase: "*les philosophes*," he wrote, "were not philosophers."[6]

Once the Romantic interpretation was fixed, little was done through the nineteenth century to change it. In fact, it was buttressed by two of the most influential writers on the eighteenth century that the nineteenth century produced: Tocqueville and Morley. There is no need for me to dwell on the merits of a man who is more worshipped than analyzed today: Tocqueville was an unmatched observer and prescient social philosopher. But he was also, I think, a much overrated historian. In his book on the Old Regime, he argued that the *philosophes* treated political questions "casually, even, one might say, toyed with them." Their "kind of abstract, literary politics found its way, in varying proportions, into all the writings of the day." They worshipped reason and intellect—their own: the ideal society, as they envisioned it, would be based on "simple, elementary rules deriving from the exercise of the human reason and natural law." This secular Utopianism was, in a sense, not their fault, it was their fate, the only political vision available to them: "living as they did, quite out of touch with practical politics, they lacked the experience which might have tempered their enthusiasms."[7] This is per-

[6] *Science and the Modern World* (1925), 86.

[7] *The Old Regime and the French Revolution*, transl. by Stuart Gilbert (1955), 138-40.

suasive, especially because it is offered without reproach, and with the large sense of human destiny that marks Tocqueville's work: the *philosophes* are not to be blamed for their irresponsibility; they were as much the victims of their society as their society was to become *their* victim. And yet, Tocqueville's analysis does grave injustice to the *philosophes:* it concentrates on the trivial side effects rather than on the central purposes of Enlightenment speculation.

From a different perspective, John Morley's biographies of the *philosophes,* sympathetic and intelligent as they were, perpetuated the misconceptions and gave weight to the kind of criticism they were designed to eradicate. Morley was an agnostic, an anticlerical, an articulate supporter of the philosophy of the Enlightenment, and in the 1860's and 1870's he wrote some lucid lives of Voltaire, Rousseau, and Diderot that embodied his radicalism. They are well informed, energetically argued, and sensitively aware of the lesser lights that surrounded these central luminaries: in separate essays, or chapters in the large biographies, Morley gave favorable accounts of Vauvenargues, Turgot, Condorcet, and others. Yet the burden of his judgment is that the *philosophes* were Utopians, addicted to "socialistic sophisms" and a certain immoral "looseness of opinion"; they were the victims of "confident exultation."[8] Morley was too much in agreement with Voltaire's anticlericalism or Diderot's political radicalism to turn his books into just another condemnation of the Enlightenment, and he was too widely read to pronounce his criticisms without reservations: if the *philosophes* in general despised the Middle Ages, Turgot at least appreciated them; if the *philosophes* in general had an unreasonable faith in rea-

[8] *Critical Miscellanies,* 3 vols. (1886), II, 71-2, 74, 76 (in his essay on Turgot).

son, Vauvenargues at least valued the passions. Yet Morley's very sympathy for the Enlightenment, and his very qualifications, strengthened the case against the *philosophes:* if a sympathizer could call the Enlightenment impractical and immoral, why should an opponent not feel free to do the same? And, as the literature shows, the opponents did feel free.

This consensus of criticism did not, of course, go unchallenged. Quite early, Kant defended Rousseau against the common imputation that he was an advocate of a return to the savage state[9]; while Goethe, a faithful reader of Rousseau, attributed the foolish and fashionable primitivism of his time to "misunderstood suggestions of Rousseau."[1] In more recent times there was even an influential textbook by Gustave Lanson, which did the *philosophes* justice—especially in the later editions written after Lanson had read the eighteenth-century writers with some care.[2] There were even specialized works, like the little book by Georges Pellissier, which accorded Voltaire the status of a philosopher.[3]

But works such as these had about as much impact on the governing interpretation as peas shot from a pea-shooter have

[9] See Ernst Cassirer: "Kant and Rousseau," in *Rousseau, Kant, Goethe*, transl. by James Gutmann, Paul O. Kristeller, John H. Randall, Jr. (1945).

[1] *Dichtung und Wahrheit*, Book VIII, *Gedenkausgabe*, X, 363.

[2] See Lanson's *Histoire de la littérature française*, first published in 1896 and many times after that, above all his 8th edition and the following. I do not want to give the impression that *no* textbooks have taken account of recent scholarship. Thus R. R. Palmer and Joel Colton, *A History of the Modern World* (ed. 1960) has a succinct chapter on the Enlightenment, and there are others. But they are a relatively small minority.

[3] *Voltaire philosophe* (1908). But characteristically enough, even this reassessment fails to place Voltaire's philosophical pronouncements in their historical context.

on the hide of an elephant. The monographs multiply, and they are duly listed in the bibliographies of our texts, but their message does not register. The specialist continues to write for other specialists who are already convinced, and on occasion he feels a little like Matthew Arnold's Byron, "a beautiful and ineffectual angel, beating in the void his luminous wings in vain"—as ineffectual, in any event, even if rather less beautiful.

This is poetic and sad. Let me be prosy and specific, and list the criticisms of the Enlightenment that are generally accepted today. First, it is argued that the *philosophes* had an unmeasured faith in reason, rigid mechanical reason. Reason, writes one recent historian of political thought, was "regarded as a panacea for all human ills."[4] And the same writer adds, presumably to lend specific gravity to his charge, "To Diderot reason was everything."[5] This is popular stuff and sounds unimpeachable, but it is nonsense. Diderot was at once the receptive medium and the revolutionary theoretician of sensibility, while his fellow *philosophes* were, on the whole, wary of treating reason as any kind of panacea at all. The *philosophes* ridiculed the rationalism of seventeenth-century philosophers as "metaphysics"; Kant spent most of his philosophical career trying to determine the limits of reason; Condillac developed a thoroughgoing empiricist psychology hostile to all rationalism; Hume made the remark that reason is, and ought to be, the slave of the passions, and constructed a theory of social behavior in which habit dominates and reason plays a subordinate part; Voltaire and d'Alembert treated reason with cautious reserve. The brilliant anticipations of modern psychology that pervade the *philosophes*' writings

[4] Lawrence C. Wanlass: *Gettell's History of Political Theory* (1953), 237.

[5] Ibid. p. 257.

sprang from their appreciation of the passions. Diderot formulated the Oedipus complex one hundred and fifty years before Freud[6]; Hume's analysis of habit was modern enough to serve John Dewey as the starting point for his social psychology[7]; Montesquieu and Gibbon made important contributions to political sociology by analyzing the nature of ideology and the devices of mass-manipulation. Sigmund Freud, the thinker who above all others is supposed to have destroyed the foundations of Enlightenment rationalism, was the greatest child of the Enlightenment our century has known.[8] In short, the Enlightenment was not an Age of Reason, but a Revolt against Rationalism.

The *philosophes*, then, may be called rationalists only if the epithet is defined in a special way. They argued that knowledge is superior to ignorance; that social problems can be solved only through reasonable action based on research and analysis rather than through prayer, renunciation, reliance on all-wise authority, or patient waiting for God; that discussion is superior to fanaticism; and that barriers to inquiry, whether barriers of religion, tradition, or philosophical dogmatism, are all pernicious barriers to understanding.

The second criticism is closely related to the first—the Enlightenment, we are told, preached the inevitability of progress: the theory of progress, "was one of the dominant ideas

[6] "If your little savage were left to himself and to his native blindness, he would in time join the infant's reasoning to the grown man's passions—he would strangle his father and sleep with his mother." *Rameau's Nephew*, in *Rameau's Nephew and Other Works*, transl. by Jacques Barzun and Ralph H. Bowen (1956), 78. Sigmund Freud quotes this passage with evident relish in his *General Introduction to Psychoanalysis* (1949), 296.

[7] *Human Nature and Conduct* (1922). For Dewey's acknowledgment of Hume's influence, see his "Foreword to the Modern Library Edition," (1930), v-vi.

[8] The relation of Freud's ideas to the Enlightenment deserves lengthier treatment than I can

of the Age of Enlightenment."[9] This notion has the status of an established truth, and yet it is a myth. Locke, Montesquieu, Hume, Diderot had no theory of progress; Rousseau's thought stressed the fact of man's retrogression and the hope for man's regeneration; Voltaire saw human history as a long string of miseries broken by four happy ages. Only Kant, with his speculative world history, Turgot with his three stages, and Condorcet with his ten epochs, may be said to have held a theory of progress, and these three thinkers stood not at the center but at the bright end of the spectrum of Enlightenment thought.

Indeed, the *philosophes* looked upon their world with sturdy, Stoic courage. They did not deny that progress is possible—some of them maintained that humanity had in fact lightened the burden of its existence through the centuries, while others were impelled by the moderate confidence that if *their* proposals were adopted, the world *would* progress. But the empirical observation that progress has occurred, or the rational opinion that progress will result from specified policies, cannot be called a theory of progress. That grandiose phrase should be reserved for the metaphysical claim that progress is an inevitable process immanent in history, and it is this claim which has been imputed to the *philosophes* with great frequency and little justice.

No doubt, some of the *philosophes*' confidence was misplaced—confidence is often misplaced. But a careful reading

---

give it here. I shall only quote one passage: ". . . after all, analysis does not set out to abolish the possibility of morbid reactions, but to give the patient's ego *freedom* to choose one way or the other." *The Ego and the Id* (1927), 72n.

[9] John H. Hallowell: *Main Currents In Modern Political Thought* (1950), 13.

of eighteenth-century writings will reveal the gloomier side of philosophic speculation. Long before the Lisbon earthquake ruined even the remnants of Voltaire's cosmic optimism, Voltaire had inveighed against the doctrine that palpable evils are really hidden goods, and that all is for the best in the best of all possible worlds. In *Candide* his savage assault on optimism was not a capricious expression of low spirits, but a reasoned philosophical position.[1] Similarly, Diderot's savage criticisms of political institutions, Holbach's pessimism about human nature, Gibbon's cynicism, or Hume's skepticism cannot be called fatuous optimism—they were neither fatuous nor optimistic. Even Condorcet, whose paean to progress is more often denounced than read, did not overlook the cruelty, the fanaticism, and the misery of men. He hoped for relief in the future, in the Tenth Epoch, but even in the present, Ninth Epoch, the most enlightened mankind had yet achieved, Condorcet saw little to cheer him: "civilization occupies only a small part of the globe," and the "number of those who are really civilized disappears before the mass of men delivered over to prejudice and ignorance. We see vast countries groaning in slavery; in one place we see nations degraded by the vices of a civilization whose corruption impedes progress; in another, nations still vegetating in the infancy of its first epochs. We see that the labors of these last ages have done much for the human spirit, little for the perfection of the human species; much for the glory of man, something for his liberty, but as yet almost nothing for his happiness. In several places our eyes are struck by a dazzling light; but dark

[1] It is worth remembering that when Voltaire's *Candide* and Samuel Johnson's *Rasselas* were published almost simultaneously in 1759, Johnson himself remarked upon the startling resemblance of the two books. Voltaire had concluded that we must cultivate our garden; Johnson, that "human life is everywhere a state, in which

shadows still cover an immense horizon. The mind of the philosopher rests with satisfaction on a small number of objects; but the spectacle of stupidity, slavery, extravagance, barbarity, afflicts him still more often; and the friend of humanity can enjoy unmixed pleasure only by surrendering to the sweet hopes of the future."[2] Whatever our views of Condorcet's categorical division of mankind into enlightened and superstitious, we will recognize this paragraph as a depressing catalogue. And, as the last sentence of the quotation shows, Condorcet's optimism is a form of therapy: he hopes that he may not despair.

Condorcet's hope was to escape from the past, and in this he was representative of the Enlightenment, which was committed to the future. This brings me to the third criticism: the *philosophes*, it is said, had no sense of history. In the light of the conclusive refutations with which this myth has been confronted, in the light of the sheer bulk of excellence in historical writings (in the light, that is, of Voltaire's *Essai sur les mœurs*, Gibbon's *Decline and Fall of the Roman Empire*, and Hume's *History of England*), this charge looks a little tarnished now. But it is not dead. As recently as 1953, a historian of political theory observed that the eighteenth century "was a time when the historical spirit was lacking and when men had little reverence for the past,"[3] and there are many today who would agree with him.

Admittedly, the rise of modern conceptions of history was

---

much is to be endured, and little to be enjoyed." Boswell quotes Johnson in his *Life* as saying that "if they had not been published so closely one after the other that there was not time for imitation, it would have been in vain to deny that the scheme of that which came latest was taken over from the other." Thus *philosophe* and anti-*philosophe* meet in a common perception of life.

[2] *Esquisse d'un Tableau historique des progrès de l'esprit humain*, in *Œuvres complètes*, 21 vols., (1804), VIII, 312-13.

[3] Wanlass: *Gettell's History of Political Thoughts*, 237. In view of

slow and tortuous; and the moralizing, relatively static histories written in the eighteenth century cannot be called unmitigated triumphs of the historical mentality. All too often, the *philosophes* turned history into propaganda—sometimes on purpose, more often unwittingly, through their very conception of the past as a struggle between rational and irrational forces. Ranke's celebrated dictum that all epochs are equally close to God, with which the modern craft of history attained maturity, was beyond the horizon of the Enlightenment. But there are many ways of expressing a sense of history. The *philosophes* were the first to treat whole cultures as a unit of historical study, and greatly improved the critical stance of historians toward their subject matter. It is true that they wanted to escape from the worship of the past because, as they rightly believed, it was used all too often as an ideological prop for reactionary policies. "At best," said Locke shrewdly, "an argument from what has been, to what should of right be, has no great force."[4] But the *philosophes* were also convinced that the only way to escape from the past was to know it.

What was the future to be like? This brings up the fourth criticism—that the *philosophes* hoped to realize the perfect society of their dreams by means of the enlightened despot. At least one respected book I know calls Napoleon's Caesaristic despotism the logical fulfillment of the *philosophes*' program,[5] and it is common property that the political theory of the Enlightenment consisted largely of d'Alembert flattering Frederick the Great, Diderot flattering Catherine the Great, and

---

Dilthey's, Cassirer's, and Meinecke's writings, such a judgment is startling. But it is not rare.

[4] *Second Treatise Of Civil Government*, paragraph 103.

[5] Geoffrey Bruun: *Europe and the French Imperium*, 1799–1814 (1938), ch. I.

Voltaire flattering both. Obviously, the *philosophes* enjoyed their proximity to power, partly because it soothed their vanity, partly because it provided them with audiences and customers, partly because it protected them from the harassment of censors. It is equally true that the close, and often informal, association of these bourgeois men of letters with royalty created intermittent fantasies. There were occasions when some of the *philosophes* dramatized themselves as modern Aristotles guiding modern Alexanders. But to take such private delusions and social aspirations for a reasoned political theory, to call Voltaire "by conviction and temperament an enthusiast of enlightened despotism,"[6] is to mistake accident for essence. In fact, the physiocrats alone advocated what they called *legal despotism.* But, in the first place, they hedged this idea with qualifications, treating this despotism as a transitional expedient to be supervised, at all times, by an alert public opinion. And, in the second place, the other *philosophes* disliked this despotism heartily. Rousseau denounced it in a violent letter to the elder Mirabeau[7]; Turgot told Du Pont that "this devil 'despotism' will forever stand in the way of the propagation of your doctrine"[8]; while Diderot asserted that "the arbitrary government of a just and enlightened prince is always bad."[9] Other *philosophes*, like Holbach, were profoundly skeptical of the benefits conferred by an omnipotent ruler, no matter how benevolent.[1] Voltaire

[6] Leo Gershoy: *From Despotism to Revolution, 1763-1789* (1944), 64. See my discussion of this view in *Voltaire's Politics*, 166-70.

[7] July 26, 1767. C. E. Vaughan, ed.: *The Political Writings of Jean-Jacques Rousseau*, 2 vols. (1915), II, 159-62.

[8] Quoted by Michel Lhéritier: "Rapport général: le despotisme éclairé, de Frédéric II à la Révolution française," *Bulletin of the International Committee of Historical Sciences*, vol. IX (1937), 188.

[9] *Réfutation de l'ouvrage d'Hel-*

is more complicated, but far from being a consistent admirer of enlightened despotism, he was a thoroughgoing relativist.

The political theory of the Enlightenment has not yet been completely explored. In the absence of such a systematic study, nothing has seemed more plausible than the picturesque scene of the all-wise, all-powerful prince laying down rational laws and dealing out rational justice with a *philosophe* by his side. The *philosophes* certainly did their part in propagating this image of themselves, and posterity has revenged itself upon them by accepting their self-portrait and not reading their writings. And yet, the notion that "enlightened despotism" was the *philosophes*' favorite form of government is simply still another myth. Few of the *philosophes* were full-fledged political theorists: generally they treated politics as though it were no more than a set of concrete controversies. This had the disadvantage of preventing them from seeing all the consequences of their positions. But it also demands that we see these positions in the context in which they were developed. When the *philosophes* favored absolutism, they did so because they were opposed to the alternative—the traditional government by a powerful aristocracy. In their eyes, absolutism was not a rationalistic scheme but a political party in the real world. They could see the virtues of British constitutionalism, or of the kind of moderate aristocracy advocated by leading Dutch or Genevan political figures. And in any event, their

---

vétius intitulé L'Homme, in *Œuvres complètes*, III, 381, and elsewhere. Diderot (as the late Walter L. Dorn suggested) came to politics late, largely as a result of his growing distaste for Frederick of Prussia, and may be quoted on several sides of the political battle. Yet his anti-authoritarianism is preponderant.

[1] See Everett C. Ladd, Jr.: "Helvétius and Holbach: *La Moralisation de la politique*," *Journal of the History of Ideas*, XXIII (April-June 1962), 221-38.

long-range program envisaged a government responsible to a wide public, and expressive of the autonomy of the citizen.

For the *philosophes*, the question of forms of government always involved the question of the masses: should ordinary men, nearly always illiterate and almost definitely unfit for self-government, be allowed a share in political life? Should they be told the truth about religion and be trusted to exercise moral self-restraint? Or should they be kept in check by politic lies, by a *religion civile?* There were few matters the *philosophes* debated more intensively and more inconclusively than this. The balance of opinion was in favor of telling the truth, not in favor of organized deceit. Even Voltaire came to place considerable trust in the rationality of the poor, as he grew older, more mellow, and more politically experienced. Montesquieu had said in 1748, in the Preface to his *Esprit des lois*, "It is not a matter of indifference that the minds of the people be enlightened."[2] And, in the second half of the eighteenth century, more and more *philosophes* could see the advantages, and were willing to take the risks, of universal enlightenment.

Behind the four criticisms I have listed, there stands a fifth which usually accompanies them: that the Enlightenment was the work of lightheaded wits who glittered in salons and invented irresponsible Utopias. A splendid recent instance, which exhibits all five of these charges together is Sir Harold Nicolson's portrait gallery of the eighteenth century, characteristically but unhappily entitled *The Age of Reason.* To Sir Harold, the *philosophes* were all rationalists, except of course Rousseau, who, he tells us, felt "distrust for and incapacity for all rational thought." They created an age of

[2] *Œuvres complètes,* ed. Roger Caillois, 2 vols. (1951), II, 230.

optimism and expected to solve all problems with a handful of rules. Sir Harold says nothing about historical writing in the eighteenth century, but this very omission from his crowded panorama suggests that he did not find the historical achievements of a Gibbon or a Voltaire worth mentioning. And, of course, the *philosophes* favored enlightened despotism. Sir Harold says many generous things about Voltaire's fight for freedom and humanitarianism, but he concludes that while "Rousseau desired the dictatorship of the proletariat, Voltaire desired the dictatorship of kings," which is to make two major errors in one sentence.[3] I need hardly add that Sir Harold's light hand, and his talent for biography by anecdote leaves untouched the accepted picture of the philosophes—they remain, in his book, earnest but not serious, impractical, witty, and shocking. The monographs grind on, telling the truth to the few who already know it. If anyone wants a refutation of the theory of progress, let him compare the popular treatment of the Enlightenment two centuries ago and today.

While scholars have valiantly directed their fire against this battery of misinterpretations, they have recently been fired upon from a new direction. I said at the beginning that the Enlightenment has been assailed for consequences it neither intended nor produced. This new attack has often been made on mutually exclusive grounds, but that has not slowed down the critics. It is becoming increasingly fashionable to criticize the Enlightenment for producing what is called "the crisis of our time." Some critics charge the *philosophes* with subverting

[3] *The Age of Reason: The Eighteenth Century in Reason and Violence* (1961), 416, 91. Sir Harold even accepts the notion of "Rousseau's theory of the noble savage" (330 and elsewhere).

stable Christian values and throwing man into the flux of relativism. Others charge them with professing Utopian goals with such grim single-mindedness that they produced the totalitarian mentality which makes our age a hell on earth. Some agile logicians have, in fact, charged the Enlightenment with both crimes at once: with one hand the infidel crew destroyed a secure religious basis for morality, and with the other it fostered a messianic attitude toward politics. The *philosophes*, in short, are widely accused today of having been cynics and fanatics at the same time.

I do not wish to minimize the horrors of our time, or to ridicule the search for their causes. The *philosophes*, great advocates of pragmatic history, would have been the first to defend the utility of such a search. I think too, that these new critics of the Enlightenment are confronting serious issues: they are trying to discard the now outworn political categories of "right" and "left," and to understand the psychological and social strains that a civilization undergoes when it secularizes its world view. I am taking issue with these critics here not because I disagree with their goals or deprecate their questions, but because I think their answers are wrong.

The most prominent advocate of the contention that the Enlightenment spawned the totalitarian view of politics is J. L. Talmon, who is now at work on a massive history of the origins of "totalitarian democracy."[4] For Talmon, our world is divided by two kinds of political positions, both democratic in resting on a mass base. The first of these, for the sake of whose preservation Talmon is obviously writing his history, is liberal democracy, which limits the competence of politics, relies on discussion, and trusts empirical scientific procedures.

[4] *The Origins of Totalitarian Democracy* (1952).

The second is totalitarian democracy, which makes every question political, believes in a single truth, divides the world into heroes who embrace this truth, and villains who reject it, and is ready to kill all the villains for the sake of the perfect world just beyond the horizon. This analysis of political fanaticism has its merits, and its importance: since the advent of Sigmund Freud and Max Weber, historians have become alert to the dangers inherent in the assumption of all virtue by political leaders. The ruthlessness of the pure in heart has been demonstrated in a variety of political climates, from Calvin's Geneva to Woodrow Wilson's Versailles.[5]

Talmon's critique is thus in the main stream of sociological history. But his search for sources is strained and, I think, wholly misleading. Far from "speaking for the eighteenth century," or even for the Enlightenment, his proto-totalitarians are exceptional men, and in exceptional moods. As Alfred Cobban has shown in a brilliant refutation of Talmon's position, "there are only incidental references to Montesquieu and Voltaire, none to the articles in the *Encyclopédie*, none to Turgot, only one to Diderot."[6] Talmon's reading of Holbach, who was a liberal, and Helvétius, who was at once second-rate and under constant criticism from other *philosophes*, is equally unfortunate. Morelly, Mably, and Rousseau, on whom Talmon rests his case, have been so variously interpreted—not only by later commentators but by their contemporaries—that it is impossible to demonstrate any single line of influence that is supposed to have sprung from them.

[5] On Woodrow Wilson, see Richard Hofstadter: *The American Political Tradition* (1948), ch. 10.

[6] *In Search of Humanity: The Role of the Enlightenment in Modern History* (1960), 183. Cobban's little book is a refreshing exception to the books I am discussing here.

Talmon's work, then, takes the unrepresentative man as representative of a movement, and unrepresentative quotations out of context as representative of a man's ideas. Even worse than that, it plays games with the subtlest of problems to which the intellectual historian must devote his best efforts: the problem of influence. Rousseau influenced the widest variety of political thinkers, and by no means all of them were extremists: reactionary counterrevolutionaries, virulent terrorists, moderate democrats, moderate aristocrats can all be shown to have read Rousseau with approval. And it is equally easy to show representatives of all these groups who read him with loathing.

I have no wish to adopt Talmon's logic here. Cobban has refuted it with an amusing argument: he has made up a chain of influence, "leading from Stalin back through Lenin, Marx, Hegel, Kant, Rousseau, Locke, and Hooker to Aquinas,"[7] a chain that might delight some anticlerical anti-communists, but that has no value as history. It would be far more respectable intellectually to show another chain of connections: some of the proto-totalitarians of the nineteenth century, planners for an industrial age governed by omnipotent technicians, men like Saint-Simon and Comte, were deeply indebted to the writings of such clerical reactionaries as de Maistre, behind whom stands the long tradition of Catholic Christianity. Would it not be far more reasonable to see the paternity of modern totalitarianism in Christianity, both Catholic and Protestant, with its sharp distinction of saved and damned, its sumptuary legislation, its authoritarian demands for subordination, its excommunications, its Inquisitions, its total view of the world, than to seek it in the Enlightenment, with its valiant efforts to

[7] Ibid.

establish a free press, general education, toleration of minorities, to lighten sentences, and to abolish penalties for whole ranges of activities regarded as criminal by the Church? Which was more totalitarian, the institutions that burned dissenters, or the movement that tried to save them?

These are rhetorical questions. I do not think we know enough to trace the intellectual pedigree of totalitarianism with any confidence; we do know enough to reject the pedigree offered by Talmon and his many supporters. For that pedigree is constructed not merely by misinterpreting the meaning, but also by overestimating the power, of ideas. No modern historian can afford to neglect the intellectual formulations that incite men to action. Even if they are rationalizations of underlying psychological pressures or economic institutions, they become autonomous historical forces. But neither the Terror in the French Revolution, nor the totalitarian regimes of our time, are merely the products of certain ideas, the "ultimate result" of speculations by eighteenth-century writers who were thinking of something else and hoped for a far different future. The pressure of events, the heritage of institutions often quite at variance with intellectual formulations, technological developments in industry or in mass-communications, changes in weaponry or developments in economics—all these brought certain ideas into prominence and, ultimately, to victory. Germany did not go Fascist because of Nietzsche, but Germans ready to go Fascist selected and distorted some of Nietzsche's teachings to suit their purposes. And what happened, in this same country, to the humane, cosmopolitan classicism of a Goethe, whom every German read and professed to worship? These are considerations so obvious that they require restatement only because they are being forgotten by the latest critics of the Enlightenment.

The flaws that vitiate Talmon's analysis of the Enlightenment as a source of totalitarianism, vitiate the criticism of writers who treat the Enlightenment as a source of modern nihilism. Lester G. Crocker's ambitious and erudite *Age of Crisis*, the first volume in a proposed trilogy on ethical thought in eighteenth-century France, treats the exceptional as typical, and the relation of ideas to facts with blithe disregard for historical realities. Crocker's thesis is announced in his dramatic title: the decline of the Christian "metaphysic" caught eighteenth-century thinkers "in the conflicts of an age of profound cultural crisis."[8] They were compelled to seek other foundations for conduct—natural law, and, increasingly as the century progressed, social utility. This breakdown of old standards caused, or at least revealed, a pervasive breakdown of moral and political decency, which resulted in the extreme philosophy of the marquis de Sade and of the Terror in the French Revolution, and which foreshadowed modern totalitarianism. History shows that "the rationalistic solutions of the middle ground have not succeeded, and have lost their formerly powerful appeal. We are impelled to extremes—to those of Sade, of Morelly, of Kant, or of the Grand Inquisitor—towards absolutes of some kind."[9] Sade is, if not Crocker's hero, certainly Crocker's protagonist: he appears in the book with strategic regularity, and is stressed because he has "an important place in the thought of his age," and has been "shamefully neglected."[1] Sade is important because he draws the "ultimate conclusions" from the "radical philosophies developed earlier in the century."[2] These radical philosophies include the right to suicide, which opens the way to Ivan

[8] *An Age of Crisis: Man and World in Eighteenth Century French Thought* (1959), 3.

[9] Ibid. 472.

[1] Ibid. 10.

[2] Ibid. 11.

Karamazov, and the "positions of Montesquieu and Hume," which obviously contain "the seed of moral nihilism."[3] Thus the Enlightenment moves on, toward nihilism, toward the Terror, toward the Crisis of our Time.

This view has its uses, if largely as a corrective. The eighteenth century was not an age of crisis—no span of a hundred years could sustain an atmosphere of perpetual emergency with any degree of cheerfulness or productivity—but it was an age of readjustment in which the decline of Christian modes of thought produced a variety of naturalistic philosophies designed to replace the dying world view. Moreover, Crocker's reminder that the *philosophes* were not always easy with themselves is of value. But it was precisely the character of the Enlightenment *not* to be "impelled to extremes." As sturdy disciples of classical antiquity (of Cicero, Seneca, and Horace) the *philosophes* took extreme care to avoid extremes. The philosophy of practical paganism—reasonable pride, moderate reform, sensible expectations—was good enough for them. It is ironic that the *philosophes* should be taken as the fathers of fanatical ideologies when they both fought fanaticism and sought to avoid fanaticism in their own thinking. It was one of their most attractive virtues that they did not draw the kind of ultimate conclusions that would subvert the humanism of their purpose. Holbach was an atheist, but did not extol crime, and did not argue that if God is dead, all is permitted. Helvétius was a utilitarian, but his psychological account of man's nature tried to lay the foundation of reasonable social policies. Diderot celebrated sexual freedom, but his ideal was the genital personality and not polymorphous perversion. Even if we concede that there were seeds of ethical nihilism in

[3] Ibid. 77.

Hume and Montesquieu, it is precisely the point of the Enlightenment that these seeds were not allowed to ripen.

When they did ripen, as with Sade, they turned into a vicious parody of the Enlightenment: Sade was not an heir but a caricature of the *philosophes*. Sade, as even some discriminating admirers will admit, was a turgid and disorganized writer,[4] and there is little point in turning a tedious voluptuary into an archetypical thinker. The philosophical disquisitions with which Sade interrupts his adolescent sexual fantasies are little more than exclamations, borrowed from the *philosophes* without being in any way philosophical themselves.

It is hardly surprising that a writer who sees the Enlightenment epitomized in Sade, will see its consequences expressed in the Terror. To be sure, Crocker hedges his analysis with a tautology: "While it would be patently absurd . . . to cast any responsibility on the *philosophes* for the complex circumstances which determined later happenings, it is nevertheless true that the intellectual climate which they helped to create was an important part of those circumstances, insofar as men's ideologies and outlooks affect their decision and their behavior,"[5] which is to say that insofar as ideology affected the Revolution it affected the Revolution. But Crocker is ready to go further, and to see the Terror as the nihilistic culmination of the Enlightenment: "Robespierre," he writes, "carried to totalitarian limits the process of conditioning that was implicit in some of the *philosophes*' theories, and furnished a model for the modern collectivist system. He caused popular clubs to be founded throughout France, in which, by speeches, songs and discussions, ideas and emotions could be manipulated and men

[4] Thus Simone de Beauvoir, whose sympathetic study of Sade is quoted in *An Age of Crisis*. See *The Marquis de Sade* (1953), 12.

[5] *An Age of Crisis*, 448.

trained to self-sacrifice for the public weal. His government sent 'commissioners' throughout the land."[6]

These are astounding sentences. The Terror was neither the culmination of the Revolution nor the ultimate consequence of the Enlightenment. And to argue, even by implication, that the very movement that devoted its vast energies and stores of wit to fight censorship, nonsense, slavery, torture, intolerance, cruelty, and war, was responsible for these horrors in our time is to stand logic on its head. Every large cluster of ideas contains within itself intimations of its own opposite—that is inevitable. But to concentrate on these intimations at the expense of the ideas themselves is to substitute fancy for history—and where history is dead, all is permitted.

There has long been a debate, started in large measure by the *philosophes*' aggressive rhetoric, over whether the Enlightenment was destructive or constructive. The *philosophes* themselves had a ready answer: demolition and construction were two aspects of the same activity. Voltaire, thinking of his gardens at Ferney, spoke for the Enlightenment as a whole when he told a correspondent in 1759 that he destroyed only

[6] Ibid. 464. Modern terms like "totalitarian" and "collectivist" suggest Crocker's preoccupation with our century. No historian will recognize in "process of conditioning" Robespierre's harangues which bored as many hearers as they fascinated. Or is Crocker referring to what he calls, on the previous page, "the systems of national education instituted by Robespierre"? (463) What systems? Again, no historian would recognize in the "model for modern collectivist systems" the network of Jacobin clubs, which Robespierre neither founded nor dominated. The word "manipulated" is hardly an apt description of the patriotic morale-building and sociability which helped the young republic win a war. Nor is the phrase "his government," which suggests that Robespierre ran a one-man dictatorship instead of participating in a willful and individualistic Committee of Public Safety.

in order to build.[7] It is just as true, I think, that before we can appreciate the real virtues of the Enlightenment, we must dispose of its imagined vices. That is why I have spent so much space on criticizing its critics.

Obviously, the Enlightenment is not beyond criticism, and I have offered some criticisms in this book. But the faults of the movement were built, I think, into their situation. The *philosophes* were pragmatic, playful, and polemical. This attitude was necessary, considering the people they wished to persuade and the authorities they had to flatter and evade. But this necessity also had some unfortunate results. The *philosophes*' fetish of practicality, their horror of speculation for its own sake, drove them close to a philistine disregard for ideas, and blinded them to the possibilities of some of the most adventurous notions produced in their own ranks. In their own devotion to literature and the arts, they avoided the separation of sensibility and energy, beauty and experience, that has haunted bourgeois culture since their days,[8] but their cult of practicality may be in part responsible for that later divorce. In addition, their moral passion, Roman in its earnestness, drove them to find moral lessons in all things, even in the universe, so that the *philosophes*, champions of science, were on the whole unappreciative of its real methods. Voltaire, d'Alembert, and Buffon were the most distinguished exceptions: the others did not fully grasp the amoral, mathematical nature of the natural sciences.

At the same time, seeking to popularize new and daring ideas, and struggling against a determined opposition, the *philosophes* were both playful and polemical. The world view

[7] Voltaire to de Brosses, January 5 (1759), *Correspondence*, XXXV, 11.

[8] See Richard Hofstadter: *Anti-intellectualism in American Life* (1963), *passim*, especially ch. 9.

they held and wished to propagate was perfectly serious, but they clothed it in dialogues, stories, didactic plays so that the charge of their irresponsibility, although unjustified, is easy to understand.

The interpreter of the Enlightenment who tries to characterize the movement after he has disposed of the myths that surround it finds the *philosophes'* style of philosophizing at once regrettable and tantalizing. For implicit in all their belligerent arguments and witty formulations there is a philosophy of real seriousness and enduring relevance. I shall do no more here than to name that philosophy, in a series of paradoxes. I have made them paradoxes because it is precisely the vision of ambiguity that has been denied the *philosophes.* Yet they had it, even if they did not clothe it in the vocabulary that is fashionable in our age.

The Enlightenment, then, was an aristocratic liberalism. In politics, as in other matters, the range of *philosophe* opinions was wide, but at the center was a program for government responsible to its citizens, governing by laws rather than arbitrary enactments, protecting the rights of civil and religious minorities. At the same time, while there were democrats among the *philosophes,* even these democrats cherished an élite of civilized men and women, who knew the classics both of ancient and modern times, loved and practiced the arts, cared for conversation, and participated in a kind of timeless assembly of the happy few.

In ethics, the Enlightenment professed an Epicurean Stoicism. The *philosophes* preached courage before death without fear of hell or hope of heaven, and those among them who knew that death was coming, like David Hume, practiced in that supreme moment what they had preached all their lives. They believed in public service—but also in pleasure. They enjoyed advising legislators, but they also enjoyed the dazzle of wit, and the play of humor in the face of grim realities.

On a deeper level, the *philosophes* glimpsed a general view of the world that I should like to call a passionate rationalism. Their rationalism, as I have said before, was not an abstract devotion to reason or a naïve trust in its omnicompetence. It was, rather, a devotion to the critical spirit that treats all positions as tentative—including their own. The *philosophes* were the enemies of myth, and the myths to which they themselves were victims were nothing more than limitations which all mortals share. Their rationalism was, one might say, programmatic: it called for debate of all issues, examination of all propositions, and penetration of all sacred precincts. But I cannot repeat often enough that this critical, scientific view of life was anything but frigid. The *philosophes* at once studied and rehabilitated the passions, tried to integrate the sexual urge into civilized life, and laid the foundation for a philosophy that would attempt to reconcile man's highest thinking with his deepest feeling.

Yet the Enlightenment did not advocate an easy, superficial reconciliation between emotion and rationality, desire and self-control. The tension between them pervades their thought and gives it the touch of tragic resignation that is so often overlooked. For—and I know that this characterization seems least credible of all—the *philosophes* professed a tragic humanism. The word humanism is rich in overtones, but the *philosophes* could claim to be humanists in all senses of that word: they believed in the cultivation of the classics, they were active in humanitarian causes, and in the widest philosophical sense, they placed man in the center of their moral universe. Yet, this humanism was also tragic. The *philosophes* were poignantly conscious of the limitations of human effort, the brevity of human life, the pervasiveness of human suffering, men's disappointed hopes, wasted lives, and undeserved misfortunes. Hence their reformist writings are a mixture of activism and acceptance: man must cultivate his garden. But to explore this saying fully is to explore the Enlightenment, and to do that—to determine its nature and speculate on its bearing for our time—will require another book.

INDEX

INDEX

19TH AND 20TH CENTURY EUROPEAN HISTORY IN NORTON PAPERBACK

THE NORTON HISTORY OF MODERN EUROPE

Rice, Eugene F., Jr. *The Foundations of Early Modern Europe, 1460–1559.*
Dunn, Richard S. *The Age of Religious Wars, 1559–1689.* (2d Ed.)
Krieger, Leonard. *Kings and Philosophers, 1689–1789.*
Woloch, Isser. *Eighteenth-Century Europe, Tradition and Progress 1715–1789.*
Breunig, Charles. *The Age of Revolution and Reaction, 1789–1850.* (2d Ed.)
Rich, Norman. *The Age of Nationalism and Reform, 1850–1890.* (2d Ed.)
Gilbert, Felix. *The End of the European Era, 1890 to the Present.* (2d Ed.)